The Scene of Harlem Cabaret

The Scene of Harlem Cabaret

Race, Sexuality, Performance

SHANE VOGEL

The University of Chicago Press

CHICAGO AND LONDON

SHANE VOGEL is assistant professor of English at Indiana University.

The University of Chicago Press, Chicago 60637
The University of Chicago Press, Ltd., London
© 2009 by The University of Chicago
All rights reserved. Published 2009
Printed in the United States of America

"Cabaret," "Summer Night," "The Cat and the Saxophone (2 a.m.),"
"Closing Time," "Sport," "Café: 3 a.m.," from *The Collected Poems of Langston Hughes* by Langston Hughes, edited by Arnold Rampersad with David Roessel, Associate Editor, copyright © 1994 by The Estate of Langston Hughes. Used by permission of Alfred A. Knopf, a division of Random House, Inc.

18 17 16 15 14 13 12 11 10 09   1 2 3 4 5

ISBN-13: 978-0-226-86251-4 (cloth)
ISBN-13: 978-0-226-86252-1 (paper)
ISBN-10: 0-226-86251-8 (cloth)
ISBN-10: 0-226-86252-6 (paper)

Library of Congress Cataloging-in-Publication Data
Vogel, Shane.
The scene of Harlem cabaret : race, sexuality, performance / Shane Vogel.
p. cm.
Includes bibliographical references and index.
ISBN-13: 978-0-226-86251-4 (cloth : alk. paper)
ISBN-10: 0-226-86251-8 (cloth : alk. paper)
ISBN-13: 978-0-226-86252-1 (paper : alk. paper)
ISBN-10: 0-226-86252-6 (paper : alk. paper)
1. Harlem (New York, N.Y.)—Social life and customs—20th century. 2. New York (N.Y.)—Social life and customs—20th century. 3. Harlem Renaissance. 4. African American entertainers—New York (State)—New York—History—20th century. 5. Music-halls (Variety-theaters, cabarets, etc.)—Social aspects— New York (State)— New York—History—20th century. 6. Performing arts—Social aspects— New York (State)— New York—History—20th century. 7. Homosexuality—Social aspects—New York (State)— New York—History—20th century. 8. African Americans—Intellectual life—20th century. 9. African Americans—Politics and government—20th century. 10. United States—Race relations—Political aspects— History—20th century. I. Title.
F128.68.H3V64 2009
306.4'8097471—dc22
2008025289

♾ The paper used in this publication
meets the minimum requirements of the American National Standard for Information Sciences—Permanence of Paper for Printed Library Materials, ANSI z39.48–1992.

For Kevin

Night Life seems to have been born with all of its people in it, the people who had never been babies, but were born *grown,* completely independent. Some of them were wonderful people, and some were just hangers-on of a sort. Some of them experienced untold misfortunes, and some of them were lucky. Some of them glittered in Night Life even more brightly than their names on the marquees. Some played sure things, others were inclined to gamble. There were a few hustlers, who depended on finding suckers for survival. And there were some who were too wise to hustle, who only wanted to have enough money to be able to afford to be a sucker. Night Life had a song and dance. Night Life was New York, Chicago, San Francisco, Paris, Berlin; uptown, downtown; Harlem, out South; anywhere they wore that gorgeous velvet mantle.

DUKE ELLINGTON
Music Is My Mistress

Contents

Illustrations

Acknowledgments

I AM grateful to those who have made writing this book so rewarding. I first want to thank Ann Pellegrini, Diana Taylor, Phillip Brian Harper, Joseph Roach, and José Muñoz, all of whom read this work in its earliest incarnation and provided suggestions and guidance on how to shape this project. Each of them has had a tremendous impact on me. I consider myself fortunate to have been given their time and engagement as readers. I want especially to thank Joe for first showing me the possibilities of performance studies and pointing the way to New York City. Once there, José inspired me, taught me how to think smarter, and always demonstrated the personal and political commitments of teaching and writing. I thank him for his guidance, direction, support, pedagogy, friendship, expectation, confidence, indulgence, and example.

Early research for this project was assisted by the Michael Kirby Dissertation Fellowship (Tisch School of the Arts/New York University), the Paulette Goddard Fellowship (Tisch School of the Arts/NYU), and a Summer Faculty Fellowship (Indiana University). A one-year residency at Emory University's Bill and Carol Fox Center for Humanistic Inquiry came at exactly the right time to immerse myself in the process of revision and to reimagine the trajectory of the book. The administrators and staff at the Fox Center—Keith Anthony, Colette Barlow, and Amy Erbil—and the center's director, Martine Brownley, cultivated a warm intellectual community that helped me to shape this book. I am particularly grateful for the advice and camaraderie of my fellow fellows there, especially Rick Rambuss, Kathryn Wilchelns, and Chad Levin. And many thanks to Michael Moon and Jonathan Goldberg, who helped me to make a temporary home in Atlanta.

As for my new home in Bloomington: my colleagues and friends at Indiana University constantly reaffirm for me the value of intellectual community and critical generosity. I especially thank Bob Bledsoe, Purnima Bose, Claudia Breger, Judith Brown (who read many versions of many pages), Linda Charnes, Ed Comentale (who saved me again and again those first few years), Margo Crawford, Denise Cruz, Jonathan Elmer, Jennifer Fleissner, Rae Greiner, Mary Gray, Susan Gubar, Paul Gutjahr, Matt Gutterl, George Hutchinson, Patty Ingham (who offered valuable comments on chapter 5), Josh Kates (who offered valuable comments on chapter 3), and Karma Lochrie. Ellen McKay and Steve Watt helped me to stay connected to performance studies and find my bearings on the terra incognita of an English department. So, too, have a handful of exceptional graduate students: Sarah Withers, Alex Dodge, Patrick Maley, Kristen Renzi, and Rebecca Peters-Golden.

Over the years a number of scholars, friends, and loved ones have supported this project, and me, as mentors and examples, including Christine Bacareza Balance, Jennifer Brody, Barbara Browning, Michael Cobb, Ann Cvetkovich, Alex Doty, Jennifer Doyle, Lisa Duggan, Penny Farfan, Licia Fiol-Matta, Sharon Holland, May Joseph, Kate Kelley, André Lepecki, Jill Lane, Anna McCarthy, Ricardo Montez, Tavia Nyong'o, Peggy Phelan, Ann Pellegrini, Eve Sedgwick, Karen Shimakawa, Rebecca Sumner-Burgos, Diana Taylor, Bob Vorlicky, Michael Warner, Steven Watson, and Ted Ziter. Their encouragement and support have meant more to me than they know. The opportunity to learn from Fred Moten while I was at NYU and since was central to this project and my own intellectual growth. Classes with him changed everything. Alexandra Vázquez has been my ideal reader and fellow traveler through the weeds and clearings. I only hope I have come to recognize what she kept telling me I was doing. David Román and E. Patrick Johnson both read the entire manuscript and offered enormously helpful suggestions and feedback. David's response to my work over the past decade has continually enriched and renewed how I think about performance. Patrick's enthusiasm and vision for this project motivated me through the final stages of revision.

Justin Bond and Kenny Mellman fundamentally shaped the way I understand performance, queerness, and history. Their performances first suggested to me what cabaret performance was and could be. I am grateful for their work and their generosity.

I thank Craig Tenney at the estate of Langston Hughes, Isaac Geweritz at the New York Public Library, Anthony Toussaint at the Schomburg Center for Research in Black Culture, Beth Howse at the John Hope and Aurelia E. Franklin Library Special Collections Department at Fisk University, and Elizabeth Campbell-Moskowitz for their help in locating materials and securing permissions. An earlier version of chapter 3 appeared in *Criticism* vol. 48, no. 3 (2007): 397–425, and is reprinted here with the permission of Wayne State University Press. An earlier version of chapter 5 appeared in *Camera Obscura* vol. 23, no. 1 (2008): 10–45, and is reprinted here with the permission of Duke University Press. I am grateful to the editors of those pieces—Jonathan Flatley and Cannon Schmitt; Alexander Doty (with valuable comments from Patricia White)—for their helpful feedback. It has been a privilege to work with Douglas Mitchell and Timothy McGovern at the University of Chicago Press. Doug's commitment to this project and his deep investment in nightlife performance and the acoustics of literature helped guide it to the end. I also thank Vivian Kirklin and Carol Saller for overseeing this process, and Marilyn Bliss for her care with the index.

To my mother and father, and to my sisters, Erin and Meghan, I am grateful for their unconditional support and unwavering belief in me. My closest friends in the world, Tara Perkins, Jason Forman, and John Srednicki, have long put up with the vicissitudes and preoccupations of a friend in academia. Their friendship over many years has been like air through a snorkel: they have given me oxygen when I've been completely submerged. Kevin Walter has read the entire book and then some. I move through the world with greater ease knowing that he is looking after me.

And I finally want to thank Scott Herring for his love and care while I worked on this book and after. His unexpected entry into this project midway through rerouted the entire thing—and me, as well. For showing me the difficult but rewarding act of revision—both on the page and off; for giving me so much time, patience, friendship, humor, support, turns of the phrase, and love; he has my deepest thanks.

——— ✳ ———

Against Uplift

Performance, Literature, and the Queer Harlem Renaissance

It's the way people look at things, not what they look at, that needs to be changed.
LANGSTON HUGHES, 1926

DUKE ELLINGTON premiered at the Cotton Club on December 4, 1927. Only a few months later, he and his orchestra began live national radio broadcasts from the nightclub's bandstand. Billed as "From the Cotton Club," these shows eventually aired nightly, beginning at 11:00, 11:30, or midnight, with occasional dinner-hour broadcasts.[1] The producers capitalized on the champagne-soaked associations of Harlem's nightclubs, with midnight broadcasts invoking an aura of cosmopolitan sophistication and illicit thrills. "By April 1933," writes John Edward Hasse, "forty-five radio stations were broadcasting Ellington around the country, reportedly a record for a dance program beginning at midnight."[2] Even though the Cotton Club did not open its doors until much later in the evening, dinner-hour transmissions allowed families across the country to imagine themselves dining there. According to drummer Sonny Greer, listeners were so eager to hear the Cotton Club broadcast that they put off their eating until it was over. Greer recalled, "We used to broadcast . . . from 6:00 to 7:00. The world was waiting for that. Everybody was waiting for that from New York to California and coast to coast, was waiting for that. Of course, you know, that's suppertime. All the people didn't anybody get anything to eat until we come off. Cats working all day, starved to death until we got off."[3] Ellington varied his set lists for the different audiences, but always managed to communicate the sexual and criminal associations of the Cotton Club. *Variety* observed that the dinner hour broadcasts were "not as 'dirty' as they are of midnights. . . . They lean more to the 'sweet' type of syncopation, but can't refrain from slipping in a real wicked ditty off and on."[4] "From the Cotton Club" carried over the airwaves not just the sound but the space of the Cotton Club as well.

These broadcasts can be understood as a kind of publicity. Though they were not the first live radio presentations of black music, nor even Ellington's first—he was broadcast locally from the Hollywood Club (later renamed Club Kentucky) as early as 1923—they helped make Ellington and the Cotton Club well known throughout the country. But the broadcasts were also publicity in another sense: they constituted a public audience that extended beyond the linen-draped tables and crowded dance floor of the Cotton Club. In doing so, the Cotton Club broadcasts suggested an architecture and atmosphere. The intimacy promised by midnight shows, Prohibition-era intoxication, and a crowded dance floor reorganized other spaces as the music of the Cotton Club filled living rooms of middle-class homes, drifted through urban tenement stairwells, and echoed down small-town streets; "the cathedral leaves its locale," writes Walter Benjamin about the effects of such technological reproduction, "to be received in the studio of a lover of art."[5] The broadcasts of Ellington's orchestrations carried with them across the nation the intimacy of the cabaret and a particular idea of black performance and Harlem nightlife.

Ellington's engagement at the Cotton Club was both part of and exceeded the "Negro vogue" of the 1920s. Growing white and corporate interest in and engagement with black music and culture, postwar economic expansion, and the relocation of vice, along with the advance of the speakeasy during National Prohibition converged to make Harlem an entertainment district rivaling those of downtown New York, Paris, and Berlin. By the end of the 1920s, *Variety* boasted, Harlem offered "11 class white trade nightclubs" and over five hundred "colored cabarets, of lower ranks."[6] At the large, extravagant nightspots like the Cotton Club or Connie's Inn, visitors to Harlem could take in spectacular Broadway-quality black revues designed to appeal to white audiences. Others sought out the smaller, less permanent clubs that featured small bands and room for social dancing, which were primarily spaces of recreation for black patrons. With their intimate interaction between performer and spectators, illicit alcohol consumption, social dancing, potential for interracial contact, public displays of sexuality, and underworld connotations, Harlem's cabarets provided a powerful symbol of the pleasure and dangers of urban life. Underneath the "sweet syncopation" of Ellington's broadcasts, the "real wicked" ditties of the cabaret always lurked, ready to corrupt the families gathered around the radio.

This commodification of black performance and recreation coincided with the literary program of racial publicity and civil rights known as the Harlem (or New Negro) Renaissance. Though shaped by a multiplicity of motives, beliefs, and objectives, the Harlem Renaissance sought on the whole to redefine the meaning of blackness and racial identity in American popular consciousness and to forcefully assert the role of African Americans in the shaping of American culture. The original architects of the Harlem Renaissance envisioned a movement that would counter images and representations of black inferiority with more "truthful" representations and evidence of serious black cultural accomplishment. Black writers would represent themselves, rather than continue being represented by the distortions of white authors, and also work across the color line with white publishers, patrons, and other supporters to reshape notions of American ethnicity and democracy. Many therefore saw the Negro vogue, with its tendency toward black sensuousness, exhibitionism, primitivism, and sensationalism, as a distraction from or, worse, an impediment to their vision of the Renaissance, one that conceded too much to "white" expectations and desires and reproduced well-entrenched stereotypes and social relations between the races. As George Hutchinson notes, "A critique of the 'Vogue' was an essential aspect of the renaissance itself . . . and infused much of its literature as well as popular performance."[7] Cabarets, and the music and performances they fostered, occupied a key place in Harlem Renaissance debates about the value of "high" and "low" cultural forms and the proper subject matter for black arts and letters. Even while black intellectuals and community leaders like W. E. B. Du Bois, Alain Locke, Charles Johnson, and Jessie Fauset capitalized in various ways on white attention, support, patronage, and curiosity to advance the Harlem Renaissance, many worried that the "Negro vogue"—and in particular its celebration of cabaret and nightlife performance—was at odds with a project of racial self-definition.

But not everyone approached the cabaret with such reticence. Like Ellington, a number of authors, artists, and performers of the Harlem Renaissance expanded the scene of the cabaret and made it available to audiences beyond Harlem's nightlife. In this book, I argue that these cultural workers used the cabaret to critique the racial and sexual normativity of uplift ideology and to imagine alternative narratives of sexual and racial selfhood. Promoted through a number of institutions, discourses, and practices, normative uplift ideology of the early twentieth century sought to ground the struggle for racial equality and the struggle against white supremacy in the material and moral achievements and possibilities of the black middle class. Structured by middle-class values and "an ethic of socially responsible individualism," uplift ideology advanced a principle of racial respectability that yoked together normative ideals of gender, sexuality, and class.[8] By the 1920s, historian Kevin Gaines writes, "uplift came to mean an emphasis on self-help, racial solidarity, temperance, thrift, chastity, social purity, patriarchal authority, and the accumulation of wealth."[9] Defining itself against an idea of the socially disorganized black masses—and especially against the urban pathologies defined by sociology in response to urbanization and African American migration—uplift ideology "devised a *moral economy* of class privilege, distinction, and even domination *within the race*, often drawing on patriarchal gender conventions as a sign of elite status and 'race progress.'"[10] This logic of uplift underlies the original impulse of the Harlem Renaissance and its politics of representation. By depicting educated and sophisticated black characters and settings and demonstrating the aesthetic integrity of the black folk, New Negro artists might differentiate themselves from the image of the uneducated masses and demonstrate, in James Weldon Johnson's words, "intellectual parity by the Negro through the production of literature and art."[11]

The writers and performers I examine in the pages that follow, however, rejected the narratives and logics of normative racial uplift and sexual respectability that initially guided the Harlem Reniassance. This "other Harlem Renaissance" turned instead to the contested space of the cabaret as material to compose alternative narratives of race and sex. The refusal to validate and valorize the values of the black middle class and the patriarchal order of family in their prose and poetry—not to mention their personal lives—led authors such as Langston Hughes, Claude McKay, Carl Van Vechten, Zora Neale Hurston, Rudolph Fisher, and Wallace Thurman, and their works, to be grouped together disparagingly as the "Cabaret School" of the Harlem Renaissance (the white Van Vechten was typically included as both origin and culmination of these tendencies). The term "Cabaret School" was used as dismissive shorthand by critics as ideologically disparate as African American educator and anthropologist Allison Davis and radical socialist Hubert Harrison. Both condemned writers whom they saw as negatively influenced by the unfortunate and distasteful sensationalism of Harlem's nightlife. "For nearly ten years," lamented Davis in 1928, "our Negro writers have been 'confessing' the distinctive sordidness and triviality of Negro life, and making an exhibition of their own unhealthy imagination, in the name of frankness and sincerity." [12] He denounced the impact of Harlem's nightlife and cabarets on African American literature, which he saw as exploiting and substantiating stereotypical images of American blackness and upturning the values of racial respectability. Harrison similarly saw the Negro vogue and cabaret craze as an effect of false consciousness, of black writers internalizing white views and subsequently creating art that had no relationship to their actual lives or lived experience. He reached the same conclusion as Davis: "On the whole, then, the influence of the cabaret, whether direct or indirect, has not been quite wholesome for Negro 'literature.' " [13]

In *The Scene of Harlem Cabaret*, I maintain that critics like Davis and Harrison described far more than they intended in their attempts to discipline and contain the cultural work of the cabaret. Such criticisms were voiced, in the context of the Negro vogue, as an attempt to diminish and trivialize this literature by linking it to notions of shallow consumption, corrupting white influence, and faddish bohemianism. However, I argue in this book that what critics dubbed Harlem's "Cabaret School" was in fact a subterranean literary tradition within the Harlem Renaissance that provided new ways of performing, witnessing, and writing the racial and sexual self. More than just an act of *épater le bourgeois,* a turn to the aesthetics of the decadents, or a devotion to the 1920s "cult of primitivism," the authors and performers denigrated as Harlem's Cabaret School consciously marked and enacted a radical break from and rebellion against the politics of normative racial uplift.

This book aims to recover the critique function of Harlem's nightlife. By "Cabaret School," then, I refer to writings and performances of the Harlem Renaissance that took up Harlem's nightlife in a critique of normalizing narratives of racial and sexual identity. This critique sometimes took the form of an explicit objection to the strictures of uplift ideology or a challenge to its dictates. But more often, the Cabaret School articulated a positive critique and affirmation that expanded the literary and performative possibilities of blackness and sexuality through the enunciation of alternative modes of thought, feeling, and existence. While the writers and performers I look at were familiar with each other's work and were in constant dialogue and debate about aesthetic matters, they did not consider themselves as belonging to a unified school of thought. Nonetheless, we can identify in their works formal and thematic affinities and a shared sensibility against the technologies, discourses, and institutions of racial and sexual normalization. *The*

Scene of Harlem Cabaret reframes the Cabaret School as a queer literary tradition that is deeply embedded within performance practices and culture. Thus my redeployment of the phrase "Cabaret School" is less an empirical or descriptive claim than it is a performative act that realigns writing and performance in the Harlem Renaissance within a queer-of-color hermeneutic.[14] While I use this phrase throughout this book, I have not attempted to write the history of all those who might fall under its rubric. Instead, I concentrate on specific instances that help us better think about the relationship between the Harlem Renaissance and black nightlife performance, and the relationship between literature and performance more generally. In the remainder of this introduction, I introduce the contexts and contours that define what I am calling the Cabaret School and the strategies that allow for the materialization of a queer Harlem Renaissance. By putting the Cabaret School in conversation with the specific performances that inspired it, we can see that these authors performed their own set of critiques — of normative uplift ideology, of racial representation, of social organization — which, though elaborated in the literary, were based primarily in the nondiscursive: the embodied practices of black performance and spectatorship that are taken up in writing but always enacted in excess of it.

OPERAS AND CABARETS: THE MORAL CALCULUS OF UPLIFT AND THE SPECTACLE OF VICE

"A race that hums operas will stay ahead of a race that simply hums the 'blues.'" So concluded a 1924 editorial in the black journal *Messenger* that compared the differences between opera houses and cabarets in order to make a larger point about cultural production and consumption. The editorial deplored the fact that while Italian, German, and Jewish immigrants could be witnessed packing the galleries of working-class opera houses, urban black youths preferred instead to listen to the blues in smoke-filled dives and basement speakeasies.[15] In the view of the *Messenger*, the opera house and the cabaret offered competing measures of the city's cultural horizon. In the first, one would find "music, light, colorful life, culture, poetry, art — all those warm and finer influences which throw a beautiful, irresistible charm over human life," and spectators would be "elevated by the drama, music, and scenery." In the other, one would be "plunged deep beneath the ground, free from ventilation, where one's clothes become thoroughly saturated with tobacco smoke and where no complaints can be made against this generally recognized impossible music." Significantly, the perceived disparity between immigrant culture and black culture was not seen here as one of economic class or working-class aesthetics. After conceding that "white people have more money than Negroes, generally speaking," the editorial observed dryly that after paying the cover charge, buying many overpriced drinks, and tipping the waiter, the average night at a cabaret is much costlier than a gallery seat at the Metropolitan Opera. In this assessment, the editorial suggests that patterns of popular black cultural production and consumption put the race at a distinct disadvantage. One way to advance the race, it concludes, would be to repudiate the deleterious effects of the nightclub and the blues and produce more enlightening and edifying musical expression. In the cabaret, the editorial exhaled, "there is little that is uplifting."[16]

There are many things to observe about this editorial. We could note, for example, the valuation of European cultural forms at the expense of black American forms and the reliance on firmly established highbrow/lowbrow cultural hierarchies. We could similarly note its attention to the spatial practices and architecture of performance and their perceived effects on the character and mind of the spectator, as well as the metaphors of firmament and underworld that underlie its moral judgments. And we could point out the editorial's distancing of cabaret attendance from economic explanations, proposing patronage of the cabaret not as an effect of class constraints but as a distinctly moral inclination that must be overcome. We could further observe the editorial's use of Progressive Era sociological notions of nightclubs and saloons as locations of community deterioration, moral misinstruction, cultural miseducation, and unproductive expenditure, in contrast with the elevating effects of the opera house. We could also note its distrust of claims for a uniquely racial art and its call for an interracial cultural consumption not at the expense of racial identity but in service of advancing an "American" cultural identity. Not least of all, we could note the editorial's explicit connection of racial advancement to cultural production and consumption rather than, say, political mobilization.

The rhetorical devices and aesthetic assumptions that shape this editorial illustrate the cultural dimensions of normative uplift ideology. Progressive Era racial uplift emerged as a response to popular cultural discourses of black inferiority and criminality, on the one hand, and social scientific discourses of black social disorganization and deviance, on the other. It interpreted the call for the collective advancement of the race as a call to increase the ranks of a visible and respectable middle class and to combat the perceived threat to the race of urban pathology. As Kevin Gaines notes, however, twentieth-century racial uplift was a philosophy and practice shaped by conflicting logics and conceptualizations: "On the one hand, a broader vision of uplift signifying collective social aspiration, advancement, and struggle had been the legacy of the emancipation era. On the other hand, black elites made uplift the basis for a racialized elite identity claiming Negro improvement through class stratification as race progress, which entailed an attenuated conception of bourgeois qualifications for rights and citizenship." [17] The tension between these overlapping yet contradictory notions of uplift produced a number of competing institutions, practices, and conceptions of black politics and culture in the early twentieth century.[18] Elite uplift ideology sought to demonstrate the black middle class's eligibility for citizenship and equality by differentiating it from those of the race who did not approximate the social and cultural norms on which such enfranchisement was premised. Cultural institutions like black newspapers, churches, and universities undertook efforts to make visible the most successful and to address the poverty and social conditions of the least successful. This version of uplift advanced a *politics of respectability* that, as Farah Jasmine Griffin puts it, "seeks to reform the behavior of individuals, and as such takes the emphasis away from the structural forms of oppression such as racism, sexism, and poverty." [19] The cultural logic of this respectability maintained that nothing less than the cultivation of a "stylized elegance" in literature, music, elocution, and photography would loosen the representational knot that tied together images of social pathology, pseudoscientific inferiority, and the minstrel stage.[20] Normative uplift was premised on the example and the exception: positive representations of the best educated and most successful of the race would counteract racist stereotypes and provide a standard to which the working class could aspire in the constant struggle to keep from sinking further down into poverty and immorality.

To redress the corrupting and community-weakening influences of low culture, elite cultural uplift promoted an educated cultural vanguard that would set an example for the black majority, produce morally and racially validating art, and lead the race into modernity. In an early sociological formulation that would shape the history of racial uplift as well as the cultural project of the Harlem Renaissance, W. E. B. Du Bois famously proposed a moral and economic distribution that set the top fraction of the race—the "Talented Tenth"—against the bottom fraction of the race—the "submerged tenth," the "lowest class of criminals, prostitutes, and loafers." [21] Through education of the mind, character, and spirit, Du Bois advocated "developing the Best of this race that they may guide the Mass away from the contamination and death of the Worst, in their own and other races." [22] Such discursive formulations defined proper racial behavior as that which conformed to the standards of modesty, decency, propriety, and conventional bourgeois morality, including, above all, proper gender and sexual comportment. Accordingly, many black intellectuals and artists who advocated the "elevation" of the race viewed nightclubs and the music performed within them as the apotheosis of "low" culture and approached them with ambivalence, embarrassment, or disapprobation. For this elite, the culture of the cabaret represented a regression and negation of the achievements of the race, one that could be opposed, it was hoped, by counternarratives of "respectful self-representation." [23]

The figure of the cabaret in the discourse of uplift was shaped by the more general Progressive Era knowledge production of social, sexual, and racial deviance. In response to the demographic shifts of migration and the late-industrial organization of the city, various movements sought to reform economic and governmental institutions, provide basic services to the urban poor, and establish a normalizing link between moral education and social organization. Such reform movements found their justification in narratives of deviance and social pathology that circulated in sensational journalism, social scientific studies, and dime-store novels in the early twentieth century. These "overlapping genres of storytelling," as Lisa Duggan describes them, helped to produce "official" knowledge of criminal, sexually deviant, and racialized subjects.[24] The late-nineteenth-century rise of sexology and criminology as scientific fields helped to medicalize and codify individuals as "deviant" or "degenerate," as well as define important distinctions between "vice" and "crime." These social scientific discourses complemented the pseudoscience of eugenics and theories of racial atavism to provide the authoritative foundation for various moral reform groups, vice squads, and sociologists in the service of managing urban spaces and bodies.[25] Whether in the service of God or greater civic order, phalanxes of antivice organizations and sociologists canvassed urban centers to catalogue and police the sexual and social threat fostered in cabarets, dance halls, and pool halls.[26]

American sociology had a central role in producing knowledge of the cabaret and urban nightlife spaces as it identified, studied, and mapped the patterns of behavior among culturally heterogeneous regions of the modern city. Sociology approached questions of standardization and deviance as aggregate trends and social configurations, undertaking studies not of individuals, but of groups, social establishments, and neighborhoods. It not only interpreted but also helped manage the local effects of successive waves of European immigration and rural African American migration to urban neighborhoods, movements that incited moral panics and inflamed nativist sentiments. In sociological terms, this urban growth and social mixture posed the threat of social disorganization—the moral chaos that occurs when social bonds and normative values are not cohesively maintained within a community. Urban nightlife districts, with their transient populations, gender and racial mixing, and underworld economies, were seen as a primary location and cause of urban social disorganization.

Scholars such as Roderick Ferguson, Marlon Ross, Kevin Mumford, and Hazel Carby have shown that American sociology, particularly as it advanced under the positivist methods of the Chicago School, racialized and sexualized this social disorganization.[27] The Chicago School of sociology refers to the social scientific program developed in the early twentieth century at the University of Chicago, an inaugural site of American sociological practice. Blending quantitative methods of statistics and numerical distribution with qualitative methods of field research and ethnography, the Chicago School mapped out the moral geographies of the urban environment and, with regard to American racial relations, undertook to "measure in material terms . . . the extent to which the Negro mass has adjusted to moral, social, and economic habits of the dominant culture."[28] These methods thus advanced findings that confirmed the assumptions of uplift ideology and shaped black social reform programs like the NAACP and the Urban League.[29]

Urban nightlife spaces such as the cabaret were understood in Progressive Era moral and social epistemologies as fostering a number of deviant sexual practices, particularly women's prostitution, homosexuality, and black/white sexual relations. Policing spaces and performances that encouraged such relations was not only a way to regulate such sexualities and reinforce the color line, but also a way to compose taxonomies and classifications of deviance that could be deployed elsewhere in the management of racially and sexually non-normative spaces and practices. In the words of one black sociologist in the 1920s, cabarets and other nightlife institutions provided sociologists and journalists with a "museum of types" for the study of antisocial behavior.[30] Peter Stallybrass contends that representations of the underclass and scenes of urban social disorder like these functioned as a "spectacle of exotic heterogeneity" by which a coherent, normalized, and homogenous bourgeois subject could be constituted.[31] During the Negro vogue of the 1920s, the multiplicity and heterogeneity of Harlem's nightlife helped to constitute both a normative white middle-class gaze and a normative black middle-class gaze. At the same time that these spectacles helped to materialize a homogenous middle-class subject, they also defined and classified the heterogeneity of the underworld to identify, categorize, and contain it more easily. This "official knowledge" of underworld practices and deviant subjectivities helped to shape the scene of Harlem's cabaret in the popular imagination as a location of sexual, criminal, and racial deviance.

Is it any wonder, then, given this framework of interpretation, that black political and cultural leaders in the 1910s and 1920s were alarmed by the popularity of nightclubs, social dancing, and jazz and blues among white and black youth cultures in the 1910s and 1920s? By the measure of uplift's moral calculus, the lures and snares of disreputable entertainments and redlight districts were seen as a problem that threatened racial advancement. To combat this social disorganization, black political and social organizations, often working across the color line with white reform organizations, generated an extensive taxonomy of proper and improper amusements, debated the value of recreation and leisure, dissected the souls of those who populate city streets, and mapped out the spaces and bodies of urban nightlife. Uplift's reliance on a moral differentiation and hierarchization as the necessary precondition to the advancement of the race produced both an economic norm—the black middle class—and a moral norm that figured the black "underworld" as a morally deficient sphere. Institutions of uplift, from black universities, community service organizations, and churches to professional clubs, newspapers, and the heteropatriarchal family, worked in concert to establish and enforce what Michel Foucault called a "normalizing judgment." A normalizing judgment "refers individual actions to a whole that is at once a field of comparison, a space of differentiation and the principle of a rule to be followed." This normalizing rule worked as a "minimal threshold, an average to be respected, and an optimum towards which one must move." [32] In early-twentieth-century America, a normalizing judgment of racial respectability established norms of familial organization, urban recreation, sexual and gender comportment, and capitalist productivity. This principle of normalization provided the basis for evaluating the advancement of the race and managing social disorganization; it produced a moral norm that "compares, differentiates, hierarchizes, homogenizes, and excludes." [33] With this process in mind, we can understand the *Messenger* editorial's appeal to opera—like the appellation "Cabaret School" and similar denunciations—less as an assimilationist appeal to European cultural norms than as an attempt to police the social spaces and expressive forms of urban black culture. It was a prescriptive address as well as a descriptive assessment, seeking to define and enforce the boundary between proper and improper racial expression.[34]

As the editorial's call for operas over cabarets suggests, the anticabaret sentiment of normative racial uplift and Progressive Era reform was shaped by a broader and more long-standing tradition of antitheatrical prejudice that was suspicious of performance's potential to influence and corrupt the moral character of its audience and apprehensive of the potential unruliness of certain forms of public congregation. At the same time, theater and performance in their higher cultural forms were seen as a potential means to improve the race spiritually and morally. Progressive Era reformers and advocates of racial uplift did not denounce performance outright but sought instead to manage it by promoting some forms of performance over others. Indeed, "respectable" performance and theater had a privileged role in the cultural movement to advance the race. The national and international popularity of many black performers could demonstrate artistic success, mark an economic advancement of the race, and counter the representational degradation of minstrelsy. Leaders of the Harlem Renaissance promoted visual arts, dramatic theater, concert dance, symphonic music, pageantry, and vaudeville as vehicles of moral education and avenues of racial representation.[35] These modes of performance were often used to ideologically manage the nightlife performances of cabarets and dance halls by enforcing hierarchies of proper and improper amusements (an idea I elaborate further in chapter 4). In contrast to the comparatively wholesome diversion of vaudeville or the racial self-determination articulated through black musical theater and drama, cabarets and dance halls represented a sexually and criminally permeated space that posed a challenge to the disciplinary goals of racial uplift.

This is a good place to stress that, although higher education was a central tenet and the primary symbol of racial uplift, to be against uplift was not necessarily to be against education, financial success, ambition, operas, individuality, or nice houses. Nor was it to be against racial affirmation, or to fetishize or romanticize poverty, criminality, or the "low." On the contrary, the Cabaret School, as we will see in chapter 2, was highly skeptical, if not critical, of the Negro vogue that spectacularized black performance and sexuality. The Cabaret School's critique should be seen alongside other postwar intraracial critiques of uplift made from the directions of black nationalism, diasporic pan-Africanism, and black Marxism, each of which reframed or eroded the terms of racial equality and self-determination as they were articulated by the elitist logics of uplift.[36] It is important here, following Gaines, to distinguish between "elite" and "popular" manifestations of uplift: that which emerges as a normative ideology in nineteenth- and twentieth-century black political and cultural discourse, and that which emerges through the local practices of "countless parents, teachers, ministers, musicians, and librarians." [37] The writers and performers of the Cabaret School—most of whom were themselves middle class and beneficiaries of uplift's institutional resources and claims to fulfillment—sought to challenge the disciplinary technologies and ways of thinking that made racial uplift into a coherent ideology. The Cabaret School undertook to recognize and enact the bodies, practices, and alternatives that were excluded from normative uplift's ideological sweep—indeed, upon which it depended. *The Scene of Harlem Cabaret* thus seeks to reframe specific works and general tendencies in Harlem Renaissance literature whose political and aesthetic effects are too often oversimplified. The cultural workers of the Cabaret School were acutely aware of the logics of racial, sexual, and gender normativity that were aligned under the banner of uplift. They not only resisted such normalizing pressures, but also made new racial, sexual, and gendered narratives and meanings out of the narratives already existing. [38]

To put it another way, unlike the Chicago School of sociology, the Cabaret School of the Harlem Renaissance took the collectivities of sexual, racial, gender, and economic heterogeneity of the underworld not as a spectacle to define or discipline but as a location of social and subjective expansion. Throughout *The Scene of Harlem Cabaret*, I show how this cabaret literature contested sociologically informed uplift narratives of black social disorganization and sexual pathology, offering instead a site for the heterogeneity of African American culture to emerge. The artists I consider offered critiques of uplift ideology, not because they were opposed to uplift's antiracist struggle or were unaware of the dominant cultural contexts and discourses in which respectability made sense as a political strategy, but because they saw antiracist struggle as inseparable from struggles against class, sexual, and gender normativity. Writers and performers like Langston Hughes, Claude McKay, Wallace Thurman, Nella Larsen, Ethel Waters, and Lena Horne untangle the normative ties of race, gender, and sexuality and imagine other models of social organization, relationality, and ethics than those deployed by the institutions of black middle-class respectability and representation. Into this field of "official" racial, sexual, and criminal knowledge, the Cabaret School propelled their own visions and revisions based on the performances and sociality of nightlife. Literature and performance were places where claims to totalizing knowledge could be undermined and spectacles of heterogeneity could be enacted in ways other than as deviance, perversion, or disorganization.[39]

Consider, as one brief example, evidence of the exchange between Langston Hughes and Havelock Ellis, the great British social scientist of deviance. Ellis was recognized as a leading figure in the production of official knowledge of sexual and social perversion, though by the mid-1920s his methods were already being superseded by the more sociocultural investigations begun by the Chicago School. In texts like *The Criminal* (1890), *Sexual Inversion* (1896), and *The Task of Social Hygiene* (1912)—all repeatedly revised and expanded throughout the early twentieth century—Ellis advanced the "incitement to discourse" of sexuality traced by Foucault.[40] The figures that populate Hughes's Harlem Renaissance poetry are the very ones taken up as case studies of deviance and pathology in sexological and criminological texts. Hughes took black nightlife and blues culture as one of his primary lyrical topics, writing poems that, as bell hooks describes them, "explore transgressive desire."[41] An early edition of *Fine Clothes to the Jew*—Hughes's second volume of verse and the one that earned him such esteemed designations as "Sewer Dweller" from Harlem's *Amsterdam News* and "poet 'low-rate'" from the *Chicago Whip*—held at the New York Public Library, is inscribed: "For Havelock Ellis, with deep admiration, these songs and poems of a simple people; Sincerely, Langston Hughes, Lincoln University, March 10, 1927" (see fig. 1).[42] This inscription demonstrates Hughes's penchant for the direction of indirection that would later find its culmination in his Simple stories—a way of defamiliarizing, undermining, and signifying on Ellis's social scientific discourse and claims to authority. Hughes's poetic inscription to Ellis reorients the location of criminal and deviant knowledge production from the objectifying gaze and scientific discourse of the investigator to the lived sounds and subjectivities of Harlem's nightlife.

It is worth noting, too, that in addition to shaping modern discourses of criminality and sexuality, Ellis also served as editor of Elizabethan and Jacobean dramatic literature for the nineteenth-century Mermaid Series and wrote extensively on modern dance. In offering *Fine Clothes to the Jew* to Ellis, Hughes interrupts and disrupts sociological discourse, enunciating a counterdiscourse to Ellis's social scientific approach and perhaps even appealing to Ellis's love of performance with his "songs . . . of a simple people." Hughes's poetry, like the other writings and performances I explore in this book, lyrically fragments the totalizing and taxonomizing drive of social science's investigations into deviant subjectivity and proudly presents nonexpert and unofficial knowledge of racial and sexual dissidence.

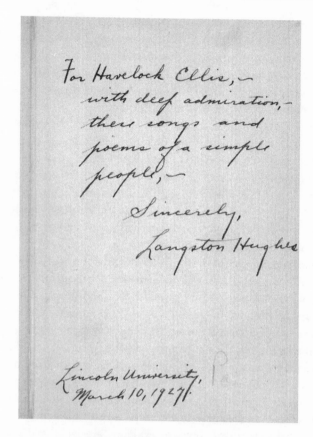

FIGURE 1 Langston Hughes's inscription to Havelock Ellis. From *Fine Clothes to the Jew*. Henry W. and Albert A. Berg Collection of English and American Literature, The New York Public Library, Astor, Lenox and Tilden Foundations.

DESPECTACULARIZATION AND EVERYNIGHT LIFE

As I described above, Progressive Era narratives of moral corruption and social disorder spectacularized vice and provided epistemological frameworks within which to situate racial and sexual underworlds in the early twentieth century. The social, historical, and theatrical events that turned Harlem into a spectacle of African American heterogeneity continue to shape interpretations of the Harlem Renaissance and especially the Cabaret School, which has often been read—at the time and since—as pandering to the Negro vogue and offering sensational, exotic, and exploitative representations of blackness.[43] Yet we will see throughout these pages that, despite its frequent recourse to primitivist language and imagery, the Cabaret School was opposed to the modernist project of spectacularizing the black body. Hughes, to take one example, was skeptical of the Negro vogue and the representational quicksand that it created—his literary use of the people, intimacies, and performances of the cabaret notwithstanding. He observed as early as 1926 that the vogue "may do as much harm as good for the colored budding artist," and ultimately looked back disillusioned, remembering Harlem's cabarets as spaces co-opted into venues where "strangers were given the best ringside tables to sit and stare at the Negro customers—like amusing animals in a zoo."[44] It was not only the performances on the stage—the syncopated steps of befeathered chorus girls or the improvisations of the jazz band—but also black patrons themselves who found themselves turned into a display for curious and adventure-seeking sightseers.[45]

The queer possibilities of Harlem's nightlife that I trace in this book were not rooted in the regenerative essentialism of primitivism but in the productive force of performance and the creation of public intimacy. Yet how does one separate the libidinal possibilities of nightlife from the 1920s' spectacularization of vice and the discourses of primitivism? How do we distinguish between the rhythms of the cabaret as stereotype and its rhythms as critique? And how might the accusation of primitivism have used race to normalize sexuality? Or, to put this question another way, how did charges of primitivism levied against some African American literature of the Harlem Renaissance function discursively to collapse sexual and gender nonconformity into racial difference? How, for example, are racial and sexual deviance mutually imagined when Allison Davis writes in his screed against the Cabaret School, "Primitivism has carried the imagination of our poets and storytellers into the unhealthy and the abnormal"?[46]

To begin to answer these questions, I detour through another spectacular event and layman's sociological venue of Harlem's nightlife: the Hamilton Club Lodge's annual drag ball, which Langston Hughes famously described as a "spectacle in color." Known in the 1920s as the Faggot's Ball, it was the "largest annual gathering of lesbian and gay men in Harlem—and the city."[47] Though not trafficking in the overt primitivism of some nightclubs, the drag ball offered another spectacularization of blackness during the Negro vogue that helped make Harlem an important tourist attraction for sightseeing slummers. "During the height of the New Negro era and the tourist invasion of Harlem," Hughes remembered in one of the balls' most enduring descriptions, "it was fashionable for the intelligentsia and social leaders of both Harlem and the downtown area to occupy boxes at this ball and look down from above at the queerly assorted throng on the dancing floor, males in flowing gowns and feathered headdresses and females in tuxedos and box-back suits." [48] These scenes of gender insubordination drew both black and white spectators of the middle and upper classes to the Hamilton Lodge's box seats. According to historian George Chauncey, though "respectable" audiences were entertained and amused, they were careful to "distinguish themselves from the queers who organized and participated in the affairs." [49] These spectacles, like the many spectacles of primitivism, helped to define the limits of proper and normal racial and sexual behavior.

But Hughes's description of the drag balls takes an unexpected turn: "From the boxes these men look for all the world like very pretty chorus girls parading across the raised platform in the center of the floor. But close up, most of them look as if they need a shave, and some of their evening gowns, cut too low, show hair on the chest." [50] In dismantling the illusion of gender transformation, Hughes may be less concerned here with calling out the bad drag of the Lodge's less-skilled queens than he is in undermining the spectatorial privilege of the audience (a project that shapes much of his autobiography). From a distance, we may think we see coherent and spectacular images of idealized race or gender—material for phantasmatic projections. But coming down from our seats and approaching the stage, we find something much more mundane and incongruous under the costumes and makeup. In this rhetorical close-up, Hughes takes us past the footlights to see the labor that goes into the performance. He despectacularizes the Hamilton Lodge's drag queens, momentarily making visible what spectacle obscures.

We will see that this same strategy of despectacularization informs the aesthetics and politics of the Cabaret School. The Cabaret School responded to the trend toward the spectacular and ahistorical simplifications of 1920s primitivism by turning instead to the historically located pleasures and labors of Harlem's everynight life. I borrow the phrase "everynight life" from Celeste Fraser Delgado and José Esteban Muñoz, who coin this neologism to link the quotidian realm of the everyday to the performances of nightlife. [51] The everyday refers to the mundane routines, habits, gestures, practices, procedures, relationships, speech acts, and performances by which unremarkable subjects negotiate the modern disciplinary organization of society through lived time and space. Everynight life, then, extends this quotidian sphere of the everyday into the nighttime, delimiting a domain where minoritarian subjects enact theories and practices of resistance and social transformation. It is in the sphere of the mundane, rather than that of spectacle, that theorists such as Henri Lefebvre, Michel de Certeau, and Robin D. G. Kelley locate the resistances and revolutionary practices that are a precondition for happiness and that offer material for imagining a better world.[52] The Cabaret School is part of such a critical tradition. Rather than offering slumming narratives or spectacular displays that would approach Harlem's nightlife as terrain to be discovered and explored—which is how most critics understood it—the Cabaret School takes up the many ways that nightlife subjects produce worlds through their everynight practices, spaces, and relationships.

Not only is the everynight life of the Harlem Renaissance opposed to the phantasmatic body constructed by primitivism, it is also at odds with the bodily abstraction longed for by the bourgeois individualism of the black middle class. What we find in Harlem's cabaret is not the uplift body—the body of proper sexual expenditure, middle-class comportment, and unviolated surfaces—nor the primitive body—the body that exists within the gaze of white spectatorial privilege and violence, the body of sexual excess, racial parody, and appropriable identity. We find instead bodies and subjects that undertake the complex negotiations and contradictions of sexual and racial self-definition in American modernity. Whether in the form of bodies on a dance floor, individuals traversing the racial boundaries of neighborhoods, fingers over piano keys, or a voice up and down the scale, the movements of everynight life and the tenor of mundaneness challenges the reification of social relations, the positivism of social scientific knowledge, and the standardization of racial and sexual norms.

CRIMINAL INTIMACIES AND FUGITIVE SOCIALITY: A QUEER HARLEM RENAISSANCE

The Harlem Renaissance was, as Henry Louis Gates Jr. famously wrote, "surely as gay as it was black, not that it was exclusively either of these."[53] Because of the same-sex object choices of many of its principal participants, its highly visible sexual subcultures, and its legibility in historical archives and records, the Harlem Renaissance has attracted considerable scholarly attention since the tenuous recognition of gay and lesbian studies in the academy.[54] Historians have excavated 1920s Harlem as a space of gay and lesbian subcultural formation, tracing the extensive social networks of drag balls, "pansy parades," buffet flats, and rent parties that provided, as I discussed above, spectacles of racialized sexual deviance and knowledge production. Furthermore, many of Harlem's most prominent writers had same-sex relationships and explored same-sex desire in their literature. Wallace Thurman's *Infants of the Spring* (1932) and his collectively edited journal *Fire!!* (1926), Richard Bruce Nugent's "Smoke, Lilies and Jade" (1926) and other writings, Angelina Weld Grimké's "The Closing Door" (1919) and posthumously published poems, Nella Larsen's *Quicksand* (1928) and *Passing* (1929), Countee Cullen's sonnets, and James Weldon Johnson's *Autobiography of an Ex-Colored Man* (1912; reprinted 1927) can all be seen to provide insights into the formation of non-normative sexual subjectivity. These sexually non-normative social and literary practices of the Renaissance typically have been understood within narratives of sexual recognition, visibility, and struggle. Historians and literary scholars have identified writers and performers who had homosexual contacts, deciphered gay and lesbian subcultural and subtextual codes, and established canons of black gay and lesbian literature. Cultural and performative spaces of sexual dissidence have been placed within easily identifiable and identitarian spaces and located within a developmental narrative of sexual history.

Just as the Cabaret School used performance to critique uplift's normalizing logics, I seek throughout *The Scene of Harlem Cabaret* to broaden what has become an increasingly narrow, increasingly normative understanding of the gay and lesbian Harlem Renaissance. While the cataloging of same-sex object choices, the deciphering of hidden codes of homosexuality, and the recovery of gay and lesbian social spaces has been valuable in establishing the existence of gay and lesbian lifeworlds and literary traditions, it has also minimized or obscured the social and literary efforts undertaken by many Harlem Renaissance cultural workers to resist the ossification of sexual and racial identity and to oppose the representational politics that organized the Harlem Renaissance. Worse, the "gay and lesbian Harlem Renaissance" can end up reducing the complexities of queer associational life while stabilizing and normalizing the terms and concepts against which uplift ideology defined itself. Suffice it to say, to be gay did not necessarily make you against uplift. Countee Cullen and Alain Locke, for example, were not ideologically aligned with the work of the Cabaret School and had little difficulty adopting the privileges and double standards of middle-class gay male identities in the early twentieth century. The Cabaret School—as we will see in discussions of Langston Hughes, Claude McKay, and Lena Horne— was less interested in presenting a fixed or transparent sexual identity than it was in challenging the calcification of racial and sexual identities and the use of those identities in strategies of social order and control by dominant white society as well as by the ideologies of normative uplift. In this fashion, the writers and performers I discuss "queer the color line" by refocusing our attention on the many ways that racial and sexual non-normativity mutually shaped each other at this specific historical moment.[55]

To be sure, the queer and fugitive scenes I explore here are readily available to readers who are looking for histories of gay and lesbian subcultural spaces. Harlem's cabarets counted among their racialized and working-class audiences those who exclusively desired people of the same sex as themselves. Nightclubs, afterhours spaces, and illicit speakeasies provided places of public sociality for sexually deviant figures such as the "fairies," "pansies," "sheiks," "bull dikes," and "wolves" who populated New York's nightlife. Daphne Duval Harrison, Angela Davis, Eric Garber, and Hazel Carby, for example, have each identified references to gay, lesbian, and bisexual identities in many urban blues songs.[56] Such sonic inscriptions of sexual deviance and criminality shaped the intimate profile of the nightclub and turned cabarets and basement dives into provisional queer counterpublics. The examples are numerous. Take one, from the autobiography of Harlem pianist Willie "the Lion" Smith, that suggests how blues music and popular performance could elaborate a sexually non-normative world. Smith describes John Wilson's performance of an instrumental piano rag called "The Bull Diker's Dream" ("a tune dedicated to lesbians," he helpfully explains). The tune was well received by patrons in the cabaret, though its performance necessitated some circumspection. It was only performed after hours, when the nightclub operated in violation of the city's laws and the boundaries between licit and illicit sexuality were less clearly drawn. Smith describes it as "one of those 'put out the lights and call the law' things and went over big just before dawn." [57]

In characterizing it as a "put out the lights and call the law thing," Smith describes a performance that is less an invitation toward visibility and community than it is one that inaugurates a moment that, in its criminality, would attempt to elude the laws intended literally and metaphorically to police boundaries, borders, and identities. Such performances may have been sites of an emergent gay and lesbian public visibility, articulation, and longing, but the possibilities of intimacy, sexuality, and libidinal exchange were not limited to the teleological direction of same-sex object choice. One of the many important contributions of George Chauncey's *Gay New York* (1994) has been the recognition that sexual subcultures of the early twentieth century did not strictly distinguish between "heterosexual" and "homosexual" identities marked by (the gender of one's) sexual object choice, but instead allowed for a range of sexual subjectivities, arrangements of masculinity and femininity, libidinal possibilities, and identificatory relationships. In Chauncey's finding, the epistemologies of (male) sexual practice were highly localized and contingent upon the class, racial, and ethnic demographics and traditions of Manhattan's neighborhoods. Accordingly, it is important to note that in Willie "the Lion" Smith's account, as in Bessie Smith's or Gladys Bentley's or Ma Rainey's performances of songs about homosexuality, the audiences were not always—nor even often—recognizable as a "gay and lesbian" audience. It is, furthermore, a mistake to think of a homosexual underworld, especially in the late nineteenth and early twentieth centuries, as segregated and isolated from an extensive heterosexual underworld. Rather, as Jonathan Ned Katz suggests, the homosexual underworld overlapped with the heterosexual underworld, "both mirroring and exaggerating its details."[58]

So how do we understand the performative address of a number such as "The Bull Diker's Dream"? In answering this question, we would not want to foreclose the range of possible effects and enactments such a performance might occasion. Such performances index the possibility of residual and emergent identifications, cross-identifications, disidentifications, and transient and provisional identifications that might exceed official—and even vernacular—taxonomies of sexual identity. In expanding the "boundaries of normalcy," in Chauncey's phrase, such performances not only shaped the emergence of a modern gay and lesbian community, but also more broadly created a space where the possibilities of momentarily close contact, psychic and physical intimacy, and affective exchange could occur.[59]

A queer Harlem Renaissance is not opposed to a gay and lesbian Harlem Renaissance, but exists in a productive relationship to it. While I am interested in Harlem nightlife's role in an emergent gay and lesbian subculture and its connection to the history and geography of gay and lesbian worlds, I am also interested in those subjectivities and experiences that do not neatly align with easy sexual identifications. Not to assume in advance whether a space or a crowd or a spectator is "gay or lesbian" or "straight" is to avoid what Eve Sedgwick warns is the risk of "reinforcing a dangerous consensus of knowingness about the genuinely *un*known."[60] It is to look at how these terms, while increasingly fixed by social scientific and popular discourse, failed to work as stable or exhaustive descriptors of the lived experiences in Harlem's everynight life. As Sedgwick suggests, such a project as the one I undertake here is less a matter of choosing between minoritizing or universalizing approaches to sexual subjectivity than it is one of investigating the "performative effects of the self-contradictory discursive field of force created by their overlap." [61] It is, in other words, to follow through on the logic of the second half of Gates's well-known assessment: the Harlem Renaissance "was surely as gay as it was black, not that it was exclusively either of these." In offering a Harlem Renaissance not containable by finite identity categories or exclusive characterizations, Gates invites us to consider the range of racial and sexual subjectivities that are at play in Harlem's cabarets. To queer the Harlem Renaissance, then, is to recognize the social and literary places where lines of sexual and racial identifications might be frustrated or undone and new social and psychic alignments made possible; spaces and practices that exceed and expand identity, rather than contract it. To queer the Harlem Renaissance, in other words, is to put out the lights and call the law.

Thus this book privileges a notion of public intimacy, rather than the related notions of sexual orientation or sexual identity, as it traces discursive and nondiscursive practices that shaped sexual subjectivity in early-twentieth-century America. The intimacy I privilege does not refer to feelings of belonging or intersubjectivity based on teleology, commitment, permanence, longevity, functionalism, or family. Rather, I refer to the contingent, provisional, and public contacts that Lauren Berlant and Michael Warner call "criminal intimacies." Criminal intimacies are relations and relational narratives that are not legible or recognized as valid by dominant discourses and social institutions. Such relations "bear no necessary relation to domestic space, to kinship, to the couple form, to property, or to the nation." [62] The cabaret is one place where these criminal, public intimacies were invented and elaborated as a collaboration between spectators and performers. They offer a horizon of possibility for social and sexual contacts that were transient, contingent, non-normative, and emergent. This is a public intimacy not defined by two coherent selves coming together or the sharing of discrete subjectivities, but an intimacy that forms subjectivity in its articulation. Such intimacies may be one precondition for a gay and lesbian subculture, but they are not coterminous with it. Criminal intimacies momentarily—and sometimes more enduringly—exceed or elude sexual categorization. This is, to be clear, not an intimacy won on the cheap, but one labored into existence against often daunting and defeating forces: they are difficult to sustain or document under the weight of normative sexual hegemony, and the institutions and practices that foster them are themselves often very fragile and susceptible to repressive acts.

The queer work of the Cabaret School compels us to ground our analysis not in the bedrooms or private lives of prominent Harlem Renaissance figures but in the public enactments of intimacy as an alternative to the emergence of a privatized sexual identity informed by white-racialized middle-class norms. The historical cabaret was a form and content that—in ways not always predictable; often in spite of itself—brought bodies, sounds, and histories together in ways that disorganized and reorganized desires, selves, time, and space. Cabaret performers, cabaret historians, and cabaret goers uniformly employ a vocabulary of intimacy to describe the style and structure of the cabaret. While a number of prominent and well-funded nightclubs manufactured a commercialized intimacy through carefully choreographed performances and the maintenance of prescribed social codes, hundreds of less remarkable nightlife spaces produced opportunities for public contact and intimacy that expanded social possibilities (and even in the most sanitized and staged cabarets, such opportunities often flourished in the gaps between prescribed and actual social practices). As I examine more closely in chapter 1, this intimacy was produced through spatial, social, historical, and performance practices. The elimination of the fourth wall and close proximity of the performers to the audience; the social interaction among the patrons before, after, and even during the show; the informality of the performance and the social codes governing the spectators (which, though informal, may still be highly choreographed); the spatial arrangements and architecture; the redirection of spectatorial sightlines; the late-night hours and consumption of food and alcohol—all work to create an effect of physical and psychic closeness and shared inwardness.

This intimacy, as Berlant and Warner's turn of the phrase suggests, is closely related to practices of literal and metaphorical criminality. The phrase "criminal intimacies" evokes the long history of the criminalization of homosexuality, the policing of minoritarian space, and the discursive maintenance of social pathology. Given these histories, we might also understand these criminal intimacies and their relationship to black nightlife performance within an oppositional rubric of fugitivity. Looking at historical studies of slavery, slave crime, and slave self-determination, for example, Fred Moten has argued that freedom was a fundamentally criminal concept. To be fully human, to be free, made the slave a criminal. (And, as Angela Davis and others have reminded us, such freedom included the liberty to choose which and how many sexual partners, if any, one might have.) This criminality is inextricably linked to ideas of publicness, intimacy, and sociality. Antebellum laws that prohibited and monitored the right of slaves to congregate and assemble criminalized black sociality for its potential for rebellion or to otherwise ameliorate the social death of slavery. Moten writes, "The definitional impossibility of a black public, on the one hand, and the fear of this impossible or unreadable black publicity, on the other, is at the heart not only of notions of black criminality but founds or constructs blackness — black social life—as criminality. To be black, to engage the ensemblic— necessarily social—performance of blackness, is to be criminal." It is this logic that made elite uplift ideology an inherently contradictory and self-deconstructing undertaking. Accordingly, Moten argues that black sociality and performance can only ever be understood in some sense as criminal precisely because it is always deeply and irrevocably tied to the notion of self-determination and freedom. Identifying the relationship between crime, rebellion, and self-determination, Moten suggests a new way of thinking about the relationship between "criminality and blackness, taking care to think criminality as, first and foremost, black sociality, social life, social organization." [63] Thus the criminal intimacy of Harlem's cabarets indexes histories of racial and sexual self-determination and self-fashioning.

"Intimacy," writes Lauren Berlant, "builds worlds." [64] But it can also tear down worlds and occasion violence. Cabaret performances were easily commodified and deployed in any number of disciplinary schemas—racial, gendered, and classed, to name only three. A primary concern of this book is to qualify the celebratory and utopic potential of the cabaret's public intimacy and intimate relations (a celebration and utopic impulse I believe in) with the ways in which this intimacy allowed for a multiplicity of psychic and physical violences. The history and dynamics of cabaret performance suggest that intimacy is also a precondition for many varieties of hostility, alienation, violation, and surveillance. Spaces like the Cotton Club, the segregated institution of black performance, remind us that intimacy, like sexuality, can be an effect of power relations, and that these relations are, as Foucault states, "matrices of transformations . . . subjected to constant modifications, continual shifts." [65] The carefully tread dialectic of hostility/ intimacy that shaped the racial and gender dynamics of segregated spectatorship is, moreover, intensified by the spectatorial relationship to live performance itself. One promise of live performance is that it might fail: the actor might forget her lines, a lighting cue might fail to execute, the performance might flop, the audience could turn. This is, in part, why people go. The relationship between the audience and the performer is structured not only by a sense of *communitas*, but also by antagonism; hostility is always present in its potentiality.

Many of the black artists and intellectuals who publicly advocated uplift were privately sympathetic to the Cabaret School's literary use of night-life performance and scenes of intimacy. As Bruce Kellner notes, however, many feared the danger "that white America might hear the wrong rhythm." [66] The rhythms of the Cabaret School and the performances and intimacies of everynight life were especially susceptible to being heard, seen, and read wrongly. The intimacy in the cabaret was not the ludic and carnivalesque free-for-all that slumming bohemians and primitivists may have seen—or, rather, invented—in their trips to the cabaret. We concede too much when such a gaze becomes the only way of understanding the complexities and contradictions of these scenes; their hasty dismissal or censure often threatens to throw out the baby with the bathtub gin. This is not to say that the writers and performers of the Cabaret School were above the temptation to exoticize or shock, or that they never romanticized the underworld or invested in metaphysical notions of racial, sexual, or social transcendence. These are critiques of Cabaret School writers that can be—and have been—made. Moreover, male writers were too frequently complicit in circumscribing and policing black women's sexual subjectivity, just as the historical cabaret, as Lewis Erenberg and Hazel Carby point out, was too often employed as a technology of gender control and a place for the refinement, rather than the disruption, of established social roles and hierarchies. [67] In acknowledging the relationship between intimacy and hostility—and the often indistinguishable line between them—we are better able to see how the Cabaret School negotiated the sexual and racial possibilities of the cabaret with its racial, gendered, and classed violences. As we will see throughout this book, the negotiation of the leisure industry does not only include the manufacture of pleasure for thrill seekers, but also, and more importantly, includes the creation of everynight networks of support and social nourishment that function outside the purview of normative social structures; in other words, the laboring into existence of queer worlds and worlds of racial amelioration through performance.

THE HARLEM RENAISSANCE AND THE POLITICS OF REPRESENTATION

To recognize the rhetorical and cultural critique of the Cabaret School, it is necessary to distinguish between two Harlem Renaissances: the historical Harlem Renaissance, the creative, political, cultural production and mode of feeling that took Harlem as its symbolic if not literal home, and the "Harlem

Renaissance," the literary institution, ideological signifier, and technology of normalization that, as a self-conscious project of racial publicity, sought to counter the overwhelming saturation of stereotypical images of African Americans in popular consciousness with positive and "proper" representations in art and literature.[68] The former was the more broad manifestation of what Houston Baker Jr. calls black renaissancism: "a resonantly and continuously productive set of tactics, strategies, and syllables that takes form at the turn of the century and extends to our own day." [69] The latter was a more focused application of one specific strategy—that of racial uplift and the politics of representation—to respond to the institutions and ideologies of white supremacy. As a literary formation, the "Harlem Renaissance" sought to channel the energies of this black renaissancism to influence and alter the image of blackness in the public sphere by demonstrating the high cultural attainments of black art. The relationship between these two senses of the Harlem Renaissance, and the way they come together and move apart from each other, produced a number of contradictions and contests over the meaning of black cultural production in the 1920s, particularly as Talented Tenth uplift elites were concerned with how a general black expressive culture was represented.

In taking up the queer intimacies of the cabaret's everynight life, the Cabaret School necessarily contested the Harlem Renaissance's politics of representation. Against the cultural logic of white supremacy and the specular legacy of the minstrel stage, the architects of the Harlem Renaissance sought to alter the way blackness and black life were presented in the public sphere through more "truthful" depictions in art, literature, and culture. Such cultural work undertook to counter stereotypical or derogatory images with more positive and accurate ones—a cultural strategy David Levering Lewis dubbed "civil rights by copyright." [70] This cultural politics informed many of the questions and debates that shaped the Harlem Renaissance: What are the obligations of literary and artistic depiction? What images are representative of blackness and black life? How would blackness be reproduced? Who is authorized to speak for black experience? The response of Renaissance leaders to such questions was a vigilant cultivation of verisimilitude, proportion, and positive and affirmative narratives: a cultural politics of representation.[71]

From the perspective of the politics of representation, the various works of the Cabaret School were a setback that impeded cultural uplift and sensationalized the lowest of the race. Literary critics during and immediately after the Harlem Renaissance sought to incorporate the Cabaret School into the parameters of the Harlem Renaissance by interpreting and managing them through the frame of literary realism. Suggesting that artists like McKay, Hughes, Fisher, and Hurston were simply depicting what they saw, literary scholars like Benjamin Brawley and Sterling Brown referred to them collectively as the "new realists" or "urban realists." This hermeneutic worked to neutralize and discipline these insurgent writers. After positing that the Cabaret School is attempting realistically to depict the experiences of the "submerged tenth," it is easy to conclude that these representations fail to represent the race adequately. Thus, Brawley decided by 1940 that the Cabaret School's realism exhibited "a preference for the sordid, unpleasant, or forbidden themes," and betrayed "a certain blatant quality, an obvious striving for effect, that frequently gave an impression of artificiality." [72] Brown similarly judged in 1937 that, as realists, they ultimately failed. Looking "for the true life of a Negro community in cabarets, most often run by white managers for white thrill-seekers," he weighed, "is like looking for the truth of slavery in the off-time banjo-plunking and capers before the big house." [73] Once framed as realist—as offering, in other words, access to what the unruly and disruptive scenes of the submerged tenth and working-class life are "really like"—such scenes work like sociological narratives to make Harlem's everynight life knowable, containable, and controllable. [74] These critical assessments helped pave the way for the narrative of literary history that finds the Harlem Renaissance superseded by the social realism of the late 1930s and 1940s as a more accurate and effective political intervention in African American literature. [75] Such assessments also shape subsequent appraisals that conclude that the Harlem Renaissance capitulated too much to the cabaret craze of the 1920s and the cult of primitivism.

In the pages that follow, however, I show that the Cabaret School should be seen within an entirely different framework of cultural politics than the politics of representation. By and large, the Cabaret School was not all that interested in literary realism. It instead actively worked to undermine the politics of representation that governed the Harlem Renaissance. Indeed, the Cabaret School substantiates literary critic Robert Bone's later assessment that "realism, however useful as a corrective to the white man's stereotypes, cannot finally cope with the ambiguities of Negro life." [76] As we will see in chapter 2, even in otherwise realist works like Larsen's *Quicksand*, Hurston's autobiographical "How It Feels to Be Colored Me," and Thurman's *The Blacker the Berry*, the scene of the cabaret is used to critique the very politics of representation that the Harlem Renaissance demanded.

Rather than engaging with the politics of representation, the Cabaret School should be seen as enacting a politics of transfiguration that operates beyond the terms of representational politics, seeking the expression of something like "truth" in an altogether different mode of inscription. Paul Gilroy defines the politics of transfiguration as

> the emergence of qualitatively new desires, social relations, and modes of association within the racial community of interpretation *and* between that group and its erstwhile oppressors. . . . This politics exists on a lower frequency, where it is played, danced, and acted as well as sung and sung about, because words, even words stretched by melisma and supplemented or mutated by the screams which still index the conspicuous power of the slave sublime, will never be enough to communicate its unsayable claims to truth.[77]

For Gilroy, such a transfigurative politics of black music and performance is often obscured, flattened, or displaced by acts of writing and textuality that cannot account for the total dramaturgy of blackness and black performance.[78] Organized by black musical production, Harlem's cabaret and its role as a potential space for a politics of transfiguration "provides a model of performance which can supplement and partially displace concern with textuality."[79] As writers and performers attuned to the criminal intimacies, fugitive sociality, and transfigural performances of Harlem's nightclubs, the Cabaret School challenged the simple referentiality of mimetic realism by highlighting the failure of mimetic representation to fix the ineffable intimacies, gestures, and performances of the cabaret and everynight life. The performative transgressions of the Cabaret School, in other words, sought to expand performance possibilities through the printed page and enact a transfigurative politics by way of and in excess of the forms and conventions of the literary. Endeavoring "to repeat the unrepeatable, to present the unpresentable," this politics brings into being new vocabularies and vantage points from which to undo and reimagine dominant models of sexuality and racial difference and provisionally to materialize and symbolize new times and places.[80] These new ways of seeing, feeling, and being were produced in and through nightlife's intimate enactments and literatures. Said Langston Hughes: "It's the way people look at things, not what they look at, that needs to be changed."[81]

Seen within the politics of transfiguration, the symbolic, social, and—yes—political interest of so many writers in Harlem's cabaret becomes a much richer subject than has been previously explored. Cabaret performance is uniquely qualified to bring such queer times and places into being. Not ordered by the logics of realism or the codes of bourgeois theater, cabaret is a nonrepresentational, nonmatrixed performance. By nonmatrixed performance, I refer to Michael Kirby's distinction between traditional theater, "where the performer always functions within (and creates) a matrix of time, place, and character," and performances where these time-place-character matrices "are neither acted nor imposed by the context," but are continuous with the performance situation. That is, the musician or performer, representing nothing other than him or herself, occupies the same time and place as the audience.[82] Kirby notes that this distinction "between matrixed and nonmatrixed performance becomes blurred in nightclubs," on those occasions when the performer might temporarily take on a fictional character in a sketch while still remaining within the time and space of the cabaret.[83] In these cases, such a matrix is "weak": unlike most dramatic theater, the impermanence and transience of a weak performance matrix prohibits the audience from fully, if at all, suspending disbelief and entering into a fictional narrative. Whether the weakly matrixed revues of *Hot Chocolates* at Connie's Inn and the Cotton Club *Parades*, or the nonmatrixed performances of Willie "the Lion" Smith playing at Pod's and Jerry's at dawn and Gladys Bentley wickedly corrupting popular songs at the Clam House, cabaret performance does not represent the world but addresses it in its local environment, incorporates the audience into its fold, and organizes social arrangements. The intimacy of such an address, as we will see, could be used as a technology of racism and sexism, but also (and sometimes at the same time) as a technology of racial and sexual self-invention. By seeing the project of the Cabaret School within the cultural politics of transfiguration, rather than in the claims to verisimilitude or authenticity of realist representation, we will see how these cultural workers responded to the contradictions of representational politics by imagining an alternative to African American literature and performance as a narrowly delimited site of either positive or negative images.

A QUEER KIND OF FORMALISM

Another way of posing the question this book asks is: Where does nightlife go when the sun comes up? Memory, of course, both individual and collective, is one key place. Nightlife performances, moreover, are not only remembered but also documented and continued beyond themselves. The rise of recording technologies like the gramophone, the nickelodeon, photographic technologies, and early motion pictures propelled nightlife sounds and sights into new media. Just as an emergent race record industry multiplied the possibilities of black sonic performance, we can find traces of nightlife in literary recordings—in autobiographies, novels, poems, stories, and song lyrics. The texts I have in mind offer not a simple or "realistic" representation of the cabaret, but another mode of performing the cabaret, an inking of the cabaret into the pages of journals, little magazines, and published volumes.[84]

Historically, the cabaret has always produced a print culture that existed in a supplemental relationship to its performances. Paris's Chat Noir, widely held to be the first avant-garde *cabaret artistique,* began publishing its own weekly magazine, *Le Chat Noir,* shortly after it opened. It contained literary compositions by contemporary writers, articles about the activities of Montmartre, stories about the cabaret itself, poems, drawings, and political caricatures. *Le Chat Noir* structurally and thematically echoed the political program that made up an evening of performance at the Chat Noir.[85] The sound poem performances and general aesthetic disruptions of dada and the Cabaret Voltaire similarly circulated in print form and in journals. (In an inversion of this tradition of the literary cabaret, the satirical Berlin magazine *Simplicissimus* inspired a cabaret after it.) The work of the Cabaret School, as we will see, is in the tradition of Montmartre's *Le Chat Noir* and Berlin's *Simplicissimus:* publications that seek to continue and expand the structure and style of Harlem cabaret culture in tone, subject matter, and style. As bound volumes and as stories and poems circulated in periodicals and journals, the work of the Cabaret School—like Ellington's Cotton Club broadcasts—created a public, an imagined community of the cabaret that produced what Benedict Anderson characterizes as a "deep, horizontal comradeship."[86]

By looking to the referential excess of this literature—to its performance—*The Scene of Harlem Cabaret* approaches Harlem cabaret and its literature both historically and formally. That is, it looks to both theatrical and literary form as well as historical context to demonstrate the queer possibilities of Harlem's nightlife. Just as the cabaret offers a formal arrangement and mode of address that places the spectators and the performer in an intimate relationship with each other, the Cabaret School uses queer manipulations of form that rupture the smooth surface of the text and think outside the confines of normative social relations and normative literary form. To put this another way, the affinities that organize the Cabaret School are legible not only by a thematic resistance to the normalizing logics of uplift in the content of their work, but also by a formal experimentation with recording and enacting the intimacy of the cabaret in the literary public sphere.

Thus, critics found not only the content of the Cabaret School disagreeable, but the formal construction of the work as well, condemning "alleged poems in which many lines consisted of one word each, and rhythm, cadence and idea were conspicuous by their absence," as Hubert Harrison charged in 1927. Or, as Benjamin Brawley lamented more succinctly in 1940, the Cabaret School "attacked the very foundations of grammar." And, as even Countee Cullen said of one of Langston Hughes's more experimental verses, "it ought never to have been done." [87] These formal insurrections are part and parcel of the queer social interventions the Cabaret School undertook. Thus, in approaching the literary aspects of Cabaret School, I attend to what literature can do, what its internal logics provide for, how those logics can be queered and racialized, and how they can in turn reflect and expand black and queer life. Attending to form in this way can help, as Hortense Spillers suggests, to explore properly "the relationship between dynamic social movement and the narratives that locate it." [88] The queer formal manipulations of the Cabaret School demand that we listen, like Ellington's radio audiences, to the sounds and sociality that African American modernism indexes. [89] They also call for us not only to recognize but also to take seriously the social, sexual, and racial possibilities that the aesthetic can enact and materialize. Such a conceptualization of the aesthetic, it is important to remember, was ultimately the project of the Harlem Renaissance itself.

Accordingly, I read the work of the Cabaret School not only as historical documents that can tell us about the mediation of criminal intimacies and fugitive sociality, but also and primarily as aesthetic performances and enactments of those intimacies and sociality. When we consider not only literary form but also theatrical form—specifically, the formal structure and style of the cabaret—form necessarily becomes a social concern. A far cry from the formalism of the New Critics, who approached the text as a unified and autotelic work of art with an autonomous meaning outside of history or politics, the queer kind of formalism I advocate in these pages looks to the ways that literary and theatrical form, questions of genre, syntactical manipulations, and modes of address might contribute to the deformation of literary structures of respectability and structures of literary respectability, confound narratives of racial and sexual uplift, disrupt the fixed and coherent subject of bourgeois realism, and materialize intimate feelings; in other words, ways the Cabaret School queers form itself. In the following chapters, for example, we will see how Langston Hughes manipulates poetic closure in order to counteract the legislative closure of cabarets, cafés, and nightclubs; how Claude McKay deformed the structure of the novel in order to unmap the sociological constructions of the underworld and syntactically effect the dynamic practices of everynight life; and how Lena Horne makes use of the theatrical form of the cabaret in order to turn away from dominant sexual narratives and withhold her sexual subjectivity from her audience in the fraught scene of segregated nightlife performance.

"WHEN THE LITTLE DAWN WAS GREY"

The snip of verse from which I take the title of this section has a rich citational history, one that helps illustrate the multiple iterations and reinscriptions of cabaret performance in the Harlem Renaissance, its role in the enforcement of uplift ideologies, and its location as a space of non-normative sexual ethics and social critique. The line concludes Langston Hughes's poem, "Cabaret," first published in 1923 in the *Crisis*, under the editorship of W. E. B. Du Bois.

> Does a jazz-band ever sob?
> They say a jazz-band's gay.
> Yet as the vulgar dancers whirled
> And the wan night wore away.
> One said she heard the jazz-band sob
> When the little dawn was grey.[90]

The poem was subsequently reprinted in 1925 in *Vanity Fair*, encouraged by the sponsorship of Carl Van Vechten, the white novelist, patron, homosexual, and friend of Hughes. Between the *Crisis* and *Vanity Fair*, the poem, like much of Hughes's writing in the twenties, reached a wide audience throughout both black urban America and fashionable white society. The poem was then included in Hughes's first collection of verse, *The Weary Blues*, published in 1926. Many of the poems in *The Weary Blues* were inspired by Harlem's nightlife and black performance (I consider these poems in detail in chapter 3), and provoked from critics qualified praise and deep ambivalence over his emphasis on performance, dancing, jazz, and nightlife.

Hughes's "Cabaret" made a second appearance in the *Crisis* in 1926, but this time it was cited by Du Bois in a review of Carl Van Vechten's novel, *Nigger Heaven* (1926). Together with his articles on the blues and black theater in *Vanity Fair*, Van Vechten's novel helped to structure the image of Harlem's cabarets in the 1920s and strengthen the connection between sexuality, criminality, and black performance. Du Bois denounced it, noting the ways that the novel used the cabaret metonymically to represent all of Harlem as fundamental otherness. He wrote that for Van Vechten, "the black cabaret *is* Harlem; around it all his characters gravitate. Here is their stage of action." Du Bois invoked Hughes's poem as a marker against which to measure Van Vechten's primitivist and fetishistic depictions of black performance and sociality:

> Both Langston Hughes and Carl Van Vechten know Harlem cabarets; but it is Hughes who whispers:
>
>> One said he heard the jazz band sob
>> When the little dawn was grey.
>
> Van Vechten never heard a sob in a cabaret. All he hears is noise and brawling.[91]

Du Bois uses Hughes's subtle representation of the psychic complexity of the cabaret to reject what he saw as the vulgarity, stereotyping, and spectacle pervading Van Vechten's cabarets. Inexplicably, in Du Bois's citation, the pronoun of the one who hears the jazz band sob is switched from feminine to masculine. It is a revealing error. As we will see, even while the urban cabaret was often a location for women blues singers to perform a narrative of sexual self-determination, the scene of Harlem cabaret was also often used to circumscribe women's social agency; for many women of color, it was also a scene of violence and limitation.

Within the citational history of this verse, we see the iteration, reinscription, and misquotation that marks the Cabaret School's textual performances. The concerns of the chapters that follow lie in the movements suggested by Hughes's "Cabaret"—between black and white media, between authenticity and stereotype, between evidence and rumor, between insider and outsider, between whisper and brawl, between sorrow and possibility. Chapter 1 undertakes to describe the cabaret and its relations of performance, a task not as simple as it might sound at first. In doing so, I map the historical relationship between black performance and the cabaret tradition to show how black cabaret in the United States emerges at the intersection of European and American traditions of cabaret performance. I then supplement this performance history with an account of how the theatrical form of cabaret—including its mode of address, architecture and spatial practices, manipulation of sightlines, and choreographic rearrangements—is productive of public intimacy and intimate formations that provide the affective framework for the Cabaret School's critique of normative uplift and possibilities for queer-of-color world making.

In the second chapter, I look more specifically at the repetition and circulation of the scene of the cabaret in the Harlem Renaissance. After 1926, at the height of the Negro vogue, two competing models of Harlem cabaret emerged in the popular landscape of Harlem's nightlife: segregated cabarets that staged scenes of blackness for the pleasure and consumption of white audiences, and "black cabarets" that were locations of performance, recreation, and sociality for primarily black patrons. This binary taxonomy, I argue, while necessary to the negotiation of Harlem's nightlife for black performers, ultimately substantiated the racial ideologies of the 1920s primitivist vogue, on the one hand, and the class-based politics of respectability of the Harlem Renaissance elite, on the other. Aware of such traps, the constellation of Cabaret School performers and writers I look at in this chapter—Duke Ellington, Ethel Waters, Lena Horne, Zora Neale Hurston, Nella Larsen, and Wallace Thurman—deconstructed such a framework and despectacularized the scene of Harlem cabaret, deploying it as a location for racial, sexual, and class critique.

The next three chapters look closely at specific texts and performances of the Cabaret School: Langston Hughes's poetry in *The Weary Blues* (1926) and *Fine Clothes to the Jew* (1927), Claude McKay's novel *Home to Harlem* (1928), and Lena Horne's performances on the segregated cabaret stage in the 1930s and 1940s. Chapter 3 examines a particular temporal moment that organizes nightlife performance: closing time. Closing time refers to the legislated hour by which nightclubs and bars must stop serving and close their doors. The enforcement of closing time produces the afterhours club, a space that unfolds in defiance of municipal and moral law, as nightlife subjects seek to continue the night beyond its regulation by the city. To elaborate this understanding of nightlife temporality, I turn to Hughes's Harlem Renaissance poetry collections. These volumes earned him both recognition and disapprobation for his depictions of Harlem's nightlife performances and made him the most prominent member of the Cabaret School. Locating his poetry in the legal and subcultural context of closing time, I show how Hughes uses this fugitive interruption into the normative temporal order to critique the clocks of bourgeois life narrative, capitalist productivity, and historical teleology. I further argue that Hughes developed formal and thematic strategies to record this elusive queer time. His lyric archive of afterhours provides counterevidence to official repositories of knowledge and gestures toward Hughes's larger relationship to the rhythms and temporalities of African American and sexual modernity.

While the previous discussion of Hughes allows us to consider the temporal profile of the cabaret and its reorganization of respectable time, chapter 4 looks to the spatial mapping and unmapping of Harlem's everynight life. Revisiting the infamous public dispute between Du Bois and McKay over McKay's novel, *Home to Harlem,* this chapter shows how the Cabaret School contested the spatial logic of uplift and the imposition of realist hermeneutics on black modernist texts. McKay's depictions of Harlem's underworld provoked many impassioned denunciations from uplift advocates, including Du Bois's assessment that the novel "for the most part nauseates me, and after the dirtier parts of its filth I feel distinctly like taking a bath."[92] Against common interpretations of the novel that see it as providing a spectacle of black exoticism and sexual excess, I argue that the novel incorporates the practices of Harlem's everynight life—specifically the practices of strolling and social dance—to undermine sociological assumptions and practices that construct Harlem nightlife as a space of social disorder. Reading *Home to Harlem* against uplift sociology, I show that McKay strategically stages the failure of realist representation to depict Harlem's everynight life, offering instead an anticartography that works not by accurate representation but by affective resonance. In the end, we also find that *Home to Harlem* exposes some of Du Bois's own contradictions and paradoxes; unlikely as it would seem, Du Bois affirmatively points to the aspects of *Home to Harlem* that most incisively shape its contribution to both a black and queer literature.

Lena Horne might seem at first to be an unlikely figure to link to the Cabaret School. Born to one of Brooklyn's most respected families, she came from a lineage firmly ensconced in traditions of racial uplift. Yet as I argue in chapter 5, the middle-class nightclub singer used the intimacy of the cabaret to highlight her alienation from both her white audience and the black majority during her career on the segregated cabaret circuit in the 1930s and 1940s, and reminds us that the Cabaret School was most often a middle-class autocritique. Some criticized Horne as a distant and cold performer who, against the expectations of black women performers at the time, resisted an affective connection with her audiences. Approaching her performance of aloofness—communicated and enacted both on film and in live cabaret performance—as an acute response to the interracial intimacy produced by performance across the color line, I argue that Horne's withholding exploited the conventions of the cabaret to resist the circumscribed roles available to black women performers on the Jim Crow stage and elaborate a gendered subjectivity that stood outside the expectations of white spectatorship and the norms of uplift respectability. In her descriptions of early nightclub performances, she embraces what I term an "unperforming of the self" through the cultivation of an impersonal intimacy that deferred a fixed subjectivity and frustrated the racial expectations of her audiences. Horne's aloofness illuminates a historically vexed connection between public intimacy and hostility to suggest that as much as intimacy could be a resource for individual and collective transformation, it was also often the precondition for varieties of hostility, alienation, violation, and surveillance.

In conclusion, I examine how the legacy of Harlem cabaret is taken up in avant-garde gay and lesbian performance, film, and literature of today. Tracing the historical and theoretical implications of the previous chapters, I consider a number of cultural enactments that continue the project of Harlem's Cabaret School in contemporary critiques of racial and sexual normativity. Building on Jean-Paul Sartre's theory of art and imagination, I suggest that these contemporary works in fact *irrealize* a queer Harlem Renaissance. That is, rather than seeking to historically locate writers and performers who had homosexual contacts, decipher gay and lesbian subcultural and subtextual codes, or establish canons of black gay and lesbian literature, these cultural works draw from a historical referent to imagine a queer Harlem Renaissance that is made anew through cultural and critical work, extending the Cabaret School into the present and the future.

As these chapters show, writers and performers of the Harlem Renaissance used the cabaret to imagine and enact alternative possibilities for racial, sexual, and socioeconomic subjectivities that resisted the normalizing imperatives of uplift ideology. The centrality of performance and its expansive possibilities to the Harlem Renaissance was something that Langston Hughes always recognized.[93] In "The Negro Artist and the Racial Mountain" (1926)—which could be read as a manifesto for the Cabaret School— he wrote:

> Let the blare of Negro jazz bands and the bellowing voice of Bessie Smith singing Blues penetrate the closed ears of the colored near-intellectual until they listen and perhaps understand. Let Paul Robeson singing "Water Boy" and Rudolph Fisher writing about the streets of Harlem, and Jean Toomer holding the heart of Georgia in his hands, and Aaron Douglas drawing strange black fantasies cause the smug Negro middle class to turn from their white, respectable, ordinary books and papers and catch a glimmer of their own beauty.[94]

Hughes's famous polemic foregrounds black performance as the site of the Harlem Renaissance. Calling for recognition of performers like Smith and Robeson, as well as for recognition of the performative lyricism of Toomer's novel *Cane,* Fisher's valuation of the practices of everyday life, and the dynamic movement of Douglas's shimmering spheres and lines, Hughes effects his own transfiguration of the Harlem Renaissance, which he insists is more expansive than what the "smug Negro middle class" guardians of uplift envisioned in "white, respectable, ordinary books and papers." Like Duke Ellington's sound, black performance in the Harlem Renaissance disorganizes—or, better, anorganizes—the exclusionary logics and spaces of racial and sexual respectability. By turning to the culture and performances of the cabaret and their deployment in literature, we can hear what Houston Baker Jr., employing a theatrical metaphor, called the "sotto voce urgings of the Harlem 1920s," which, it turns out, were not so sotto after all.[95]

——— ✳ ———

CHAPTER ONE

American Cabaret Performance and the Production of Intimacy

LET'S BEGIN with two cabaret scenes:

In his autobiography, Hollywood mogul and former vaudeville impresario Jesse Lasky recounts how he "introduced" cabaret performance to the United States in 1911. He had been dazzled by the opulent cabarets and dance halls he attended on trips to Europe and aspired to bring such entertainment to an American public. Lasky's entrepreneurial undertaking, with his partner Henry Harris, sought to offer "revues comparable to the Ziegfeld Follies, in combination with a cuisine in the class of Delmonico's," the renowned institution of nineteenth-century upper-class dining.[1] He imagined that successful productions at his cabaret would tour on the vaudeville circuits, further increasing revenues for investors. Lasky commissioned a Broadway theater, which he christened the Folies Bergère after the lavish Parisian music hall, and imported acts from Paris, Berlin, and London to supplement local talent. The event was, according to Lasky, a wholly novel phenomenon:

> Everything about the Folies Bergère was unheard of in New York, including the prices! It had a champagne bar, a balcony promenade, the first midnight performance in this country, at which an expanding stage slid out over the orchestra pit and put the performers on handshaking intimacy with the first row patrons. Such now-commonplace service items as glass-topped tables with doilies under the plates, silent flag signals on silver ash trays to call waiters without disturbing performers or other diners, and sealed programs for sale were so novel in 1911 as to be conversation pieces.

Lasky recalls, "Even the word *cabaret* was so strange that we felt obliged to specify in advertisements that it was 'pronounced cabaray.'"[2] The fact that the Théâtre des Folies-Bergère in Paris was not what anybody considered a cabaret, but a music hall, hardly seems to have concerned Lasky; he was not one to let such genre rules get in the way of making a profit.[3] Alas, though met with widespread excitement, the Folies proved too expensive to maintain. It closed after five months, but it heralded, so the story goes, a new and modern era in New York's nightlife.

Lasky's tale contains many elements that have shaped the historical understanding of American cabaret performance: a tangential, even strictly nominal, relationship to European cabaret; an image of middle-class sophistication and consumerism; the cultivation of intimacy between performers and spectators; an emphasis on architecture and spatial practices as a way of characterizing the cabaret; performances that borrowed from the styles of vaudeville, music halls, and other popular amusements; and an excited self-consciousness about the new and modern character of the night. American cabaret was thus imagined as an institution of cosmopolitanism, a place, as Lasky described the Folies Bergère, "more Parisian than Paris."[4]

Alongside Lasky's description, I want to juxtapose another scene of cabaret performance, this one from the autobiography of Langston Hughes. Hughes worked for several months in 1924 as a dishwasher, waiter, and cook at Le Grand Duc, a nightclub in the Montmartre district of Paris, the bohemian neighborhood that is credited with cultivating in the 1880s the first European cabarets. While Hughes worked at the Grand Duc, it became a center for black American musicians in Paris to gather after performing elsewhere, a place to eat, drink (always, Hughes noted, at "professional rates"), and play some more after hours:

> When all the other clubs were closed, the best of the musicians and entertainers from various other smart places would often drop into the Grand Duc, and there'd be a jam session until seven or eight in the morning—only in 1924 they had no such name for it. They'd just get together and the music would be on. The cream of the Negro musicians then in France, like Cricket Smith on the trumpet, Louis Jones on the violin, Palmer Jones at the piano, Frank Withers on the clarinet, and Buddy Gilmore at the drums, would weave out music that would almost make your heart stand still at dawn in a Paris night club in the rue Pigalle, when most of the guests were gone and you were washing the last pots and pans in a two-by-four kitchen, with the fire in the range dying and the one window letting in soft light.[5]

In this passage, Hughes marks the zigzag movement of the cabaret back across the Atlantic from New York to Paris, a movement that brought black

American performance with it. Like Lasky, he is conscious of the newness and improvisation that structures the sociality of the cabaret, experiences, he notes, that did not even have a name yet (this question of naming will take on greater significance in the discussion below). And just as Lasky attempts to recreate what he takes to be a now-familiar scene as if we are visiting it for the first time, Hughes's memory seeks to conjure the feelings of a past experience as if it occurs in the present. Locating himself in the small kitchen, he suggests how such musical performances might transfigure and revalue otherwise exhausting acts of labor. The almost breathless momentum of his final run-on sentence relates the elements that align—sonic, spatial, temporal, social—in order for this experience to have the physical and psychic effect it has on Hughes. In an act of writerly intimacy, Hughes narrates this scene in the second person, inviting the reader into the space, rhetorically allowing "you" to be part of the in-crowd, one of the guests who remain when most of the guests are gone.

This chapter takes the chiasmus of these two anecdotes—the first of, but not in Paris; the second in, but not of Paris; both indelibly stamped, in different ways, American—to examine the problems and possibilities of intimacy posed by the cabaret during the Harlem Renaissance. Together, these autobiographical scenes point us toward some dimensions of public intimacy that are central to the history of the cabaret and were a key resource of Cabaret School critique in the Harlem Renaissance. My aim here is twofold: first, to outline a provisional understanding of cabaret performance that can begin to address the conventions of intimacy that have shaped its historical experience, and second, to deepen our understanding of the role that performance and public intimacy plays in black and queer cultural histories. As we saw in the introduction, forms of public intimacy have long provided a context for subjective and social possibilities foreclosed by the privatized relationships of home and work, creating, as Lauren Berlant proposes, types of attachment that "make persons public and collective and that make collective scenes intimate spaces."[6] If we understand intimacy not simply as an ideal to strive for but as an index of a variety of public relationships, feelings, and narratives that can be—and are—transformative in both positive and negative ways, we can better understand the constrictions and expansions of subjectivity that shape the forms of public intimacy produced in and through cabaret performance.[7]

Intimacy, as Harlem's history attests, is a kind of trespass: the intimacy-effects of the cabaret make conscious the boundaries between self and other as well as the conditions for their crossing. In thinking of intimacy in this way, I follow the literary critic Michael Cooke, who suggests that intimacy, rather than a private emotion or individualized affect, "takes the form of reaching, or being invited, out of the self and into an unguarded and uncircumscribable engagement with the world." Cooke identifies the search for this intimacy as the driving impetus of twentieth-century African American literature. As black writers increasingly exceeded the double consciousness, existential depletion, and material constraints of previous generations, he argues, the arc of this literature came to achieve a fuller expression of intimacy. The achievement of intimacy, Cooke argues, is "a process, an experiment in human modality, and it is laden with risk. Implicitly it takes away the protections, learned and instinctive, with which the personality routinely operates, and in return holds out as much prospect of exhaustion and rebuff and ridicule as it does an enhancement of the spirit and the terms of life. There need be no surprise, then, that intimacy should be risked most by those with the least to lose."[8] Intimacy, in other words, threatens (promises?) to undo the routines and routes, the familiar patterns and rote narratives, that organize psychic and social lives. For those already excluded from dominant narratives and normative systems of kinship, family, and social belonging, the rewards of such risks in forging public intimacies can be nothing less than a vital mode of existence. This is not a state-sanctioned, familially organized, or economically privatized intimacy, but an intimacy that Cooke defines more expansively as the "acceptance of depth along with openness of engagement."[9]

The everynight improvisations and provisional intimacies of Harlem nightlife invite us to see what Cooke calls the achievement of intimacy not only as literary teleology but also as performed enactments that bring people together and provide occasions for such expansions of selfhood. The history of American cabaret, that is, offers us an opportunity to consider the transitivity of intimacy, its hazards and its promises, the ease with which the play of looks becomes the play of encounter and, quite often, of contact. It also allows us to consider the central role of performance in maintaining intimate social formations. All performance, arguably, produces intimacy, whether a naturalist drama, a religious ritual, a stadium rock concert, or a sporting event. In presenting a focused event around which to direct our attention and organize a shared experience, performance turns a public into an audience with a common point of reference, even while the meaning of that shared experience may vary widely from spectator to spectator.

Such copresence is a necessary aspect of any theatrical event or live performance. Yet from the time of its emergence, the cabaret's shared experience was recognized as a more intimate mode than that of its theatrical cousins. The cabaret's double identity as a restaurant/bar and as a performance space called for highly specific codes of spectatorship and participation. For sociologist Erving Goffman, as we will further see below, the kind of copresence such as that occasioned by the cabaret "renders persons uniquely accessible, available, and subject to one another."[10] During the Harlem Renaissance, this copresence would prove to be a crucial resource for black and queer subjects. It offered alternatives to uplift narratives of sexual and racial individuality and enabled writers and performers to theorize new forms of subjecthood and social relations. Such availability and accessibility to one another made possible by participation in the cabaret, however, was not always transformative or critical of racial and sexual hegemonies; intimacy is just as likely to function as a means to maintain the status quo as it as a means to challenge it. But our queer histories are enriched when we train our senses on those moments in even dominant and normalizing performances when intimacy exceeds what is expected or comfortable, the criminal intimacies and fugitive socialities that even the most hegemonic of performances can occasion.

In this chapter my goal is deceptively straightforward: to describe the American cabaret, with an aim toward understanding its relationship to black performance practices in the first half of the twentieth century and its organization of intimate social formations. Historicizing and theorizing the kinds of performances and relationships that occur under the name *cabaret* will require sharpening some distinctions and blurring others; like intimacy itself, cabaret does not always mean what it says. Drawing on the methodological insights of theater and performance studies, my aim is to anatomize the conditions of cabaret's production of intimacy and examine what performance theorist Gay McAuley calls "the spatial condition itself."[11] The path of this chapter will veer away from the specificities of Harlem in the first part, only to return to the very local spaces, practices, and acts through which the Cabaret School would elaborate its critiques. I first sketch the transformations of the word *cabaret* as it appears in different times and places in the six decades between 1880 and 1940. This tour will take us from the bohemian streets of Paris to the jook joints of the Deep South before finally settling in Harlem, where it was rearticulated in a framework of black performance. Given this genealogical account, I then propose that to understand the social and performative effects of the cabaret, we should look not only to generic distinctions, sociohistorical context, and discursive formations that shape the cabaret, but also to the spatial practices and relations of performance that produce the cabaret as an intimate formation. It is precisely these felt experiences that would enable the Cabaret School to theorize and inhabit the cabaret as a place of collectivity and community, one that offered alternative structures of intimacy, relationality, and sociality to those advanced by the official spokespersons of uplift: its race men and race women, its sociologists and its preachers.

A PREHISTORY OF HARLEM CABARET:
BLACK PERFORMANCE AND THE CABARET TRADITION

Much has been written about night clubs. Their origin, their history, their methods. How, stemming from Bowery concert saloons, they progressed by steps to the cabaret and thence to the current product. Much indeed has been written, but still they remain a puzzle.

NIGHTLIFE: VANITY FAIR'S INTIMATE GUIDE TO NEW YORK
AFTER DARK (1931), A GUIDE FOR WHITE READERS

Many kinds of performance, often with little formal resemblance to each other, have appeared under the name *cabaret*, from avant-garde sound poems and shadow plays to vaudeville sketches and political parodies to French *chansons*, Cuban *sones*, and African American blues.[12] In an attempt to analytically untangle the array of performances that have shaped the cabaret tradition, I proceed here by methods both philological and genealogical, tracking both the word *cabaret* and the performances that appeared under its name as it traveled and changed over the modern era. This approach allows me to identify multiple, even conflicting, influences and sources that have shaped cabaret's history and cultural meaning without recourse to narratives of origin that would falsely privilege some traditions or exclude others.[13] While following these genealogical and philological transmutations highlights the differences and divergences in *cabaret*'s promiscuous use, it also reveals unlikely similarities and reverberations between performances that seem otherwise unconnected. By excavating the historicity of *cabaret*, we can see how the word accrued new meanings and new performances even as it carried in its morphology the residue of previous ones, expanding what theater historian Barbara Webb calls the "grammatical options with which we can articulate the always-incomplete contexts of African American performance and American performance" in the early twentieth century.[14] In the final analysis, it may turn out that *cabaret* will better describe a mode of performance and social possibility—a particular "style and structure," in the words of nightlife historian Lewis Erenberg—than it does the fixed and necessary conventions of "cabaret performance" as such.

Modern cabaret performance's official history begins with the Chat Noir in the Montmartre district of Paris in 1881. A loose literary club of poets and artists refashioned a bohemian tavern in the impoverished neighborhood as a meeting place where they would share their work through public readings and performances. The Chat Noir borrowed the word *cabaret,* which had been used since the seventeenth century to describe a small drinking house or tavern, often featuring informal performances. Distinguishing themselves as a *cabaret artistique,* the Chat Noir and subsequent imitators adapted minor forms of popular entertainment—popular songs, shadow plays, marionette shows, pantomimes, dances, and skits—and endowed them with an oppositional edge in modernist performances of political and social satire, cultural commentary, and aesthetic critique. As word of the exclusive cabaret spread around Europe, it soon drew not only artists and bohemians, but also members of the Paris establishment, the middle class, and the fashionable and cosmopolitan—those who were often the very targets of the performances' parodies.[15]

The Chat Noir established many of the conventions that would come to define *cabaret.* It combined the social setting of the café or tavern with the stage of popular amusements. The performance program eschewed a singular narrative, offering a collage of forms, voices, and acts. In this way it resembled the structure of the music hall or variety theater, but on a much more intimate scale. The cabaret's small stage placed the audience and the performers into close proximity, and there was no backstage to speak of. Indeed, in the first years of its operation, the audience of writers and artists performed for itself, taking turns on the stage to share their work. Moreover, unlike the variety theater, the *cabaret artistique* relied on a more literary style of performance notable for its valorization of wordplay, sharp wit, ironic punchlines, and modernist inscriptions of French folk forms like the *chanson.* Such a program was at first loosely structured and gradually became more formalized as the Chat Noir's audience grew.

The Chat Noir closed in 1897 after a sixteen-year lifespan uncharacteristically long for a cabaret. But other *cabarets artistiques* sprouted in Montmartre, Barcelona, Berlin, Vienna, Zurich, Munich, and Moscow. The Chat Noir and these European successors—places such as Le Mirliton, the Quatre Gats, the Lapin Agile, the Cabaret of the Eleven Executioners, Sound and Smoke, the Fledermaus, and Dada's Cabaret Voltaire—shaped the institutions and aesthetic principles of the Continental avant-garde in the decades before the First World War. The combination of artistic quality, aesthetic experimentation, intellectual engagement, anticommercialism, and social critique gave the word *cabaret* an exclusive, oppositional, and elite connotation that distinguished it from popular and commercial entertainments like the café concert, the variety show, or the music hall—places that, as historian Harold Segel put it, made "no pretensions to serious art." [16] Such distinctions were reinforced by state regulations as well as popular perception. Theater historian Laurence Senelick reports that "when the minister of public education asked the prefecture of police in 1897 why cabarets were not subject to preliminary censorship like theatre and music-halls, he was told that the personnel of the Chat Noir and Le Mirliton were 'composed of poets and song-writers whose works had artistic value and who do not seek the vogue enjoyed by smutty productions.'" [17]

Yet already by the turn of the century, these distinctions between the "serious art" of the cabaret and the popular art of the music hall were becoming diluted. The *cabaret artistique* shed much of its exclusivity and began to compete with the music hall as an institution of popular entertainment. Announcing it as a "sign of the theatrical times," one account on the eve of the twentieth century predicted that the cabaret's rising popularity and increased accessibility would remap the landscape of Paris's popular performance: "Acrobats will be relegated to the circus, the music halls will have killed the theatres, and the cabarets, in their turn, will have killed the music halls." [18] Its new popularity altered the nature of the performances themselves as they became more professionalized. To the extent that cabarets retained their political edge, their critique tended toward more palatable and less threatening parody. Though cabarets after the First World War continued to offer a stage for political satire, aesthetic experimentation, and bohemian voices, "their spirit," Segel concludes, "transformed from artistic exclusivity and experimentation to commercial divertissement." [19]

American cabaret performance evokes but reorients this European tradition. While European cabaret was distinguished from popular amusements by its association with the modernist avant-garde, its performances of political satire and cultural critique, and its bohemian audience, cabaret in the United States was initially associated with commercialism, spectacle, and popular consumption. (It would not be until 1938, when Barney Josephson opened the integrated, leftist Café Society in Greenwich Village that the American tradition of jazz and popular music merged with the explicit political parody and critique of the European cabaret tradition.) The cabaret was a central institution of American nightlife that used the combination of performance and late-night dining to create an atmosphere that brought people together in new public formations of intimacy and sociality.

In following the word *cabaret* across the Atlantic, we find it settling at

Jesse Lasky and his partner Henry Harris's entrepreneurial nightlife experiment, the Folies Bergère, an institution that warrants as prominent a place in cabaret's American tradition as the Chat Noir occupies in the European.[20] A far cry from Montmartre's Chat Noir, this "first" American cabaret more closely resembled Paris's popular music halls than its artistic cabarets. Lasky and Harris imported the word *cabaret* in an attempt to elevate the popular performances of American vaudeville by appealing to a more fashionable middle-class audience. The pair opened the Folies Bergère in New York City's theater district in 1911 (at Forty-sixth Street and Broadway), borrowing the name from the opulent Parisian music hall that had inspired the Ziegfeld *Follies* and at which Josephine Baker would in 1925 debut her infamous "banana dance" after American cabaret—and its performers—traveled back to Montmartre.[21] I will have more to say about that journey below. Here, however, I want to dwell for a moment on the opening-night performance of Lasky and Harris's Folies Bergère. A closer look at its aesthetic specificities, its deployment of the name *cabaret*, and its manipulation of space and performance offer important insight into the style and structure of American cabaret performance as it developed in the first three decades of the twentieth century.

April 27, 1911, drew an overflowing audience of New York society to the Folies Bergère, enticed by the novelty of a theater combined with an upscale restaurant. The spacious, carpeted theater, decorated in shades of gray, pink, and gold, had both a main floor and a balcony. Spectators on the main floor dined at small tables with pink-shaded table lamps and movable chairs. Each section of tables was arranged on a slightly raised platform, "so that the orchestra floor presents a series of terraces." [22] Diners, seated at the proper dinner hour of 6:30 p.m., were entertained by two groups of musicians while they ate, a Hungarian orchestra on the stage and a string quartet at the back of the main floor. Following dinner (at around 8:30 p.m.), a theatrical program made up of two vaudeville revues and a ballet began. The first revue was a "profane burlesque" that satirized prominent public officials and well-known names. The fast-paced performance featured opening comments by the Statue of Liberty, a marching parade of dancers representing various parts of the world, a skit involving Mephistopheles and his wife, extravagant chorus lines, women vocalists, acrobats, pantomimes, and French *danseuses*. The second act featured a visiting *corps de ballet* from London, numbering sixty, who performed *Temptations*, a ballet about the vices and seductions of modern nightlife. A third act concluded the show with another satirical vaudeville revue that featured European acts and

American chorus numbers. This program made use of topical parody and local critique to entertain the audience, even incorporating them into the spectacle. During one of the early dance numbers, for example, "messenger boys" were sent from the stage to retrieve "pretended notes" from those in the audience addressed to the chorus girls, a contrivance that allowed the performers to burlesque some of the better-known spectators in attendance. Similarly, later in the show, three "policemen" interrupted the performance in the name of decency and threatened to close down the theater if Salome, a figure in one of the dance routines, was not driven off the stage. These "policemen" were given buckets and mops and, in a parody of the puritanical morals reformers, were made to "clean up the stage."

This three-part vaudeville program, however, was only the first performance of the evening. Around midnight, the second performance began. In a marketing decision that would have important consequences for the texture and shape of American nightlife, Lasky called this entertainment a "cabaret show." The distinction Lasky sought to make between the vaudeville revue of the first half of the night and the cabaret show of the second was one of scale, tone, and theatrical posture. One account described the cabaret show as a "sublimated vaudeville"; that is, it featured musical and dance routines that relied on the smaller and more restrained gestures of a much smaller cast, inviting the audience into the performance through more subtle acts of communication. To that end, the producers drew a platform across the orchestra pit to create "a sort of extended 'apron' that brought the performers very close to the audience."[23] The cabaret show had ten acts that performed informally while audiences were served a late supper. Unlike the earlier performances, which occurred after dinner, the audience ate their midnight meal during the cabaret show. The accompanying musicians performed on the stage itself, visible and part of the spectacle rather than hidden from view in the theater's orchestra pit as in the previous portion of the evening. Flirting with a Continental naughtiness, the cabaret show also included "living sculptures," barely dressed women posing in three-dimensional tableaus in proscenium boxes at each side of the stage.[24] The production and cabaret show ran for four months and was followed by a second production that began a six-week run beginning in August. For this second production, Lasky and Harris recruited the acclaimed composer J. Rosamond Johnson (brother of James Weldon Johnson) to write the music and conduct the orchestra for the satirical revue *Hello, Paris*—the first time a black conductor led a white orchestra for a white-cast production in New York City.[25] (The program for this second production also included Mae

West among the principals.) In the end, the Folies was too extravagant to be financially sustainable. But in its short existence, this theatrical experiment inspired numerous imitators and helped establish a new mode of nightlife entertainment in the 1910s for the middle classes, one that expanded the social, economic, and aesthetic possibilities of nighttime.[26]

Lasky's claim to have introduced the word—if not the idea of—*cabaret* to the United States, however, overstates the case. As early as 1896, Casino Chambers at Thirty-ninth Street and Broadway promoted the Cabaret du Neant, "the Parisian Sensation" with performances every half hour until midnight.[27] Another midtown café, invoking the crooked streets of Montmartre, called itself the "Cabaret du Chat Noir." This restaurant, advertising itself specifically to after-theater crowds, offered food "a la Carte at all hours" and musical performances late into the night.[28] European immigrant communities who brought their own popular amusements with them further established early cabaret performances in ethnic enclaves throughout the city. In 1907, for example, the *New York Times* celebrated a downtown German theater for its "cabaret show." The paper described the informal atmosphere and the blurred boundaries between the stage and the spectators as "nothing so much as the assemblage of good friends where the people without 'talents' are heartily thankful to those who provide the entertainment."[29] Given these earlier establishments, we can revise Lasky's claim. His Folies Bergère inaugurated the first "American" cabaret in the sense that it was a late-night amusement that did not arise organically from the performance cultures of European immigrants nor appeal to ethnic immigrant, African American, or working-class audiences, but offered such amusements to a mixed-gender, middle-class American audience. It incorporated a Continental veneer, but was, in Lasky's words, "a European production, produced by an American for an American audience."[30] His Folies Bergère played a key role in bringing the word *cabaret* across ethnic, racial, and class lines, so that New York's respectable society, particularly its women, could legitimately take part in a midnight sociality that was previously not widely available.

In casting his transatlantic gaze toward the spaces of European popular performance, Lasky pointedly elides his cabaret's relationship to American popular performances of the lower classes—the kinds of spaces from which he sought to differentiate his own venture with the imported word *cabaret*. That is to say, in addition to the middle-class vaudeville tradition indexed by Lasky's Folies Bergère, there are traces of other, subterranean, traditions that haunt and shape American cabaret's midnight congregations and performances. It is necessary, then, to supplement this account with some of the institutions of nineteenth-century working-class and black amusements—the concert saloon, the black and tan saloon, the professional club, and the jook joint—whose genealogical traces shaped the performance practices and nightlife ethos of the modern American cabaret.

Nineteenth-century working-class saloon culture provided comradeship, recreation, and leisure for men and, less often, women. While a black saloon culture existed in New York City since at least the mid-eighteenth century, it increased and expanded rapidly following New York State's emancipation of slaves in 1827.[31] Many saloons included musical entertainment or small ensembles in order to attract customers and shape the atmosphere of the scene. Increasingly, saloons that featured entertainment and shows became more professionally organized and efficiently run, evolving into the concert saloon. A fixture of urban American nightlife from the 1860s through the 1890s, the concert saloon was a male-oriented commercial drinking house that added musical and sometimes theatrical entertainment in order to attract customers. Theater historian Brooks McNamara has excavated the remains of the concert saloon, reconstructing the architecture and atmosphere of these performance spaces.[32] They had a basic stage area, sometimes with footlights, a drop curtain, and scenic flats. Performances combined musical acts, dance routines, minstrel performances, parodies, and comedy sketches loosely organized by a master of ceremonies who would also perform on occasion. Audiences sat at tables where they were served by "waiter girls," female employees who in some cases filled in as theatrical entertainment. Waiter girls sometimes provided commercial sex (concert saloons occasionally doubled as prostitution houses), but more often offered commercial intimacy: sitting and chatting with customers, serving drinks, and earning tips for their friendliness throughout the show. Like the master of ceremonies, the waiter girls were part of the structure of the concert saloon that contributed to the direct exchange between performer and spectator and the mood of participation, rather than passive observation, of the patrons.

Concert saloons and their immediate offshoots, wrote popular commentator Herbert Asbury in 1928, "were precursors of the modern night clubs and cabarets, though they lacked the ornateness of the present-day jazz palaces."[33] Asbury was not alone in this assessment. Many twentieth-century commentators and performers traced the origins of the cabaret of the 1910s and 1920s to the nineteenth-century concert saloon. According to nightclub veteran Jimmy Durante, cabaret could trace its origins to the Melodeon, a concert saloon opened in Chinatown in 1859 by a Philadelphian named

Frank Rivers. "In launching his idea on the restless sea of pleasure," Durante memorializes, "Frank Rivers became the responsible agent for all the sin cellars, honky-tonks, and joints that followed for seventy years in the placid steps of the Melodeon."[34] Another claim finds the origins of cabaret in the basement of a Greenwich Village house opened to the neighborhood by black proprietor and entertainer Isaac "Ike" Hines. The entertainment at Ike Hines's was informal: anybody who could sing, dance, or play an instrument was invited to put on a show for a crowd of spectators gathered around tables night after night to socialize and relax. First dubbed Ike's Rathskeller (in the tradition of the German basement tavern) and later renamed Ike's Professional Club, it was one of the hottest nightspots in Greenwich Village in the 1880s, a role it maintained when it relocated to the black entertainment district in the West Fifties at the turn of the century.[35] A third entry in this origins-of-cabaret sweepstakes suggests that the Marshall Hotel, the black rooming house and gathering space that opened on West Fifty-third Street in 1899, was "the birthplace" of the modern, informal entertainments of American cabaret.[36] Marshall's was neither a concert saloon nor a cabaret, but like these it served food and drink during musical performance and functioned primarily as a kind of leisure space for those in the performance industry. Marshall's, like Ike's and the Melodeon before it, consolidated nightlife performance and late-night eating and drinking in a common event.

While the concert saloon and saloon culture in the urban context shaped the contours of an emergent American cabaret tradition, so too did the performances and ethics of the rural jook joint of the southern United States. The jook was a central institution of secular black dance and music developed during and after Reconstruction by rural sharecroppers and migratory workers in the South. Defining the jook as "a Negro pleasure house . . . set apart on public works where the men and women dance, drink, and gamble," Zora Neale Hurston placed them within the genealogy of black urban cabarets as the "primitive rural counterparts of resort night clubs, where turpentine workers take their evening relaxation deep in the pine forest."[37] Throughout the early twentieth century, black southern migrants brought with them the practices, sounds, sensibilities, atmosphere, movements, and food of the jook as they traveled from the rural south to the urban north. This cultural migration—what Farah Jasmine Griffin calls "the south in the city"—significantly shaped the character of black northern nightlife performance.[38]

The pathways and theater circuits of traveling black performance in the late nineteenth and early twentieth centuries further connected the performance practices of the rural jook to the black concert saloon and established movement between them. Because New York City was the starting point and terminal destination for many touring black vaudeville shows and musical theater in the decades surrounding the turn of the century, the city was home to a critical mass of performers looking for temporary work between or after a show's run.[39] Ike Hines, for example, was a banjo player with Charles Hicks's Georgia Minstrels, a black-managed and black-performed touring minstrel company, before he settled in lower Manhattan and opened his Rathskeller. Hines brought to his concert saloon the entertainment connections, performance skills, and business sense he cultivated on the road shows that toured across the country. From urban concert saloons to rural jook joints to regional theater circuits, nineteenth-century institutions of black performance and recreation were connected by the musicians and patrons who moved in and through them, carrying related but disparate influences of performance and sociality into twentieth-century black nightlife districts.

Just as it was instructive above to dwell briefly on the performance of Lasky's Folies Bergère, it is also helpful to describe Ike Hines's club at its midtown location in order to get a sense of black saloon performance as it began to intersect with the cabaret tradition. With the increasing professionalization of black popular performance circuits and their centralization in New York City, Ike's club transitioned from a midcentury concert saloon to a late-century professional club. Professional clubs catered first to those in the business, providing afterhours amusements for actors and entertainers as well as work and recreation for performers traveling through the city. After passing through a carpeted parlor with a few tables, visitors would enter a back room with tables that lined the walls and a small piano in the corner. The arrangement of the room left a small bare floor for singers or entertainers. The tables would often be stacked or pushed aside to make room for patrons to dance. The second level had a room for private parties as well as rehearsal space, which was available to local performers for developing and honing new acts. Above that, rooms were available for boarders. Having performers and others in the fast set as the primary customer base brought a new dimension to the intimate atmosphere and the performances at Ike's. As a social space for "notables of the ring, the turf, and the stage," Ike's attracted not only professional entertainers and musicians but also those who like to be around professional entertainers.[40] This dynamic created its own hierarchy of regulars and outsiders that was organized by familiarity, recognition, and accumulated knowledge. Codes of racial belonging also shaped these social hierarchies. Ike's typically drew a small number of white visitors, either middle-class adventure seekers or white performers there to lift sounds and gestures for their blackface imitations, with both varieties registering as outsiders. This notion of familiarity with actors and entertainers would come to inform the intimate formations of Harlem nightlife in the 1920s.[41]

Into late-nineteenth-century saloon culture, another institution emerged that played a central role in the margins of urban recreation: the "black and tan" saloon. This designation described working-class concert saloons or bars that encouraged black-white social mixing and opportunities for interracial public dancing. At the end of the nineteenth and early twentieth century, black and tans were nightlife spaces on the margins of the margin. In his 1890 muckraking exposé of New York tenement life, *How the Other Half Lives,* Jacob Riis wrote that the "border-land where the white and black races meet in common debauch . . . has always been the worst of the desperately bad. Than this commingling of the utterly depraved of both sexes, white and black, on such ground, there can be no greater abomination."[42] Even as cabarets and dance halls became a respectable option for amusement and leisure among the middle classes throughout the early twentieth century, the black and tan remained the symbol of the limits of moral corruption. As historian Kevin Mumford shows, the black and tan helped in part to make other popular amusements more respectable after World War I, as dance halls demonstrated their propriety by "subtly interspersing the culture of antimiscegenation — that is, by consistently contrasting their institutions with the Black and Tans."[43] By the late 1920s, as covert vices became popular fads, midnight shows became acceptable affairs, and black culture became a hotly consumed commodity, such interracial mixing was as often a manufactured performance for a more modern audience as it was a social transgression. A far cry from Riis's "commingling of the utterly depraved," Harlem's elegant white-marketed cabarets were sometimes referred to as black and tans not as a moral judgment but as a cynical attempt to market the putative thrill of interracial intimacy for a middle-class audience, effectively evacuating the term of its class specificity though retaining its racial connotation.[44]

The purpose of this genealogical discussion is not to determine whether American cabaret originates with the Melodeon in 1859, Ike's Rathskeller in 1883, Marshall's in 1899, or the Folies Bergère in 1911. Nor is it to trace American cabaret's origins to the concert saloon, the jook joint, the black and tan, or the nightspots of Paris. Beyond pointing to the impossibilities of identifying singular origins or direct influences, this prehistory of Harlem cabaret helps us see a family of late-night performances and performance spaces that all fed into and shaped the idea of *cabaret* in the 1910s and 1920s as the name was popularly attached to a variety of nightlife establishments in the United States. These establishments proffered a cultural reservoir of spaces, experiences, and performances that shaped the meanings variously affixed—by performers and entrepreneurs, by critics and morals reformers—to the cabaret during Prohibition and the Harlem Renaissance.

From Lasky onward, what is important to remember is that *cabaret* attempted to codify a mode of American nightlife performance in respectable terms; what was previously denounced as the questionable morality of the lower classes could now be acceptably consumed under the banner of European sophistication. The first two decades of the twentieth century, as nightlife historians such as Lewis Erenberg and Kathy Peiss have shown, marked a transformation in the institutions of urban nightlife as entrepreneurs made concerted efforts to adapt working-class and immigrant amusements into "respectable" forms suitable for the middle classes. The cabaret, for example, rose in popularity alongside the dance hall, which facilitated new expressive possibilities for middle-class (and working-class) youth. Unlike formal dances like the waltz, modern popular dance of this era featured a high degree of lingering bodily contact, informal gestures and movements, hip- and pelvis-centered rhythms, and generally encouraged the "centrifugal tendencies" of the dancing body to proceed unrestrained.[45] Such dancing contributed to the sense of nightlife as a space of social and sexual transgression and earned the denunciations of already suspicious morals reform organizations. Casting strangers together in familiar interaction, this kind of dancing had previously occurred in backrooms of concert saloons and in cellar dives; now it was featured prominently in the city's more upscale cabarets and nightclubs and was especially alarming for the possible corruption of otherwise upstanding young women, who were increasingly invited to attend unescorted. For many, the only difference between a *dance hall* and a *cabaret* was simply the degree of sexual transgression that was permitted. While the dance halls at least had the potential, properly operated, to be used for respectable social interactions (sometimes even functioning in the daylight hours), from the perspective of morals reformers and Progressive Era uplift, the cabaret was simply a more extreme version of a dance hall, where sexual expression was much more explicit and encouraged by the late-night milieu and the consumption of alcohol.[46]

This transformation of nightlife entertainment from disreputable to respectable suggests one of the central paradoxes of New York nightlife in the Progressive Era. In the words of Erenberg, "the elegant cabarets were not bohemian because, rather than being a rejection of the values of success, the cabaret was pictured as its reward." [47] As nightlife amusements gained respectability, they traded on a carefully managed and organized notion of transgression and a manufactured experience of intimacy, retaining the allure of the underclass but within highly scripted social scenes. Upscale cabarets were less often an expression of the city's carnivalesque inversion of morality than they were a staging of it for visitors looking for bohemian experience. True enough, in New York, the cabaret was often the destination of tourists seeking to consume sexual, racial, and class difference. Moreover, many establishments and individuals were happy to oblige such pursuits for their own advancement or gain. A rejection of middle-class mores was not likely to be found in such respectable nightclubs, which became so precisely by excising any possibility for challenges to middle-class norms. Middle-class social values were, in fact, typically reinforced and enlarged by such consumption.

Yet this transformation was never wholly accomplished. The cabaret's historical and geographic proximity to supposedly debased underworld performances and populations left a stain that could never be fully rinsed away. Its relationship to actors and showfolk, nonwhite racialized and working-class cultures, and underworld economies caused these "respectable" nightclubs to brush up against the less respectable people, places, and practices in their orbit. Thriving middle-class entertainment districts like Times Square and, later, Harlem, provided opportunities for the expansion of middle-class subjectivity, but in doing so they also altered the ecology of more marginal nightclubs, whose demographics were affected by middle-class patrons looking for something "more authentic" and by a police force protecting middle-class social and business interests. From Paris to New York, through concert saloon and jook joint, the cabaret was shaped by an overdetermined relationship to class-bounded recreation that made it a contradictory site of both (middle-)class ideology and (middle-)class critique. Thus, the very class and moral structures that the name *cabaret* was invoked to purge in order to make nightlife performance and sociality viable for mixed-gendered middle-class consumption were not erased, but only rendered into more complex systems of contradiction and disavowal.

National Prohibition only exacerbated these contradictions. The 1920s marked a promiscuous dispersal of the word *cabaret* as it came to be applied indiscriminately to a range of spaces that featured late-night performance in combination with food and drink. Beginning with the passage of the Volstead Act in 1919, the threat of federal raids initially necessitated a more mobile and discreet nightlife space that could function by word of mouth beneath the notice of the police. Full-scale kitchens, large stages, and terraced tables gave way to more furtive patterns of consumption and pared-down performances that recalled the concert saloons of the nineteenth century. By the mid-1920s, when Prohibition became easier to navigate and New York City's local enforcement of federal law waned, larger nightclubs began to reopen, especially around commercial hubs and entertainment districts like Times Square and Harlem (where black musicians and soldiers returning from France after World War I similarly redeployed the name *cabaret* in their own cosmopolitan remapping of Harlem's streets).

The word *nightclub* was itself a neologism that gained currency in the 1910s as a clever loophole used to circumvent in the statutory regulations on closing time. Bars and cabarets could exempt themselves from legal closing time and curfew laws by declaring themselves "private" membership clubs (which were not under the same regulations as commercial establishments), closing their doors at the designated hour and continuing operations.[48] *Nightclub* and *cabaret* were used interchangeably during Prohibition to describe not only those large nightclubs with elaborate revues but also the speakeasies, basement dives, and improvised cabarets that honeycombed Manhattan and provided small ensembles, the occasional singer, and space for social dancing. In Harlem, the institutions, practices, and ethics that organized urban commercial nightlife ranged from large nightclubs like the Cotton Club and Connie's Inn, which produced two productions a year featuring dozens of performers in vaudeville-like musical revues that attracted a largely white upscale audience, to smaller spaces like the Capitol Palace and the Catagonia Club, which offered more intimate musical numbers and a social scene that drew posttheater patrons, off-shift musicians, and afterhours crowds. This spectrum of performance styles and spaces, as we will see in more detail in the next chapter, organized the meanings of 1920s Harlem cabaret.

In a reverse translation that stands out among the many ironic twists of cabaret's history, post–World War I black expatriation brought *cabaret*, in its American guise, back to its birthplace: the triangular intersections of Montmartre where the Chat Noir and other *cabarets artistiques* first developed. The musical and social opportunities of postwar Paris brought large numbers of not only black Americans but also Antilleans and North Africans to France. Before and during the war, black American musicians like Louis Mitchell, Will Marion Cook, and Eugene Bullard laid the groundwork for later international stars like Florence Jones, Ada "Bricktop" Smith, and Josephine Baker.[49] As in Harlem, black performance appeared not only in large-scale theatrical revues (the most famous being Baker's *La Revue Nègre*), but also by itinerant musicians and small ensembles looking for gigs in the cafés and clubs that dotted the bohemian hills. Surveying the range of 1920s African American nightclubs in Montmartre, art historian Jody Blake writes: "Including the Abbaye Thélème, Bricktop's, Chez Florence, the Grand Duc, the Perroquet, the Plantation, and Zelli's, these establishments gave visitors the impression that they had suddenly stepped into Harlem."[50] These spaces brought blues, dance, popular song, and jazz to Paris and were a location for the larger production of a black Atlantic intimacy and aesthetics. The musical center of black expatriate Paris was Le Grand Duc, where Langston Hughes worked as a dishwasher in 1924. As we saw at the beginning of this chapter, Hughes drew affective nourishment from the performances he witnessed while working there. As Hughes wrote in his autobiography, such performances connected him across the Atlantic to the United States: "Blues in the rue Pigalle. Black and laughing, heartbreaking blues in the Paris dawn, pounding like a pulse beat, moving like the Mississippi!"[51] The confluence of the Seine and the Mississippi within the crowded walls of the tiny club points to the movements and intersections of European and American cabaret, nightclub and jook joint, as they echoed and reverberated across the ocean, across the room, and across the page.

One consequence of cabaret's multiple influences—and *cabaret*'s multiple uses—has been the persistent image of American cabaret as a performance of commercial leisure and popular entertainment as opposed to the explicit political performances and avant-garde experimentation of the European *cabaret artistique*. It would, however, be a mistake to think of American cabaret as "not political" or to make *a priori* or arbitrary distinctions between political cabaret and the cabaret of feeling, sentiment, and character. Such distinctions, while useful for discursively policing the boundaries between high and low, black and white, European and American, masculine and feminine, production and expenditure, politics and culture, and so on, are less helpful in describing the ways that nightlife performances were actually enacted and experienced. We need only look to the classic blues in performance for an explicit instance of both a formal challenge to dominant musical aesthetics and a thematic critique of gender, racial, and labor relations in the United States. And, as we will see in chapter 5 when we turn to Lena Horne's performances, even more standardized cabaret compositions could provide models of cultural resistance. These black interventions into aesthetic, political, and social form—examples of what Fred Moten, in a formulation that deconstructs some of the geographical, racial, and teleological assumptions of the historical avant-garde, calls the "sentimental avant-garde" of the 1950s and 1960s that was prefigured by black Harlem/Paris—suggest one way that the cabaret of sentiment, feeling, and character was available as a mode of critique. Moreover, cabaret's "other performance," those social performances among the spectators who attend the cabaret, often continued traditions of counterpublic collectivity and expression for sexual and racial minorities, those of the urban lower classes, and those who otherwise find themselves rendered incomplete by the public sphere's dominant narratives.[52]

These examples of the racial, sexual, gender, and class politics of the cabaret suggest why, as we will see in the pages ahead, the cabaret was so readily marshaled in debates about racial uplift and moral reform. The rise of the speakeasy during Prohibition and the growth of Harlem as an entertainment district contributed to the more general moral panic that took nightlife culture as a primary site of anxiety in the early twentieth century. This panic refracted larger American anxieties around race, sex, and modern life through the spectacle and sound of black performance.[53] In response to the threat of black performance and jazz sociality, New York City passed ordinances in 1926 requiring any establishment that offered musical entertainment or dancing in combination with food and drink to be licensed by the city. These ordinances, which exempted the more "respectable" entertainment provided in New York's luxury hotels, were "largely directed at the black music and dance that was performed in the Harlem clubs, as well as the social mixing of the races."[54] Known informally as the "cabaret laws," they inscribed into the city bureaucracy another definition of *cabaret* (one still on the books today): "Any room, place or space in the city in which any musical entertainment, singing, dancing, or other form of amusement is permitted in connection with the restaurant business or the business of directly or indirectly selling to the public food or drink."[55] This legal definition of the word both complements and competes with the popular, theatrical, and historical meanings of *cabaret* we have traced so far, stepping in at a late date to clarify and explain with the utilitarian efficiency of urban administration and to shape, in very material ways, the contours of the cabaret tradition—at least for performers and nightclub owners, who were forced to comply with new conditions and constraints on their livelihood.[56]

A final word on the morphology of *cabaret*. As a word imported from Paris less for its exact meaning than its aura, *cabaret* invited users to modify and adapt it. In particular, Harlem Renaissance writers peppered their writing with the popular nightlife colloquialism *cabareting*. To cite some examples, novelist Nella Larsen used this gerund in each of her two novels, *Quicksand* (1928) and *Passing* (1929); Rudolph Fisher used it in his essay "The Caucasian Storms Harlem" (1927); and Wallace Thurman used it in his 1926 review of Carl Van Vechten's novel, *Nigger Heaven*. In each of these cases, *cabareting* describes middle-class patrons who begin their evening at one of the city's more respectable nightclubs before searching elsewhere for more authentic, fateful, and intimate spaces. The earliest use I have found of this verb form of the noun *cabaret* is in a poem by Thomas R. Ybarra called "Cabaretting" published in the *New York Times* in 1912, which playfully announces in short, staccato lines the unstoppable progression of the cabaret over the landscape of modern urban nightlife. The final verse, which captures the momentum of the new nightlife spirit that threatens to enlist even your dinner in its march of singing and dancing, reads:

> But should steak
> The echoes wake
> With a tune,
> Do not swoon;
> Should the soup
> With a whoop
> Do a dance—
> Should a plate of chicken salad
> Sing a sentimental ballad
> Don't be fretting,
> Cabaretting
> MUST advance![57]

Ybarra knowingly rhymes "cabaretting" with "fretting," playing on the newness of the word and Americanizing, at the level of verbal play, the French tradition. Two years later, Irving Berlin rhymed it more properly with "playing" in his lyric to "This Is the Life" (1914), a Tin Pan Alley ditty about a farmer who arrives in New York City and decides to abandon his rural life (and wife) for the life of cabareting. This verb form, first appearing about a year after Lasky's Folies Bergère opened and used frequently in the second half of the 1920s in the context of the Negro vogue, marks the participatory aspect of the cabaret, carrying the notion of hopping from one spot to another throughout the night and expanding the use of the word to mean not only a place you go to but also a thing you do. The lexical expansion of *cabaret* in the urban nightlife of the 1920s, evidenced not only in the license of poets and songwriters but also in the genealogical influences I have traced above, provided a vocabulary and a history that performers and writers of the Harlem Renaissance used to describe performances of public intimacy that, as we will see, were central to queer and black expressive culture and cultural critique.

CABARET AND THE RELATIONS OF PERFORMANCE

Perhaps there are certain rendezvous that feign a sinister look. For Harlem, like other places, is not without its sham and if a touch (however fake) of crime be required, there are always those to furnish it. Which in no sense means that all is unreal. On the contrary.

NIGHTLIFE: VANITY FAIR'S
INTIMATE GUIDE TO NEW YORK AFTER DARK

Another scene: one that echoes Ike Hines's Rathskeller and anticipates Hughes's Le Grand Duc; one that points toward what is at stake in Michael Cooke's formulation of the achievement of intimacy. In his well-known account of Ethel Waters's early performance at Edmond's Cellar, a working-class black nightspot in Harlem, writer Rudolph Fisher describes the specific relations of performance that shape and are shaped by the conventions, associations, and spatial practices of the cabaret. Edmond's was a crowded, low-ceilinged basement cabaret that had to close in the summer months because it "became a furnace that could melt your bones." According to Waters, the crowd there was made up of "the sporting men, the hookers, and other assorted underworld characters," cross-dressers, "male queers," and "he-she-and-what-is-it types."[58] Night after night at Edmond's, Fisher writes, singers "wore themselves ragged trying to rise above the inattentive din of conversation, and soon, literally, yelled themselves hoarse." This, he suggests in a playfully denaturalizing aside, was the cause of the "familiar throaty roughness" that most white people associate with blues singers: "though admired as characteristically African, [it] is as a matter of fact nothing but a form of chronic laryngitis." Waters, unlike these less remarkable performers, "would stride with great leisure and self assurance to the center of the floor, stand there with a half-contemptuous nonchalance, and wait. All would become silent at once. Then she'd begin her song."[59] Fisher's description of Waters's performance draws attention to the totality of stage practice and the context of audience reception, taking into account a performance vocabulary that includes gesture, movement, stillness, lighting, music, space, and architecture in addition to the words spoken or songs sung on the stage. Such legendary accounts—which are legion in the history of cabaret—illustrate the peculiar dynamic of cabaret's relations of performance. The social interruption occasioned by the performance at the cabaret required, as Waters well knew, a stance or disposition that could manipulate the distracted spectatorship of the audience.

I find in this description of Waters's mastery of cabaret's mode of performance some possibilities for thinking through the cabaret as an intimate formation. The genealogy in the previous section points toward some of the ways the form of cabaret, in its multiple genres and guises, developed as a uniquely intimate performance event. Observing that "cabaret's history is closely tied to the problem of genre," performance historian David Román cautions that "part of the challenge for theatre historians interested in cabaret has to do with sorting through the various popular performances from different historical periods and distinct cultural traditions associated with the form."[60] As Román indicates, *cabaret* implies a specific form and spatial practice in which a number of performance genres and cultural traditions have developed in different times and places, each modifying or expanding the style and structure of cabaret and imprinting it with its own local stamp. A consideration of cabaret's form points us toward the structural aspects of the cabaret performance that have shaped the experience of public intimacy. The movement and use of *cabaret* through its different contexts, in other words, maps more than a simple nominalism, tangential correspondence, or strategic misnaming of cabaret performance in the United States (though it was at times each of these things). Rather, *cabaret* both names and indexes the development of a specific framework and context for affective experience and social relations. *Cabaret*, like *theater*, refers to both a kind of performance and the room or building where such a performance takes place. We will see in subsequent chapters how performance genres, subaltern histories, and sociological discourse shape the cabaret as an intimate formation. Here, following Waters and building on the genealogy charted above, I turn to a closer consideration of the cabaret's spatial and performance practices and their role in shaping an intimate social formation.

While theater scholars such as Marvin Carlson, Susan Bennett, and Gay

McAuley have theorized and analyzed theatrical space and its role in shaping performance relations, the characteristics of the cabaret pose a different set of problems that make theories developed for the theater an ill fit.[61] Unlike the naturalist or bourgeois theater, the relations of cabaret performance are shaped by the cabaret's double identity as both a restaurant/drinking place and a place of performance. *Cabaret,* in other words, describes a specific arrangement of nightlife performance as it intersects, interfaces, and interferes with a specific social arrangement. This double identity joins the sociality and intimacy of the drinking establishment to the sociality and intimacy of the variety theater or dance hall, producing a sphere of informality and participation where the audience and the performer occupy the same space as coequal inhabitants, each making a competing claim over the control and use of the space. The cabaret audience gathers not only to see a show, but also for the conversation, contact, and social encounters provided by the cabaret as a drinking and dining place. The cabaret performer, meanwhile, does not create and operate within a fictional world separate from that of the audience, as the performer of a dramatic performance might. Rather, the cabaret performer addresses the audience from a position continuous with the audience's time and place. The dual intimacies produced by a dining establishment and by a performance space often become dueling intimacies as these axes intersect and interrupt each other, provoking an underlying tension between performer and audience that reveals intimacy to often be coterminous with hostility.

This status of the audience and its relationship to the performance can be usefully contrasted with two other modes of theatrical performance that address the spectator in particular ways: naturalist theater, on the one hand, and environmental theater, on the other. In naturalist theater, technical and performance conventions situate the audience as relatively passive observers to the characters of the story (even as the performers are highly attuned to the presence and mood of the audience), separated by footlights, orchestra pits, and theatrical conventions like the fourth wall. The principles of the environmental theater developed in the 1960s avant-garde, by contrast, seek to engage and address the audience by enfolding the performance around the audience and involving it in the space of the actor. Unlike either of these, the cabaret performer must enter into a space already being produced by the audience for its own uses. The cabaret performer, that is, addresses her audience from within the audience's space, rather than her own. If environmental theater seeks to immerse the audience in the performance, the cabaret poses the much more daunting situation of immersing the performance in the audience.[62]

The act of becoming an audience is, perhaps, the theater's first act of intimacy. Theater theorist and director Herbert Blau reminds us that the audience "does not exist before the play but is *initiated* or *precipitated* by it; it is not an entity to begin with, but a consciousness constructed." [63] Yet how does this work in the cabaret, where a public exists with its own social consciousness prior to the performance and, indeed, quasi-independently of it? How does a cabaret performer, in other words, wrangle this public into an audience? And how does this dynamic shape what comes to be understood as cabaret's intimacy? Unlike the conventional spatial regions of both legitimate and popular theater, the cabaret did not always delineate a performer-only space separate from the space of the audience. Small or improvised cabarets did not always have a backstage area or dressing rooms, and it was not uncommon for performers to sit at the bar or a table among the audience before and after performing. The audience was encouraged—by food and drink, by tables, by dancing in the same space that would later be occupied by professional performers, by arriving substantially before and staying long past the "official" performance—to relate to the cabaret as its own social space. Before and after the show (and throughout the evening, when cabarets provided occasion for public dancing), patrons and waiters would often occupy the very playing area where actors, dancers, or bands would perform. Their social practices were not put on hold when the show began, as they were in the naturalist theater, but were continued—sometimes amplified, sometimes muted, but continued nonetheless. Thus not only was the audience focused on the "official" performance on the cabaret floor, but they were engaged by what McAuley calls the theater's "other performance" and what Erenberg calls cabaret's "action environment": the public display, self-fashioning, and self-reflexivity of the audience for itself.[64] For these reasons, argued Cabaret School writer Rudolph Fisher, cabaret attendance was a different kind of spectatorship than that of the theater or concert hall: "You don't just go to a cabaret and sit back and wait to be entertained. You get out on the floor and join the pow-wow and help entertain yourself." [65]

These "other performances" were encouraged by the cabaret's seating arrangement, which decentered the location of performance. The arrangement of the spectators around tables, rather than in fixed rows, expanded the field of perception beyond the unidirectional sightlines of naturalist or popular theater. Each table constituted a compass rose of vision, with some spectators placed with their backs to the performance but facing other patrons and spectators, some of whom in turn faced them. The commencement of the "official" performance occasioned new arrangements of the body, which further made spectators aware of their presence in the scene as they turned and twisted to view the show. Unlike naturalist theater—even theater in the round, where spectators are visible to each other through the performance—the cabaret did not provide a common and constant focus for the audience's gaze. Instead, the performance refracted the audience's gaze, prism-like, throughout the space, creating multiple focuses.

This rearrangement and scattering of sightlines expanded the field of vision to implicate and involve the spectator in the scene of performance as one who not only watched but was watched by others—what McAuley calls the "play of looks" that crisscross the space between spectators, on the one hand, and between spectator and performer, on the other.[66] This play of looks finely tuned cabaret's dynamics of copresence. Goffman describes the self-consciousness and intersubjective openness that such scopic matrices effect: "Each individual can *see* that he is being experienced in some way, and he will guide at least some of his conduct according to the perceived identity and initial response of his audience. Further, he can be seen to be seeing this, and can see that he has been seen to be seeing this."[67] The amplified self-consciousness of cabaret spectatorship and the rituals of participation that produce an intimate public authorize claims of rapid familiarity and mutual recognition. In most cases, the performer, too, is implicated in this expanded field of vision, caught in the same circuits of recognition and self-reflexivity. The cabaret's distracted spectatorship is thus not a lack of attention but a multiplication of it, one that opens and activates the peripheral range and sensations of the audience.

The cabaret simultaneously truncated and expanded the nightlife sociality practiced in the traditional saloon or drinking establishment. Bar sociality, as we saw in our earlier discussion of saloons and jook joints, is defined in part by the opportunities and spatial practices that allow bar patrons to approach, encounter, or engage with each other in a socially open and accessible context.[68] While cabarets to varying degrees also have such opportunities, they appear much more limited vis-à-vis a bar because of the official performance of the cabaret, which interrupts such sociality, and the conventions of table seating, which though increasing mobility from the point of view of proscenium theater, limit mobility from the point of view of the bar. Sociologist Shari Cavan, for example, reports in her classic study *Liquor License: An Ethnography of Bar Behavior* that in a nightclub with a formal performance, "the proprieties of audience demeanor restrict the extent to which the spectators of the production may involve themselves in sociability within the setting [while] the expectation that patrons will show involvement in and deference to production restricts the extent to which other activities may be engaged." [69] The regulation of social behavior and restrictions on complete mobility by the most respectable cabarets was one of the factors that made it more acceptable for middle-class women to attend late-night amusements in mixed-gender company, as their location at a table could partially close off their social accessibility. By a similar logic, some of Harlem's upscale, white-marketed cabarets were more tolerant of racially mixed crowds when they were seated at different tables, but often barred mixed-race parties from sitting and socializing together.

Yet though nightclub sociality may be more constrained than that of a bar, it is for the same reasons a more intimate experience. The collective address to, and the instantiation of, a public available to a shared and focused event transforms the public into an audience, a provisional collective that is produced in relation to the performance itself. In seeing the intimate formation of the cabaret as one that produces social relations, identities, and communities through performance, I build on the work of queer performance theorist Miranda Joseph, who has argued that performance, like other kinds of labor, produces such relations through its collective consumption. In doing so, she makes an important distinction between consumption and consumerism that helps to recast the devalued status of American cabaret as "merely" entertainment. In demonstrating the performativity of production and the productivity of performance, Joseph argues that the consumption of a performance is itself a kind of productive labor, recognizing "*consumption, not merely as consumerism,* but rather as a site of performative production, that is, as a highly constrained site of collective as well as individual subject constitution." [70] For Joseph, the audience's act of witness and the consumption of performance are productive of subjectivities and collectivities, intimate relations, and affective worlds. This understanding of the audience helps explain how the shared focus of nightlife performance produces the cabaret as a space not only of physical intimacy—a matter of social availability, spatial arrangements, and bodily proxemics—but also of psychic intimacy—produced by and producing a structure of experience and affective connection between those gathered, a framework within which nightlife relations are formed and re-formed. And, arguably, this is what makes the experience of the cabaret or nightclub more intimate than a drinking establishment without a performance, the constrained codes of mobility and choreographic limitations of sociality described by Cavan notwithstanding.

Publicity photographs taken of the interiors of some of Harlem's better-known cabarets in the 1920s can help illustrate some of these claims about the cabaret's relations of performance. I turn to these images not in an at-

FIGURE 2 Interior of the Cotton Club. Michael Ochs Archives/Getty Images.

tempt to historically reconstruct these scenes but to index the general architecture of intimacy and the articulation of space that is repeated and inhabited within specific and local conditions. The first two images show the
interiors of two of Harlem's largest, upscale, primarily segregated cabarets:
the Cotton Club (fig. 2) and Connie's Inn (fig. 3). These clubs offered world-
famous musical revues and late-night dining to some of cabaret's biggest
audiences. The Cotton Club, for example, managed to crowd in about 700
people on busy nights, seated at tables on two tiers and in walls lined with
booths. This was, by comparison, about half the size of the average vaudeville or variety theater, and the performance style, spectatorial conventions,
and spatial arrangement created the illusion of an even smaller space.[71] The
swirling murals on the wall and ceiling at Connie's Inn contribute to a sensation of movement and motion, just as stage lights fixed in each of the four
pillars cut bright diagonals across the dance floor, illuminating the tables
and the patrons as well as any performance in their glare. (I will discuss the
murals and mise-en-scène of the Cotton Club, with their southern planta-

tion motifs, and performances at other white-marketed cabarets in the next chapter.) The photograph of Small's Paradise (fig. 4), one of Harlem's large cabarets, which cultivated a more racially mixed audience, similarly provides a view of the stage across a sea of menus and table settings.

These clubs were at once atypical and representative of Harlem's cabarets: they were among a handful of clubs that had the capital and the longevity to allow for their photographic documentation, and an even smaller number for whom drawing attention to themselves invited more patrons, rather than increased scrutiny from law enforcement. Yet for exactly these reasons, this trio was among the most visible and iconic of Harlem's nightclubs and can offer us a general sense of cabaret's spatial practices. Another photograph shows the interior of the Nest Club (fig. 5), a smaller, primarily black-attended cabaret that featured "more music than floorshow" and drew an afterhours crowd of musicians and show folk after their places

FIGURE 3 Interior of Connie's Inn. Photograph and Prints Division, Schomburg Center for Research in Black Culture, The New York Public Library, Astor, Lenox and Tilden Foundations.

FIGURE 4 Interior of Small's Paradise. Photograph and Prints Division, Schomburg Center for Research in Black Culture, The New York Public Library, Astor, Lenox and Tilden Foundations.

of employment closed around 2:00 a.m.[72] As in the other photographs, an "official" performance area is designated in the center of the room. In the Cotton Club and Small's, this performance area is raised one step and demarcated by railings. Open gaps on each side of these railings allowed performers to circulate among the spectators, and, in a reverse flow, allowed spectators to take a turn on the dance floor. Less fixed demarcations set off the floor at Connie's and the Nest Club, but lighting cues, the floor's polished wood (as opposed to the carpeted areas where tables were arranged), and the tables themselves serve as the ring that defines the area of performance.

Like most cabarets, these four all make use of the thrust stage arrangement that locates tables around three sides of the dance floor, with the fourth side of the rectangle given over to the bandstand. The narrow bandstand in each nightclub occupies one side of the dance floor, in these cases large enough for a baby grand piano, drum kit, and an orchestra of at least a dozen musicians who would give an "official performance" or provide dining entertainment and music for the social dancing of the patrons. The

tight placement of tables pushed snugly against the dance floor and leaving as little room as practicable between tables for waiters to pass further
suggests how the manipulation and reorganization of sightlines and bodily
comportment contributes to the sense of copresence. Unfixed seating allowed patrons to turn inward toward their table or readjust their chairs
to join other parties or better view the performance. Despite their large
seating capacity, spaces like the Cotton Club nonetheless managed to generate a sense of closeness and intimacy for its spectators through relations
of performance that designated the performance space as the domain of the
audience. Low ceilings and flat auditoria further created a sense of hori-
zontality that stood in contrast to the verticality of both Broadway stages
and, increasingly, the city itself, as skyscrapers reshaped the urban skyline.
The inhabited tightness of these spaces is finally insinuated by the mounted

FIGURE 5 Interior of the Nest Club. Photograph and Prints Division, Schomburg
Center for Research in Black Culture, The New York Public Library, Astor, Lenox
and Tilden Foundations.

cooling fans that appear on pillars, in corners, or on walls, which were as much for the performers, cast under hot spotlights, as they were for the packed-in audiences.

Together, these images point to the social and spatial circumstances of cabaret's relations of performance. The trespass of the performance is structural: even when—especially when—the audience is most anticipating the performance, the performer represents an interruption into their social organization, an interruption that is continually enacted and mended. The very modality of performance that brings the performer closer to the audience both physically and psychically makes that shared terrain a potentially contentious one. It is this interplay of closeness and distance, acceptance and refusal, connection and disconnection, concentration and distraction that shapes the cabaret as an intimate formation, the perpetual disorganization and reorganization of sound, bodies, sightlines, and feelings as the performer competes with the audience itself for its attention. Thus, for the popular performer, write Stuart Hall and Paddy Whannel, "the making of rapid connections with the audience was not—as it may have been for the second-raters—a quick way of ingratiating themselves with their fans, but something else, *a condition of the kind of art* in which they were engaged." [73] This mode of popular entertainment was common to illegitimate theater (i.e., non dramatic, non text-based, or non-licensed), from cabaret to vaudeville to the music hall. Indeed, it was a kind of illegitimate form that required new gestures and technologies, new tones and sounds, new negotiations of space and spatial practices to traverse, or at least occupy, the distance between audience and performer enacted by modern popular performance. This distracted spectatorship and its structure of interruption— what cabaret historian Lisa Appignanesi characterizes as the cabaret's "nodal point of participation and provocation"—help better explain the dialectics of intimacy and alienation between performer and audience that uneasily shape the cohabitation of space and the achievement of intimacy. [74] As Ethel Waters demonstrated, standing silent on the small stage in "contemptuous nonchalance" amid the din at Edmond's, cabaret performance is rupture and repair at once.

The intimate strategies and gestures that cabaret workers such as Waters developed were important not only for the integrity of the performance but also for earning a living. As a space of entertainment in an emergent middle-class leisure industry, the cabaret developed in a structural relationship to work. This made the cabaret's intimacy deeply entangled with, and often inseparable from, economic production and wage labor. Against romantic notions of intimacy as a sphere of relations or feelings outside of market forces, the intimacy of the cabaret is not only taken up within commercial practices and exchange value, but is often produced through them. To take just one example, cabaret performance was often structured by a tip economy in which performers and hosts "work the room." This tip economy had its own codes, strategies, and risks. Offering advice to new performers, bandleader Louis Mitchell warned that "When you sit too long drinking with people, you get too intimate. Then they're embarrassed about giving you a tip. It's all right to sit down and have a drink, but excuse yourself as soon as possible and say you have to get back to the door. And even at the door, be careful. Never raise your hand to shake a customer's, let him raise his hand first." [75] In this account, intimacy is both physical proximity and social familiarity. It becomes a necessary tool of remuneration for the performer, and overfamiliarity becomes a professional liability. In a similar vein, Ada "Bricktop" Smith describes the wage arrangements in some of the clubs in which she worked. At one nightspot, "entertainers were given a choice: they could be paid a straight twenty-one dollars a week or take twelve dollars and split the tips the customers threw on the floor." She started out taking a weekly wage, but soon learned that tips from eager patrons allowed her to take home significantly more money. The club owner, too, benefited from such an arrangement, since he did not need to pay the performers, but could rely on the patrons to support them. [76] Tip economies often created competition among performers and other employers, especially at nightspots that tried to distribute tips equally to the entire working staff. Waitresses and bartenders learned to palm tips that were supposed to go in the general pool. At Harlem's Capitol Palace, things could get so bad that pianist Willie "the Lion" Smith requested a mirror placed above his piano so he could survey the scene as he performed, keeping an eye on his coworkers and adding another layer to the play of looks that crisscrossed the cabaret. [77] These economies that support nightlife—and that nightlife supports—were as crucial a part of the production of intimacy as any dance floor trespass or sideways glance.

Having outlined the cabaret's general relations of performance, it is important to remember that the intimacy produced by cabaret performance is not a product of abstract spatial relations but of how those abstract conditions were inhabited and embodied in specific local and national contexts. The internal relations of performance shaped and were shaped by external relations, ideologies, discourses, and histories. This is another way of pointing out that the photographs of Harlem's cabaret we saw above show caba-

FIGURE 6 "Dancing in a Café." Photograph and Prints Division, Schomburg Center for Research in Black Culture, The New York Public Library, Astor, Lenox and Tilden Foundations.

rets in unused states. They were likely taken in the daytime, before open-ing. The orderly arrangement and totalizing view anticipates the actual use of the space that would reorder such organization in the evening and belies the messy heterogeneity of cabaret sociality. The empty tables evoke what stage vernacular called "snow blindness"—the experience had by many a second-rate performer of looking out during a show and seeing the glare of clean tablecloths on unused tables reflecting back at them. And in the case of Harlem's nightlife during the Negro vogue, snow blindness takes on a second meaning, referring not only to clean tablecloths on empty tables, but also, in many nightclubs, to the sea of white faces that filled the room.

Let's turn, then, to one more photograph of a cabaret interior in order to mark what these other photographs fail to convey, a rare snapshot taken of a Harlem basement cabaret at night. Titled "Dancing in a Café" by archivists at New York Public Library's Schomburg Center for Black Research, the image is undated and unidentified; it is a piece of ephemera from Harlem's everynight life (fig. 6). In the foreground are white-linened tables and open bottles of champagne recently abandoned for the movements of the dance floor. Beyond the tables, couples dance together to the sound of the small ensemble in the background. Filled with movement and sound, the cabaret invites this crossing of space and boundaries, the turning of chairs, the play of looks, the circulation, drinking, and dancing of the crowd. This intimate formation promises to continually exceed itself, organizing and reorganizing bodily configurations, sightlines, identities, experiences, and desires. Yet although "Dancing in a Café" might offer a useful corrective to the abstract discussion of spatial practices above, it too cannot help but to freeze and immobilize the dynamic production of intimacy that it documents in its photographic trace. Despite this, such photographs, like the texts and performances we will examine in subsequent chapters, can continue beyond their initial enactment or audience to create new intimate formations and public intimacies as they are taken up in new contexts and circulate across different times and spaces.

This chapter's outline of cabaret performance—its genealogical influences and relations of performance—suggests some of the ways that *cabaret* has signified and functioned in different times and places. It also describes the development of a performance framework for feelings of belonging and connection as well as alienation and interruption. More specifically, as the cabaret tradition converged with the history of black performance in the United States, intimacy emerged as a specific nightlife experience and technology, constituting an affective domain for the intersecting fields of racial and sexual knowledge production. It is to the queer and nonwhite racialized uses of this structure and style of performance during the Harlem Renaissance that I turn next. During the Harlem Renaissance, the cabaret's production of intimacy was a crucial resource for a queer-of-color critique that was both part of and exceeded the Harlem Renaissance: part of the Harlem Renaissance in that it critiqued the white supremacist ideologies and racist iconographies of U.S. popular and literary cultures; in excess of it in that it constituted a location for intraracial critique of the Harlem Renaissance's limiting politics of respectability. We will see in the chapters that follow how black writers and performers made use of cabaret's mode of address and relations of performance in order to elaborate this critique and enact new possibilities for social relations and public intimacy in both print culture and performance culture, often crossing the boundaries between the two.

———— ✳ ————

CHAPTER TWO

The Scene of Harlem Cabaret

1926 and After

When I sit in the drafty basement that is the New World Cabaret with a white person, my color comes.

ZORA NEALE HURSTON,
"HOW IT FEELS TO BE COLORED ME"

"What?" Arline was genuinely surprised. "You in Harlem and never been to a cabaret? Why I thought all colored people went." Emma Lou bristled. White people were so stupid.

WALLACE THURMAN, THE BLACKER THE BERRY

If Bessie Smith had killed some white people she wouldn't have needed that music.

AMIRI BARAKA, DUTCHMAN

IN THE 1920s a very specific image of Harlem cabaret was crafted, an image that still structures how black urban performance in that decade is understood. James Weldon Johnson identified the 1920s as the era "when Harlem was made known as the scene of laughter, singing, dancing, and primitive passions, and as the center of the New Negro literature and art." This scene became a formula, even a cliché, repeated and refined not just in the nightclub and on the Broadway stage, but in novels, short stories, film, poetry, journalism, and historical and sociological studies. In his assessment of this scene—where it came from; what it meant—Johnson proposes that "the picturesque Harlem was real, but it was the writers who discovered its artistic values and, in giving literary expression to them, actually created the Harlem that caught the world's imagination."[1] It was between the "literary" and the "real," between discursive and nondiscursive practices, that the scene of Harlem cabaret becomes legible *as* a scene.

Johnson was in a good position to recognize this interplay of text and performance. He was part of the turn-of-the-century scene at the Marshall Hotel, the Black Bohemia rooming house, barroom, and professional club where a generation of stage and musical performers such as Bert Williams, George Walker, Aida Overton Walker, Will Marion Cook, and Johnson's brother, J. Rosamond Johnson, congregated, celebrated, and commiserated over the conditions and opportunities for black performance. Despite his own commitment to Progressive Era racial uplift, Johnson was always sympathetic to the ethics, sociality, and creative labor of the urban underworld and rejected the moralizing and pathologizing precepts of uplift ideology. His genre-bending, anonymously published novel *The Autobiography of an Ex-Colored Man* (1912) offered detailed descriptions of Marshall's and the midtown Ike Hines's club that were so ethnographically accurate that he reprinted passages verbatim in *Black Manhattan* (1930), his sociological history of black performance in New York City. Together, these two books plumbed the depth and range of musical work, stage life, and the "sporting world" at the turn of the century, offering a complex image of nightlife ethics and insisting on the black nightclub as a context where "new artistic ideas were born and developed."[2]

As such, Johnson's *Autobiography of an Ex-Colored Man* was an important precursor to the project the Cabaret School would develop, in a much different context, after 1926. (Johnson's novel, in fact, was republished under his own name in 1927, making it simultaneously prior to and part of the Harlem Renaissance's Cabaret School.) The year 1926 saw a critical shift in Harlem Renaissance debates over the politics of representation and the appropriate subject matter for black literature as younger writers challenged the literary prescriptions of the civil rights establishment.[3] This shift coincided with the rise of the Negro vogue and another wave of crackdowns on Harlem's nightlife by the city, which passed new licensing regulations and initiated a campaign against racial intermingling in Harlem nightclubs.[4] These shifts in the worlds of literature and nightlife performance were in part a response to the appearance that year of two works by white writers, which profoundly shaped the representational terrain of Harlem's cabaret: Carl Van Vechten's novel *Nigger Heaven* (1926) and Edward Sheldon and Charles MacArthur's Broadway play *Lulu Belle* (1926). The wide literary and theatrical success of these works (*Nigger Heaven* went through fourteen printings in a little over a year; *Lulu Belle* had a run of 461 performances on Broadway and was revived in Los Angeles later in the decade) helped to fix Harlem in the national and international imaginary as an entertainment district. Both works featured key scenes that consolidated a narrative of primitivism and exoticism around the bits of Harlem and black performance that had seeped into white consciousness through race records, radio broadcasts, newspaper articles, and performance reviews. In so visibly taking up Harlem's nightlife, *Nigger Heaven* and *Lulu Belle* informed the emergence and formation of something loosely described as the Cabaret School, the multiple texts and performances that took up Harlem's cabaret in order to critique the imperatives of racial and sexual normativity.[5]

Long before *Nigger Heaven* was published, Van Vechten wrote about Harlem's nightlife and black performance in his journalism and promoted black writers such as Langston Hughes in white publications — to the suspicion of some Harlem Renaissance leaders. In his 1925 "Prescription for the Negro Theatre" (published in the trendsetting *Vanity Fair*) he issued a plea for black theatrical revues, which he found increasingly formulaic and sanitized, to turn to the scene of the cabaret and the "spirit of the frequenters" in Harlem's nightlife in the hope that they would reinvigorate the perfunctory performances of blackness on the Broadway stage:

> The reproduction of a scene in an authentic Negro cabaret, such as Small's (if it could be reproduced), would be another excellent plan. Naturally it would not bear the slightest resemblance to the cabaret scene ordinarily exhibited on the stage. The difficulty would not be to match the ebullient entertainers, or the dancing waiters, or the eccentric jazz band, with its mad drummer, who might all be transplanted successfully in person, but to recapture the spirit of the frequenters of the resort as they go through the paces of the Black Bottom, the Hey Hey, the Scronch, and the gestures of the Itch and the Picking Cherries, and all the other gestures and paces that accompany the insane trappings of the drum, the moans of the hatted trumpet, and the harmonious thumpings of the piano.

This cabaret scene, he suggests, should be staged along with other spectacles of stereotyped blackness and primitivism, culminating "with a wild pantomimic drama set in an African forest with the men and women nearly nude as the law allows."[6] Van Vechten's ideal black performance was one in which (white) spectators participated vicariously in the experience of blackness through the gestures and paces of black spectators, which in this description become an extension of the "insane trappings," moans, and thumpings of the jazz band—gestures which draw a direct line from the cabaret to the jungle. His novel *Nigger Heaven* amplified this call in literary form. Largely about the frustrated romance between a middle-class black librarian and an aspiring writer in Harlem society, the novel advanced the Negro vogue with sensational scenes of fictional cabarets like the Winter Palace and the Black Venus. The novel's final cabaret scene descends into a cocaine-induced nightmarescape in an underground cabaret-turned-catacomb called the Black Mass, where the line between human and inhuman, life and death, pleasure and pain, blurs in a frenzy of black performance that culminates with sexual orgies, sadomasochistic abjection, spirit possession, and ritual sacrifice. With such characteristic excess, Van Vechten often made a case for the cultural politics of representation more persuasively than its own boosters could.

Just as significant—possibly more—to the heightened fascination with Harlem's cabaret in 1926 was Edward Sheldon and Charles MacArthur's *Lulu Belle,* a "mulatta melodrama" dubbed by one reviewer as "the Carmen of Harlem."[7] The play follows the career of Lulu Belle, a calculating and capricious light-skinned nightclub entertainer and dancer (played on Broadway by the white actress Lenore Ulric in blackface) who achieves world fame but is, in the end, murdered by one of her many discarded suitors. Critics were less impressed with *Lulu Belle's* plot or acting than they were with the verisimilitude of its staging: a black street scene (complete with a four-story tenement, functioning fire escapes, and a Ford automobile), a Harlem boarding house, a luxurious Parisian apartment, and, most highly praised, a recreation of a Harlem cabaret, where the performance of the Charleston was a show-stopping number. The play not only directed downtown audiences uptown to see Harlem's cabarets firsthand, but also inspired a cabaret after it: queer-of-color subcultures in Harlem adopted the tragic Lulu Belle as a camp icon and staged drag shows at the newly christened Lulu Belle Club.[8]

As was usually the case with Negro vogue narratives of the cabaret, both *Lulu Belle* and *Nigger Heaven* pivot on a notion of a corrupted and corrupting black female sexuality. Like Lulu Belle, Lasca Sartoris, the campy sexual predator of Van Vechten's novel, condensed sociological stereotypes of nightlife's moral pathology and cultural stereotypes of the light-complexioned or "mulatta" temptress into a singular sexual and racial threat. These two works suggest some of the representations of blackness that Harlem Renaissance leaders sought to counter. The narrative pleasure both stories provided relied upon suspicions of black female sexuality and the moral consequences of its enactment, whether in the staging of Lulu Belle's death at the hands of a scorned suitor or the slow torment and destruction of *Nigger Heaven*'s male protagonist at the hands of Lasca Sartoris. The sexual distortions of such depictions ultimately reinscribed a moral judgment on expressions of female sexuality, spectacularized and racialized its embodiment, and turned the scene of the cabaret into something like a morality tale. It is no wonder, then, that such hyperbole and excess lent itself to camp reappropriation. The cross-gendered rewriting of Lulu Belle and her sexual immorality by male queers of color was one way that those who found community and intimacy in Harlem's everynight life disrupted and parodied such narratives. Drag performances and other acts of gender insubordination at the Lulu Belle Club resurrected the maligned Lulu Belle to deliver a new verdict on her transgressions.[9] Cabaret School writers, too, as we will see in more detail below, similarly contended with this construction of deviant or unrestrained black female sexuality as they frequented the scene of Harlem cabaret after 1926.

Twentieth-century black literature had, of course, depicted nightlife prior to *Lulu Belle* and *Nigger Heaven*. Passages in Paul Laurence Dunbar's *The Sport of the Gods* (1902), Johnson's *Autobiography* (1912), Jean Toomer's *Cane* (1923), Langston Hughes's cabaret poetry (which appeared in both black and white publications in the three years before 1926), and urban blues lyrics all examined the social and sexual complexities of the scene of black urban performance and entertainment. But *Nigger Heaven* and *Lulu Belle* gave the screw of representational politics another turn, so to speak, and after these works, the cabaret took on a particularly contentious cast within the Harlem Renaissance. While *Nigger Heaven*'s influence on the Harlem Renaissance is often overstated, its impact on the landscape of Harlem's nightlife was significant. Few readers believed that *Nigger Heaven* or *Lulu Belle* offered realistic depictions of Harlem's nightlife, but the play and the novel, popular sensations both, further established the image of Harlem as an interracial entertainment district.[10] Moreover, they shaped how the cabaret was—and could be—described. As we will see below, an easily gendered, sexualized, and racialized taxonomy began to shape the catalogue of Harlem's cabarets as ambitious entrepreneurs capitalized on the burgeoning entertainment scene: on one hand, those segregated cabarets that cultivated a primarily—though not exclusively—white audience for black performance, and on the other, those "black cabarets" that provided a space of sociality, intimacy, and performance for primarily—though not exclusively—black audiences and performers.

As Johnson maintained, the relationship between performance and text was not one of source material to fiction, but one that mutually shaped the perceptions, experiences, and spectatorial and performance practices of the cabaret. By approaching the relationship between the literary cabaret and cabaret performances as reciprocal and dynamic, we can better understand how the scene of Harlem cabaret performed and resonated in Harlem Renaissance writing. In what follows, I first look at the binary of segregated cabarets/"black cabarets" that structured the conceptual organization of Harlem nightlife during the 1920s. Even as this dualistic taxonomy affirmed many of the central assumptions of the Negro vogue and its desire for "authentic" blackness and black sexuality, it provided some necessary and practical generalizations about Harlem's audiences, aesthetics, and history for those nonwhite subjects moving through it. It helped guide black performers to specific places of employment or enjoyment, for example, and signaled the social and aesthetic codes that made navigating Jim Crow performance culture possible. Yet like all binaries, the taxonomy of segregated cabarets/"black cabarets" does not permit the analytic nuance or flexibility that would help us begin to account for the unsystematic ways that Harlem's everynight life was experienced. Indeed, this binary often renders such everynight experiences unintelligible. In the second section, then, I look at the way this binary was lived, negotiated, and deconstructed by the everynight subjects who crossed its respective thresholds and inhabited its recesses. To do so, I turn to sociologist Erving Goffman, by way of Houston Baker Jr. to suggest a model of situational "tightness" and "looseness" as a way to understand the scene of Harlem cabaret. Within this framework, I then look specifically to how the tight scenes of Harlem's everynight life were loosened and expanded by the black writers of the Cabaret School. In particular, a cluster of writings after 1926—Nella Larsen's *Quicksand* (1928), Zora Neale Hurston's "How It Feels to Be Colored Me" (1928), and Wallace Thurman's *The Blacker the Berry* (1929)—took up the scene of Harlem cabaret as a location from which to critique both the racial and sexual normativity of uplift elites and the racial and sexual subjection of white spectatorial practices.

Critics have often assumed that the Cabaret School contributed to the Negro vogue and the cult of primitivism consolidated around Harlem's entertainment district by works like *Nigger Heaven* and *Lulu Belle*. On closer examination, however, we will see that these scenes were engaged in a deep tradition of exploring the racial, sexual, and social possibilities of black urban nightlife performance and worked to continue and expand that tradition when faced with the simplifications and fetishizations of the Negro vogue. This is another way of saying that the writers and performers of the Cabaret School voiced a critique of the vogue while maintaining a fidelity to the possibilities of black performance and the intimacies of everynight life.

SEGREGATED CABARETS AND "BLACK CABARETS"

Nigger Heaven and *Lulu Belle* lifted the curtain on the recently opened clubs in Harlem, not so much exposing a hidden secret as codifying an interpretation that had already begun to achieve some currency in the preceding years. The vicissitudes of the color line as it was drawn and redrawn through Harlem's nightlife sorted its nightclubs to one side or the other, causing two distinct kinds of cabaret performances to appear in the social and literary generalizations of the decade. The first were those that staged spectacular productions of black performance primarily for the white, middle-class audiences that had emerged in the 1910s as public amusements rose in prominence and acceptability. With large orchestras and extravagant revues, Harlem's biggest nightclubs were sometimes officially, sometimes unofficially whites-only establishments. Except for those light-skinned patrons who could pass as white or those with the money or clout to make it past the doorman, these clubs welcomed African Americans only as waiters, busboys, cooks, and, above all, entertainers. Though it billed itself as a "colored club," Barron Wilkins's Exclusive Club (at 134th Street and Seventh Avenue) opened in 1915 and was one of the first cabarets in Harlem to begin catering to white and very light-skinned patrons. Harlem Renaissance writer Rudolph Fisher was once turned away from Barron's because he was too dark; he wrote that Barron's "simply wasn't a Negro cabaret; it was a cabaret run by Negroes for whites."[11] Ethel Waters likewise maintained that "the ordinary working colored people weren't wanted there and knew better than to try and get in."[12] Connie's Inn (at 131st Street and Seventh Avenue), was described by one white nightlife guide as "rambling, subterranean, and black as an African coal mine"—though the guide immediately reassured its readers that the "clientele is wholly white and, for the most part, dressy."[13] It drew a white audience in the hundreds for premier floorshows, like *Keep Shufflin'* (1928) and *Hot Chocolates* (1929), that brought dozens of light-skinned chorus girls to tableside proximity. Small's Paradise (at 135th Street and Seventh Avenue), the cabaret Van Vechten wanted to see translated to the Broadway stage, allowed for a mixed audience, though its high prices and white-marketed performances made it an unlikely destination for most working-class Harlem residents. Its more relaxed admission policy was a selling point for many white visitors, who were promised actual racial intermingling along with the all-black floorshow (and by the late 1920s, Small's even began employing black writers and composers). On weekends the large basement cabaret crowded in some 1,200 to 1,500 people for its late-night shows.[14]

Performances at these segregated cabarets functioned as what Saidiya Hartman calls a "scene of subjection," a historical staging of blackness that depends on the complicity of enjoyment, entertainment, and spectatorship for the subjugation of black Americans. Such scenes "outline a problematic of enjoyment in which pleasure is inseparable from subjection, will indistinguishable from submission, and bodily integrity bound to violence."[15] Opening in 1923, the Cotton Club (at 142nd Street and Lenox Avenue) was perhaps the most famous of these white-marketed cabarets, nightly staging such scenes of subjection. While the actual practice of segregation at this cabaret was far from absolute, I take the Cotton Club as an exemplary manifestation of what we could think of as "Jim Crow cosmopolitanism" in the U.S. North: a white relationship to the color line that imagines itself, against the explicit barbarism of southern Jim Crow, in terms of urbane sophistication, benevolent patronage, and flirtatious transgression. New York City politicians, Wall Street financiers, Hollywood movie stars, and elite society figures flocked in their jewels and costly cars to this Harlem nightclub. Once inside, the Cotton Club staged an entire mise-en-scène of antebellum nostalgia and modernist primitivism, setting jungle designs alongside plantation motifs. Duke Ellington's son, Mercer, recalled that "the stage was set up to represent the Land of Cotton, with a plantation cabin, rows of cotton bushes, and trees that shot up when the show started."[16] Cab Calloway commented dryly, "I suppose the idea was to make whites who came to the club feel like they were being catered to and entertained by black slaves."[17] By the mid-1920s, over seven hundred people crowded inside on the weekends to dine, dance, mix, mingle, see, be seen, and catch the renowned performances.

These antebellum set pieces and interior designs shaped the spectatorial cues and theatrical possibilities of the all-black nightclub revue throughout the 1920s and 1930s. The nightclub revue was a plotless performance mode built around vaudeville-inspired acts, ribald comedy sketches, spectacular chorus numbers, and popular songs. Like Harlem's other segregated cabarets, the Cotton Club produced two Broadway-style revues a year, lavish productions with scores of cast members, musicians, and light-skinned chorus girls. These shows, known as the *Cotton Club Parades* after 1931, showcased black performance and choreography primarily scripted, designed, and staged by white writers, composers, and directors.[18] The *Parades* competed with other well-known revue franchises like Lew Leslie's *Blackbird* revues, Florenz Ziegfeld's *Follies,* George White's *Scandals,* and Earl Carroll's *Vanities.* The *Cotton Club Parades* distinguished themselves by consistently featuring the nation's most famous black entertainers. The revue was an ideal form for the performances at Harlem's white-marketed cabarets, offering blackness as spectacle and surface and allowing white audiences a carefully choreographed and controlled access to blackness and black sexuality under terms that were ultimately unthreatening to their own social position or sense of self. As kinetic, spectacle-driven performances, with neither narrative nor psychological realism, there was little need for interpretive work from either the spectator or, sometimes, the performer, who often saw such gigs as nothing more than a job.[19]

Hartman's analysis of such scenes of subjection draws from antebellum stagings of black amusement and contentment on the auction block, the coffle, and the blackface stage of minstrelsy and melodrama. She identifies the many ways that pleasure and pain, amusement and suffering, were inextricably linked in slave subjectivity and performance. While the scene of Harlem's segregated cabarets resembles these antebellum amusements, there are important differences between the minstrelsy and melodrama of the nineteenth century and 1920s cabaret revue. Located after Reconstruction's failure and within Jim Crow–era ideology, the cabaret is an emblem of a different historical moment and a different mode of popular amusement than slave amusements. In minstrel shows, the black body was posed as a figure of ridicule and mockery. In melodrama, the black body was also posed as a figure of virtue and suffering. In both of these popular amusements, as opposed to Harlem cabaret, the black body was performed by white actors in blackface (though Ulric's performance in *Lulu Belle* reminds us that blackface continued well into the 1920s and beyond). On the white-marketed cabaret stage of the 1920s, black performers had significant opportunities to push against the tight constraints of white-authored performance conventions and, as we will see below, develop and refine urban musical traditions and gain some access to and influence within the music, recording, and popular performance industries.

Nonetheless, performative vestiges of both the minstrel stage and the melodrama could be found in the "innocent amusements" of the segregated cabaret revues of the 1920s, not least in the creation of a spectatorial field where black performers filled the stage for the pleasure of a white audience variously as spectacles of sexuality and athleticism, as images of comic and grotesque buffoonery, and as figures on a pastoral landscape of plantation nostalgia.[20] The celebrated waiters at Small's Paradise, for example, delivered drinks while doing the Charleston. According to one account, recorded by the Federal Writers' Project: "Twirling trays high above the heads of the customers and balancing them precariously on one or two fingers, they danced between dancing couples where paper could hardly have been passed. Their journey ended, they contrived a special flourish of the tray, an intricate flurry of dance steps, and deposited a pitcher of raw gin on a customer's table."[21] Such spectacularization allowed white patrons proximity to the sexuality and physicality of blackness that also unfolded on the cabaret stage, while at the same time effacing labor with entertainment and service with enjoyment. The mise-en-scène of the Cotton Club and the dancing waiters at Small's thus literalized Sterling Brown's observation in 1933 that "a kinship exists between this stereotype [of the exotic primitive] and that of the contented slave; one is merely a 'jazzed up' version of the other, with cabarets supplanting cabins, and Harlemized 'blues,' instead of the spirituals and slave reels."[22] The scene of Harlem cabaret in the 1920s continued to depend upon such nineteenth-century discourses of black contentment and amusement, while modifying and adapting them within a modernist aesthetic and a cosmopolitan mindset.

"Scene," however, has a double sense as both a frame of performance and spectacle circumscribed by certain theatrical and spectatorial conventions, as in the discussion above, and as a hot spot, a sphere of activity, a place where *things happen* (these two connotations, I hasten to add, are far from mutually exclusive). The second kind of cabaret and cabaret performances that emerges in descriptions of Harlem's nightlife are those spaces of black performance that were locations for the dance, sociality, and good times that Albert Murray calls the "Saturday Night Function."[23] The Saturday Night Function—whichever day of the week—was a scene of black vernacular world making. These performances, which flourished alongside the scenes of subjection in segregated clubs, had genealogical traces in the brief allowances of dance and sociality by slave owners, antebellum practices of "stealing away," church dances, and the development of the jook joint. Cabaret School writer Claude McKay placed these clubs in the geography of black economic and social solidarity: "between Seventh Avenue and Eighth the population was still white. The saloons were run by the Irish, the restaurants by the Greeks, the ice and fruit stands by the Italians, the grocery and haberdashery by the Jews. The only Negro businesses, excepting barber

shops, were the churches and the cabarets."[24] Each of these social spaces—
barber shops, churches, and "black cabarets"—offered variations of racial
community for black Harlem. These clubs were sometimes advertised in the
black press, but more often thrived by word-of-mouth publicity spread by
musicians traveling through and locals who would initiate new visitors into
the geography of nightlife.

Harlem's "black cabarets" were typically small, working-class establishments that could not support the extravagant floorshows of a Cotton Club
or Connie's Inn. They more often had a three- or five-piece band in the
corner of a makeshift dance floor. They were, in the words of James Weldon Johnson, places of musical "emulation and guildship"—locations of
pleasure, instruction, networking, and professionalization for performers
and musicians.[25] The Rhythm Club (at 131st Street and Seventh Avenue),
for example, had no singers or floorshow, but drew a late-night crowd after performers got off work at the white-trade clubs. Ambitious musicians
would play informally, hoping for an opportunity to sit in for a number
with established performers or to be heard by a bandleader looking for side-
men (Duke Ellington often found players there). The Nest Club (at 133rd
Street and Lenox Avenue) was similarly "more music than floorshow," and
like many of Harlem's "black cabarets" was an economically and socially
supportive environment for newly arrived musicians.[26] The Lenox Club (at
143rd Street and Lenox Avenue) was slightly more theatrical, with three
musical sets a night that included a small floorshow of eight chorus girls, as
well as its popular Breakfast Dances on Sunday mornings from 7:00 a.m.
until 11:00 a.m. The Lenox was primarily a black space but occasionally
attracted white spectators from the Cotton Club down the block who were
not ready to head home at closing time.[27]

Paradoxically, there is a crucial relationship between the intimate and
crowded scale of these clubs and the possibilities for black subjective expansion. The Capitol Palace (at 139th Street and Lenox Avenue) could com-
fortably accommodate about forty couples on its basement dance floor—a
fraction of the crowd that would fill Connie's Inn or Small's Paradise—
though according to pianist Willie "the Lion" Smith, "on Saturday night
they would try to squeeze a thousand people into the room."[28] Yet such
crowded conditions were in practice more socially loose and comfortable for
many black patrons and performers than the much larger white-marketed
nightclubs. Singer Ethel Waters first made her name in Harlem at Edmond's Cellar (at 133rd Street and Fifth Avenue), which was typical of many
small, basement cabarets. It seated between 150 and 200 patrons at small
tables wedged around what Waters described as a "handkerchief-size dance

floor" and a three-piece band.[29] Such clubs were often the location of after-hours "cutting sessions," musically expansive jam sessions where performers staged improvisational duels to show each other up. At Mexico's (at 133rd Street and Seventh Avenue), cutting contests were organized around instruments: one night might be devoted to the trumpet, another to piano. Duke Ellington recalled the tuba cutting one night at Mexico's: "The joint was small and it had a hard turn as you walked downstairs to get it. The cats who weren't actually playing all stood out on the sidewalk with their big tubas. It was too dangerous to fight your way through that hall and all those drunks with that big, valuable thing in your arms."[30] Intimacy, improvisation, and aesthetic movement occurred both in spite of and by way of the crowded arrangements of these clubs.

If the Cotton Club and other segregated cabarets were constructed scenes of black performance, the smaller, "black cabarets" like Mexico's or the Capitol Palace were no less constructed, though the constructions themselves were not alike. The relationship between the aural and the visual, for example, was different in the "black cabarets" than it was in the segregated cabarets. The black bodies in the spectacular revues and chorus lines in the segregated cabarets were prepared for performance according to racial aesthetics and theatrical conventions that reinscribed the "truth" of blackness for a white audience as either primitive or sexually and socially deviant. The spectacle in the segregated cabarets emphasized the visual display of excessive embodiment, and the sound of jazz or blues was often naturalized as black authenticity by such kinesthetic performances. The performances in the "black cabarets" were no less spectacular or sexual, but the spectacle of the band in performance emphasized instead the production of sound and a reciprocity between performers and audience. In so doing it marked a counterhistory to the "truth" of blackness naturalized in the white-marketed cabarets. Yet while these two institutions—segregated cabarets and "black cabarets"—cultivated different kinds of sounds and performances that advanced very different performance traditions, and while they allowed for necessary generalizations for those performers and spectators navigating Harlem's nightlife, we will see that the actual practices and performances in these spaces were rarely so easily codified.

BREATHING SPACE AND WIGGLE ROOM

As nightlife receded with the rising sun, the veil came down on Harlem. Critics then and now have been quick to point out that Harlem was not only an entertainment district but also, and primarily, a residential neighborhood.

While downtown tourists flocked to 142nd Street and Seventh Avenue for midnight shows, their taxis rarely ventured down the side streets where the majority of Harlem's residents lived and worked. W. E. B. Du Bois made this point in 1926 when he wrote that "the overwhelming majority of black folk [in Harlem] never go to cabarets. The average colored man in Harlem is an everyday laborer, attending church, lodge and movie and is as conservative and as conventional as ordinary working folk everywhere." [31] James Weldon Johnson seconded him in 1933 when he noted that downtown visitors would be unlikely to see "the other, real and overshadowing Harlem. The commonplace, work-a-day Harlem. The Harlem of the doubly handicapped black masses engaged in the grim, daily struggle for existence in the midst of this whirlpool of white civilization." [32] Hughes more succinctly reminded readers in 1940 that "most of the whites saw nothing but the cabarets, not the houses." [33] This refrain from Renaissance writers was later reprised by a subsequent generation of historians. In his landmark history of the Harlem Renaissance, Nathan Irvin Huggins wrote that "the white hunter in New York's heart of darkness would not see (doubtless, would not recognize) his 'savage-primitive' drummer and dancer, on sore, bunioned feet picking their way on morning's concrete to cold-water flats, to lose their rhythm-weary bodies in sexless sleep." [34] Historian David Levering Lewis later echoed these sentiments: "People rose in Harlem each day to go to work, many of them before the last white revelers had careened homeward. The great majority never saw the interior of a nightclub." [35] This recurrent critique necessarily recalls the material and social realities of Harlem: the high cost of living and extraordinary rents, combined with low wages and employment discrimination, made the neighborhood's streets, row houses, and tenement complexes cramped and crowded spaces that belied the expressive freedom of the cabaret, segregated or otherwise. [36]

Occasionally, cabaret performers made the tensions between the fantasy of the nightclub stage and the reality of tenement dwellings the subject of formal critique in their musical productions. In 1940, Duke Ellington recorded a swing symphony whose title, *Harlem Air Shaft*, directly invoked the image of poverty and tenement living. The air shaft was introduced into the architecture of urban housing in order to ameliorate the living conditions of the immigrant poor and improve social hygiene in slum areas by bringing a modicum of ventilation, sunlight, and (especially in the hot summer months) a little extra breathing room into dark and stagnant corners of tenement housing. It was a well-intentioned but fundamentally flawed concept. The narrow shafts guaranteed that those on the bottom floors received little sunlight, and the shafts often became repositories for garbage and debris. And, by focusing reformist energies on architectural concerns, they displaced attention from the structural causes of misery and scarcity. From sociological and public policy perspectives, the air shaft has been since its deployment a symbol of the tight space of urban crowding, poverty, and confinement.

This, however, was not the experience of the air shaft that inspired Ellington's symphony. Foregrounding the experience of the air shaft as a vector, not of disease, but of sound, smell, touch, contact, intimacy, and publicness, Ellington described the mood of *Harlem Air Shaft* as an attempt to conjure the mundane sociality of tenement living: "So much goes on in a Harlem air shaft. . . . You hear fights, you smell dinner, you hear people making love. You hear intimate gossip floating down. You hear the radio. An air shaft is one great big loudspeaker. You see your neighbors' laundry. You hear the janitor's dogs. The man upstairs' aerial falls down and breaks your window. You smell coffee. A wonderful thing, that smell. An air shaft has got every contrast. One guy is cooking dried fish and rice and another guy's got a great big turkey. . . . You hear people praying, fighting, snoring. . . . I tried to put all that in *Harlem Air Shaft*." [37] Ellington takes the confines of the air shaft, an enclosed and claustrophobic symbol of poverty and slum living, and turns it inside out, pushing against confining material conditions to signify opportunities for social and subjective expansion.

Ethel Waters described a similar relationship between her performances in the tight space of Edmond's Cellar and the crowded intimacy of urban poverty. Waters's early reputation and fame came from her unequaled ability to create narratives in her performances of otherwise banal popular standards by treating each song as a minor affective drama. She based these dramas on the everyday life of the tenement: "I'd hear a couple in another flat arguing, for instance. Their voices would come up the air shaft and I'd listen making up stories about their spats and their love life. I could hear such an argument in the afternoon and that night sing a whole song about it. I'd sing out their woes to the tune of my blues music." [38] Like Ellington, Waters turns inside out the confines of the air shaft on the nightclub stage. Their formal transformations of the air shaft reflect their respective modes of performance. Conducting an orchestra, Ellington organized the multiple sounds of the tenement into a symphonic composition by layering the distinctive tones and sounds of his band's individual instruments into a single sound that nevertheless retains its particularities—the experience that his protégé Billy Strayhorn called the "Ellington Effect." [39] Singing blues as a vocalist, Waters drew upon the emotional register of individual experience to translate the bits of sound and intimacy that echoed in the air shaft into public expressions of private feelings collectively shared by the audience. Both Ellington's arrangement and Waters's blues amplified the heteroglossia of city life and expanded movement, narrative, and intimacy beyond the narrow vertical hold of tenement walls.

Drawing a line from the air shaft as a space for the performance of everyday life and the cellar as a space for the performance of everynight life, both Ellington and Waters describe acts of composition that formally expanded tight spaces and created moments of looseness for men and women. I want to suggest this modulation between tightness and looseness — at once spatial and social, discursive and nondiscursive, sonic and kinesthetic, performative and ontological — as one way to think about black performance in Jim Crow America.[40] Sociologist Erving Goffman classifies tight spaces as those gatherings, settings, and relationships of social life where codes of comportment, behavior, expression, speech, situational obligations, and appearance are tightly scripted and dictated. Tight spaces may produce a feeling of social claustrophobia. Figuratively speaking, there is not a lot of room to move. Loose spaces, on the other hand, are those gatherings and settings where such codes are more informal, where air flows, and there is more freedom to improvise.[41] For Goffman, nightclubs and cabarets in general should qualify as loose spaces, given their relaxed codes of participation, increased informality, and cultivation of recreation and play. But when contextualized within Jim Crow performance history and plotted within the racial and gender coordinates of early-twentieth-century nightlife, the cabaret can be seen as a much more complex scene of social constriction and expansion.

Ellington and Waters were both familiar with the tight confines of the Cotton Club bandstand, where each performed white-authored music for white audiences, and the crowded but looser floors of Edmond's Cellar or the Rhythm Club, where they each played black-authored music and improvised their own sounds for working-class black audiences. Their performances point to some of the ways that tightness-looseness might be a more useful and accurate way of describing the affective geographies of Harlem's everynight life than notions of authentic-inauthentic, true-false, or real-staged. In the language of speech-act theory, tightness-looseness directs us to a performative model of racial production — one that elaborates itself through its doing, thus allowing for improvisation and novel productions — rather than a constative model — one that refers a performer or performance to a preexisting conception in order to evaluate its authenticity.[42] Though Harlem's nightlife was described and necessarily navigated in the dualistic terms of segregated cabarets and "black cabarets," these two categories too easily reify valued oppositions that have structured the historiography of the Harlem Renaissance and of black performance more generally: good versus bad, authenticity versus inauthenticity, purity versus contamination, solidarity versus exploitation, creation versus appropriation. Such conceptualizations make it easy to romanticize the "black cabaret" as a mythic space of racial solidarity and "real" blackness and to dismiss the segregated cabaret simply as a racist institution for the exploitation of black culture and labor.

Segregated cabarets and "black cabarets" existed in a dialectical relationship to each other, affecting each other's development. These two categories had an important function as pragmatic generalizations that made managing and negotiating Harlem's nightlife possible for black performers and participants. But when, as categories, they become fixed or cease functioning generically, they foreclose a nuanced understanding of the multiplicity of racial performances that shaped both of these spaces and obscure the dynamic practices that occurred within and between them. There were, of course, groups of white spectators in black nightclubs long before the Negro vogue in the late 1920s (Rudolph Fisher characterized them as "incidental white people"—usually no more obtrusive than background music).[43] White-marketed cabarets, even the Cotton Club, were similarly known to admit black spectators on occasion. And, more to the point, Harlem's segregated clubs were important institutions of artistic creation and an elaboration of blackness that was never only a performance of exploitation, appropriation, and subjection. The conceptual possibilities offered by a notion of tightness-looseness, suggesting not an either-or system of evaluation but a spectrum of degree and a calculus of mobility, can help us to recognize the performances and social rearrangements of Harlem's everynight life. The tighter a space, the more likely it will substantiate and reinforce existing social and discursive structures. The looser a space, the more likely it will provide opportunities to imagine or enact alternative structures. Such a framework thus invites us to look for loose pockets within tight spaces, those moments of social or musical performance when subjective expansion was—openly or furtively, individually or collectively—cultivated in the Jim Crow United States.[44]

Performing the music of white composers or the dance of white choreographers at segregated clubs limited and constrained opportunities for self-expression, demanding a highly circumscribed performance of blackness and sexuality. Yet even at the Cotton Club and other white-marketed night-clubs, black performers found ways to loosen such tight performance conventions. We might think of Waters's genre-defying rendition of "Stormy Weather" in the *Cotton Club Parade of 1933*, in which she brought psychological realism to the segregated stage, as well as her unprecedented contractual demand to perform once each night rather than the usual three shows a night required of other performers, claiming the right to emotional and physical rest.[45] In a similar vein, Ellington was occasionally able to relax the segregation policy of the Cotton Club in order to allow friends and family to hear him perform, altering the spectatorial makeup of his audience and multiplying the modes of reception for his performance.[46]

By the time they headlined on the stage of the Cotton Club, of course, Ellington and Waters were nationally renowned. As tight as the conventions of white-marketed nightclub revues were for them, those conventions were even more confining for Harlem's less celebrated performers. Lena Horne, who began her career as a dancer at the Cotton Club (and whose negotiations of that tight space I examine further in chapter 5), noted that while the stars at the Cotton Club had small dressing rooms, the chorus girls were herded into one unventilated room backstage before and during shows. Horne later described this backstage region and the working conditions of the Cotton Club that simultaneously belied and realized the frontstage plantation nostalgia. As she moved backstage, cosmopolitan glitz and murals of cotton fields stretching into the horizon gave way to the cramped dressing room that accommodated all twenty-five dancers, "in which we had barely space enough to sit before our makeup mirror." Horne continues:

> I saw that it was littered with loaded ash-trays, coffee containers, newspapers, make-up, fan magazines, the half-eaten sandwiches and cartons of chop suey we were too tired to gulp down, and the bags in which some of the girls brought their knitting or mending. I realized that it reeked of perfume and cigarette smoke, stale perspiration, ad the mingled odors of our many meals. And I longed for a breath of fresh air and some place I could stretch my aching limbs and go to sleep.[47]

The dancers were discouraged from using the club's only women's bathroom because it was for white audience members. Looking back, she acknowledged the Cotton Club as an important institution in the history of black performance, but she tempered that acknowledgment with attention to the experiences of unremarkable performers:

I suppose it is possible to say that the bands and the performers who used the club as a jumping off place for their careers were exploiting as much as they were exploited; that, on balance, the club contributed a great deal to the development of their talents and to the development of an audience for those talents. But those of us on the lower levels were in no position to appreciate such subtleties. All we knew was that we were underpaid and overworked in the most miserable conditions.[48]

Despectacularizing the Cotton Club and drawing attention to the every-night life of unremarkable performers, Horne points out one way that caba-ret's performance conventions and situational obligations apply differently depending on one's location in the nightlife economy.

Similarly, Harlem's "black cabarets," rather than referring to spaces of "actual" blackness or "real" black performance, more precisely reference spaces where the situational obligations and social requirements enforced by the color line were less constricted by the performance of race and music prescribed by white-marketed nightspots. Reed player Cecil Scott remem-bered the Capitol Palace as a place musicians would head to after playing at the white-trade clubs "eager to blow since on their regular jobs they were restricted from righteous playing because they would have to play stock arrangements for floor shows."[49] Scott's "righteous playing" describes not only the sounds of the trumpet or saxophone but the social and subjective space that such sounds brought into being. These clubs and their perfor-mances countered the aesthetic violences of white-authored black revues, provided greater social and regulatory freedom for racial and sexual impro-visation, and offered opportunities to replenish oneself from the quotidian wear and tear of the city or the toil of Jim Crow performance. The situa-tional obligations and performance idioms of Harlem's basement speakeas-ies reveal the paradox that sometimes the more crowded a space, the more possibilities for psychic and aesthetic mobility.

In 1926, *Nigger Heaven* and *Lulu Belle* significantly contributed to the construction of Harlem as a loose space for white bohemians. But as they wove the color line through more of Harlem's nightlife, they simultane-ously produced it as a tighter space for black performers, spectators, and residents. The aesthetic principles and performance conventions of Har-lem's segregated cabarets not only imposed limits on creative possibilities for black performers, but also fetishized and spectacularized a primitivist construction of blackness that the New Negro movement committed itself to undo. The representational policing of the scene of Harlem cabaret by black uplift advocates and Negro vogue tourists—not to mention its literal policing by the city's investigative and administrative powers—tightened those pockets of looseness folded into Harlem's everynight life by black and queer subjects. As we will see, many writers followed the path of Harlem's performers by critiquing the tight conditions of both the Negro vogue and of uplift ideology in order to preserve the cabaret as a space where new social configurations and musical sounds could be assembled.

VARIATIONS ON THE SCENE

In the three years following the popular success of *Nigger Heaven* and *Lulu Belle*, writers of the Harlem Renaissance turned again and again to the scene of Harlem cabaret.[50] These iterations implicitly and often explicitly engaged with the spectacle and rhetoric of white-marketed nightclubs and the social possibilities of "black cabarets" and afterhours clubs. I turn now to three such scenes—one from Larsen's *Quicksand*, another from Hurston's "How It Feels to Be Colored Me," and a third from Thurman's *The Blacker the Berry*—that each offer narratives of the cabaret after *Nigger Heaven* and *Lulu Belle* in order to critique and expand the representational parameters of Harlem's nightlife. As these writers take up the spectacle and rhetoric of white-marketed nightclubs, they suggest that Harlem cabaret in the literature of the 1920s was less often a trope or a metaphor than it was an index of spaces, sounds, and experiences, even as they helped to construct and deconstruct those very experiences. Read intertextually, the echoes and resonances between them allow us to see how they collectively contributed to the meaning of Harlem's nightlife and attempted to secure a little wiggle room in some tight social, literary, and historical situations.

These three passages also serve to remind us that one of the things at stake in the scene of Harlem cabaret after *Nigger Heaven*, *Lulu Belle*, and the long history of uplift's moral policing is the meaning and enactment of women's sexuality. "Some evidence suggests," Goffman notes with the air of hypothesis, "that women, in general, are more tightly defined than men."[51] The social codes that govern women's public behavior are applied more strictly and more forcefully than the codes imposed on men, producing highly gendered relationships to public space, bodily comportment, and norms of sexual respectability. We hear this especially in the sexual and class-coded connotations of the "loose woman" and her "uptight" inverse: vernacular charges that work in concert to discursively circumscribe sexual agency and redefine sexual self-determination in patriarchal interests. Larsen, Hurston, and Thurman each revise this gender construction, using and subverting the representational conventions of Harlem cabaret to loosen the tight confines of racial and sexual normativity in Jim Crow America. All three of these scenes insist upon the cabaret as a space of subjective complexity rather than simplicity, density rather than exposure, performativity rather than truth. They push against the tight constraints of uplift morality and slumming primitivism, offering a more complicated theorization of racialized spectatorship and black performance for a post–Van Vechten, post-*Lulu Belle* Harlem.

In *Quicksand*, Nella Larsen — a close friend of Van Vechten's — chronicles Helga Crane's conflicted navigation of the color line and her untenable status as a biracial woman within Western racial epistemology.[52] Even as it issued a damning critique of the gendered logic of uplift ideology, the novel was widely praised by Harlem Renaissance leaders for its psychological complexity and for refusing the trend toward Harlem's underworld stereotypes — at least for the most part, since the book exemplifies the sort of tightness-looseness dialectic that I discussed above. In the middle of the novel, Helga reluctantly finds herself uptown with friends after a dinner party for a night of Harlem cabareting. Maneuvering through a post-*Nigger Heaven* cabaret scene, Helga is transported from the dance floor by the "savage" sounds of the jazz band in a sequence that begins by echoing Van Vechten's Black Mass only to discard it by the end of the paragraph:

> They danced, ambling lazily to a crooning melody, or violently twisting their bodies, like whirling leaves, to a sudden streaming rhythm, or shaking themselves ecstatically to a thumping of unseen tomtoms. For the while Helga was oblivious to the reek of flesh, smoke, and alcohol, oblivious of the oblivion of the other gyrating pairs, oblivious of the color, the noise, and the grand distorted childishness of it all. She was drugged, lifted, sustained, by the extraordinary music, blown out, ripped out, beaten out, by the joyous, wild, murky orchestra. The essence of life seemed bodily motion. And when suddenly the music died, she dragged herself back to the present with a conscious effort; and a shameful certainty that not only had she been in the jungle, but that she enjoyed it, began to taunt her. She hardened her determination to get away. She wasn't, she told herself, a jungle creature. She cloaked herself in a faint disgust as she watched the entertainers throw themselves about to the bursts of syncopated jangle, and when the time came again for the patrons to dance, she declined.[53]

Though Helga declines a return to the jungle when the band resumes, Larsen stops short of embracing a middle-class critique of the cabaret that would view it as a space of commercialized vice or as an easily condemned location of primitivist stereotype. Instead of the jungle promised by the

Negro vogue, *Quicksand*'s cabaret turns out to be a battleground over which the values of black middle-class morality are waged against the criminal intimacies and fugitive socialities of Harlem's nightlife, with the meaning of Helga's sexual subjectivity hanging in the balance.

To wit: the most captivating figure in the cabaret—for Helga as well as the reader—is not Helga's former employer and possible romantic interest Robert Anderson, who is unexpectedly there, but his companion, Audrey Denney, a light-skinned woman who has earned the reproach of Helga's female friends for associating with white men and frequenting racially mixed downtown parties. Audrey provides a different model of race and sexuality than that imagined by the representational schemas of either the Negro vogue or uplift ideology. She is sexually and racially suspect, inspiring the censure of the women in Helga's party (especially Helga's strident friend Anne Grey, who calls Audrey "treacherous" and suggests she should be ostracized from the black community) and the attention and curiosity of the men. Helga, however, finds herself on the wrong side of racial and sexual identification in this scene, seeing in Audrey not an enemy but a possible model of selfhood. She feels admiration for the "beautiful, calm, cool girl who had the assurance, the courage, so placidly to ignore racial barriers and give her attention to people."[54] Yet the reputation-damaging gossip of Anne quickly disciplines Helga's admiration, which she keeps to herself as she jealously watches Audrey Denney and Dr. Anderson cling tightly on the dance floor:

> Her long, slender body swayed with an eager pulsing motion. She danced with grace and abandon, gravely yet with obvious pleasure, her legs, her hips, her back, all swaying gently, swung by that wild music from the heart of the jungle. Helga turned her glance to Dr. Anderson. Her disinterested curiosity passed. While she still felt for the girl envious admiration, that feeling was now augmented by another, more primitive emotion. She forgot the garish crowded room. She forgot her friends. She saw only two figures, closely clinging. She felt her heart throbbing. She felt the room receding. She went out the door. She climbed the endless stairs.[55]

In this passage, Audrey becomes the cabaret scene. She replaces—even obliterates—the tight scene from which Helga views her. Larsen's invention of Audrey Denney draws from stereotyped images of sexually predatory and treacherous light-skinned cabaret women, like Lulu Belle or Van Vechten's antiheroine Lasca Sartoris, who destroy their male companions, either out of whimsy or malice.[56] But unlike Van Vechten, Larsen takes pains to show that Audrey is known only through the policing discourse of gossip through which she is narrated. In other words, we never see the cabaret from Audrey's point of view, nor do we ever learn about her background or inner life. While Van Vechten creates a compelling but finally grotesque caricature, Larsen is more interested in the way that such caricatures get imagined in the first place and their function within larger ideological regimes. The "truth" of Audrey Denney is never revealed or verified; she performs in the scene as a fantasy, a projection of the sexual and racial transgressions that pose a threat to the politics of respectability and the integrity of normative uplift ideology.

But Larsen's scene is also more complex than a simple critique of uplift's gendered logic. Here, as in her second novel, *Passing* (1929), Larsen depicts a woman protagonist attracted to another woman whose ability to realize the choices that the protagonist can only fantasize about confounds the circuits of desire and identification. Prefiguring the queer desire that Deborah McDowell argues is more strongly present in *Passing*, Helga's sense of sexual and racial selfhood—understood in this scene as a horizon of possibility activated and enacted by Audrey Denney—is at once recognized and disavowed.[57] This identification affects her much more deeply than the simple identification with the "jungle creature" she brushed off at the beginning of the scene. Unable to reassure herself so easily that she is *not* Audrey Denney—that she is not, in other words, made up of the complex, messy, and socially unsanctioned racial and sexual subjectivity that is earlier deemed "treacherous" by an uplifting Anne—Helga feels her own sense of self begin to unravel. The cabaret's promised rupture in consciousness occurs not in the movement toward the "jungle" and an unrepressed state of primitive blackness, but in the dissolution of the epistemological foundations of racial respectability as Helga identifies with Audrey Denney. Seeing herself as Audrey, another possibility of racial and sexual subjectivity opens up for her in the space of desire between women—and in the face of both Anne's petty viciousness and the primitivist stereotypes of the Negro vogue. Larsen cements her critique with Helga's flight up the cabaret's "endless stairs" (a continuation of the novel's general theme of perpetual flight from untenable tight spaces), unable to meet the indictment that Audrey Denney makes just by her defiant comfort, sexual self-determination, and sheer existence.

Zora Neale Hurston presents a similar cabaret scene in her autobiographical essay, "How It Feels to Be Colored Me," which appeared in the white monthly *The World Tomorrow* two months after *Quicksand* was published. This essay is a collage of scenes—from her childhood performances on the front porch of her Eatonville home, to the very white campus at Barnard, to a mixed-race table at a basement cabaret, to a stroll down Seventh Avenue—within which Hurston (or at least the "Zora Neale Hurston" constructed in this first-person essay) feels racial difference and racial identity. The juxtaposition of these scenes suggests that racial feeling for Hurston is contextual and relational. While she often feels "surged upon, and overswept" by whiteness at Barnard, Hurston describes a similar contrast when she brings a white friend to the New World Cabaret, setting him in a black environment.[58] Drawing a sharp distinction between her friend's response to the performance and her own, Hurston raises specific questions not only of spectatorship but also auditorship—how different practices of listening and hearing shape one's relationship to Harlem's cabaret traditions. Just as the sight of Audrey Denney allowed Helga to momentarily glimpse something beyond herself, the sound of the jazz band expands the cabaret for Hurston:

> When I sit in the drafty basement that is the New World Cabaret with a white person, my color comes. We enter chatting about any little nothing that we have in common and are seated by the jazz waiters. In the abrupt way that jazz orchestras have, this one plunges into a number. It loses no time in circumlocutions but gets right down to business. It constricts the thorax and splits the heart with its tempo and narcotic harmonies. The orchestra grows rambunctious and rears on its hind legs and attacks the tonal veil with primitive fury, rending it, clawing it until it breaks through to the jungle beyond. I follow those heathen—follow them exultingly. I dance wildly inside myself; I yell within, I whoop; I shake my assegai above my head, I hurl it true to the mark *yeeeeooww!* I am in the jungle and living in the jungle way. My face is painted red and yellow and my body is painted blue. My pulse is throbbing like a war drum. I want to slaughter something—give pain, give death to what, I do not know. But the piece ends. The men of the orchestra wipe their lips and rest their fingers. I creep back slowly to the veneer we call civilization with the last tone and find the white friend sitting motionless in his seat, smoking calmly.
>
> "Good music they have here," he remarks, drumming the table with his fingertips.
>
> Music. The great blobs of purple and red emotion have not touched him. He has only heard what I felt. He is far away and I see him but dimly across the ocean and the continent that have fallen between us. He is so pale with his whiteness then, and I am so colored.[59]

Hurston's move into the jungle is not repudiated, as it was by Helga Crane in Larsen's cabaret scene. Many scholars have criticized Hurston for this choice, seeing this scene as an especially egregious capitulation to stereotypes of racial atavism and positioning Hurston as the antithesis to what they view as Larsen's more complex depictions of racial and sexual subjectivity.[60] Other critics, Barbara Johnson most extensively, have argued that Hurston's over-the-top rhetoric—from the same sardonic writer who coined the phrases "Negrotarian" and "Niggeratti" to name white Harlem Renaissance patrons and black literary intelligentsia, respectively—should be read as both parody and deconstruction of cabaret primitivism.[61] Hurston's direct engagement with the Negro vogue and its primitivist prescriptions is immediately apparent, but a closer reading suggests that Hurston may be launching an additional, more subtle critique that is easily missed amid all the whooping and yelling. I would suggest that, in addition to echoing someone like Van Vechten, Hurston's scene also reverberates with the work of W. E. B. Du Bois and reconfigures the musical horizon of his Talented Tenth and their uplift charge.

In describing the rending of the "tonal veil," an image that suggests both musical tone and skin tone, Hurston invokes Du Bois's well-known metaphor of the color line as a veil that separates knowledge and contact between black and white. As the leading figure in African American letters at the time and editor of the *Crisis*, Du Bois was a profound influence on all the writers of the Harlem Renaissance, especially with *The Souls of Black Folk* (1903), the text in which he most fully develops the metaphor of the Veil. Hurston invites us to think her cabaret scene alongside and against a particular scene from the final pages of *The Souls of Black Folk*, where Du Bois offers his own description of what a "rending of the Veil" would look and sound like: "If somewhere in this whirl and chaos of things there dwells Eternal Good, pitiful yet masterful, then anon in his good time America shall rend the Veil and the prisoned shall go free. Free, free from the sunshine trickling down the morning into these high windows of mine, free as yonder fresh young voices welling up to me from the caverns of brick and mortar below—swelling with song, instinct with life, tremulous treble and darkening bass. My children, my little children, are singing to the sunshine, and thus they sing:" The text breaks off as Du Bois follows the colon with a printed musical score for the spiritual "Let Us Cheer the Weary Traveler."[62] For Du Bois, it is the sound of the enslaved (and that sound's preservation and continuation by the Fisk Jubilee Singers) that he finds both in and as the rending of the Veil.

Read through Du Bois's scene, we can understand another possible effect of Hurston's scene, within another tradition besides that of primitivism—a tradition of black musical production and its politics of transfiguration.

Like Du Bois, Hurston too imagines a "rending of the Veil" and the sounding of racial subjective expansion that both ruptures and surpasses it. But she rescores Du Bois's vision, taking it out of the context of racial uplift and resituating it in the very kind of scene that Du Bois, in the late 1920s, abhorred.[63] In the act of revising the moralism and elitism that subtends Du Bois's Renaissance conception of black cultural politics, Hurston finds more possibility in Harlem's cabaret than that imagined by Van Vechten in his sensory journey to the jungle or sought after by tourists as they cabbed uptown.

Hurston conceptualizes the Veil (here and throughout her essay) less as a boundary that separates than as a stage where difference is performed and knowledge is produced. When "Zora Neale Hurston," Helga Crane, and, below, Thurman's Emma Lou, all describe the "jungle scene" of the cabaret, they expose it not as a reversion to natural type, but as the careful construction and staging of a performance. Listening to this scene, we find that the "tonal veil" also refers to some specific musical experimentation and sonic expansion. Hurston's move into the jungle suggests not only the mise-en-scènes of white-marketed clubs and primitivist narratives of literary modernism, but also the sound and theatrical style of so-called "jungle music," which was developed and refined by Duke Ellington at the Cotton Club. Ellington's jungle music complemented the club's primitivist ethos and was characterized by what one music dictionary describes as "pseudo-African musical effects—especially pounding tom-toms, unusual harmonies, 'primitive' scales (usually pentatonic and whole-tone), and muted, growling brass lines."[64] Working within the tight theatrical constraints and the audience expectations of the white-marketed Cotton Club for "jungle music," Ellington and his orchestra pushed sound, rhythm, and instrumentation into more stylistically experimental registers. In a generous tone, and from some historical distance, Ellington himself described these demands on his band's sound as "both educative and enriching, and it brought about a further broadening of the music's scope."[65] Hurston's rending of the tonal veil reflects a similar broadening—or loosening—of textual and performative tightness. Her move into the jungle, in other words, is too often only read silently, within a literary tradition of modernist primitivism. But it should also be heard within a musical tradition that represented both the discursive constraints of the Negro vogue and simultaneously the creative expansion and loosening of those constraints. Up against the theatrical conventions and audience expectations of Harlem's nightlife, the writers and performers of the Cabaret School—like Ellington and Hurston—found ways to creatively expand and broaden such tight spaces.

Wallace Thurman's *The Blacker the Berry* addresses this project of critique and revision even more directly as it confronts post-*Nigger Heaven* and post-*Lulu Belle* Harlem nightlife. His 1929 novel about intraracial color discrimination and the psychology of race shame details an evening at Small's Paradise from the point of view of the protagonist Emma Lou, who is conscious of being one of the only black patrons, and the darkest, in the entire cabaret.[66] Foregrounding questions of perspective and point of view, Thurman imagines the Negro vogue not from a seat in the audience but from the theatrical vantage point of backstage, where the labor of creating nightlife scenes of blackness is rendered visible. Specifically, Emma Lou, in a clear reference to *Lulu Belle*, gains employment as a dresser for a white actress starring as the "mulatto Carmen" in a fictional Broadway show called "Cabaret Gal," an "alleged melodrama of Negro life in Harlem."[67] Part of her job involves helping to darken Arline Strange's face for the role each night (even as she spends evenings off bleaching and peroxiding her own face in a futile attempt to lighten it). Peeking from backstage into the theater, Emma Lou watches the white audience watching a white actress in blackface dancing in an imitation of a Harlem cabaret. As she observes their delight in the show, she wonders with mild disdain if any such scenes really exist.

She soon finds out. After the show one night, Arline enlists Emma Lou to act as a guide for Arline's visiting brother, who wants to see an "authentic" black cabaret while he is visiting New York. She accompanies the white revelers uptown to Small's Paradise—the first time she has ever been to a cabaret. Emma Lou, this scene's consummate spectator, watches her party dance until they return to the table to make room for the floorshow entertainment. The show consists of two women dancers who provide a comic physical juxtaposition for the mostly white audience—one skinny, one fat—as they obscenely thrust and undulate their bodies around the cabaret for tips:

> Emma Lou, all of her, watched and listened. As they approached her table, she sat as one mesmerized. Something in her seemed to be trying to give way. Her insides were stirred, and tingled. The two entertainers circled their table; Arline's brother held out a dollar bill. The fat, chocolate-colored girl leaned over the table, her hand touched his, she exercised the muscles of her stomach, muttered a guttural "thank you" in between notes and moved away, moaning "Muddy Waters," rolling her eyes, shaking her hips.
>
> Emma Lou had turned completely around in her chair, watching the progress of that wah-wahing, jello-like chocolate hulk, and her slim, light-brown-skin companion. Finally they completed their rounds of the tables and returned to the dance floor. Red and blue spotlights played upon their dis-

similar figures, the orchestra increased the tempo and lessened the intensity of its playing. The swaying entertainers pulled up their dresses, exposing the lace trimmed stepins and an island of flesh. Their stockings were rolled down below their knees, their stepins discreetly short and delicate. They shimmied and whirled, charlestoned and black-bottomed. Their terpsichorean ensemble was melodramatic and absurd. Their execution easy and emphatic. Emma Lou forgot herself. She gaped, giggled, and applauded like the rest of the audience, and only as they let their legs separate, preparatory to doing one final split to the floor, did Emma Lou come to herself long enough to wonder if the fat one could achieve it without seriously endangering those ever tightening stepins.

"Dam' good, I'll say," a slender white youth at the next table asseverated, as he lifted an amber-filled glass to his lips. . . .

Emma Lou blinked guiltily as the lights were turned up. She had been immersed in something disturbingly pleasant. Idiot, she berated herself, just because you've had one drink and seen your first cabaret entertainer, must your mind and body feel all aflame.[68]

There is much that needs to be said about this scene, but for now I want to focus on the technological details by which Thurman marks the performance of blackness and the performativity of race as so many devices of stagecraft. The "red and blue spotlights" that "played upon" the bodies of the dancers in Thurman's scene should remind us of Hurston's face "painted red and yellow" and her body "painted blue" in "How It Feels to Be Colored Me." Barbara Johnson notes that Hurston's description of skin paint in that scene, rather than skin complexion, indicates that "the move into the jungle is the move into mask; the return to civilization is the return to veneer. Either way, what is at stake is an artificial, ornamental surface."[69] It is also likely, taking a cue from Thurman, that Hurston's red and blue body are not only metaphorical but point to the technical effects and lighting gels that cast cabaret performers in various hues. Hurston, like Thurman, brings to our attention the technologies that, quite literally, mediated and staged the performance of exoticism (and I might point out here that Thurman worked at *The World Tomorrow* when Hurston published her essay and that the two of them had previously collaborated on the avant-garde journal *Fire!!*). This same awareness of the theatrical production of skin color occurs later in the novel, when Emma Lou watches the light-skinned chorus girls of "Cabaret Gal" from back stage. She notes once again from the wings that "despite many layers of liquid powder she could see that they were not all one color, but that they were either mulatto or light-brown skin. Their makeup and the lights gave them an appearance of sameness."[70] The manipulation of makeup and lighting effects reveals much of Harlem to be a stage, much of racial representation to be melodrama and absurdism; even the promise of full sexual exposure reveals only stepins—a show undergarment designed for modesty, merely part of the costume. These lighting effects and makeup, all of primitivism as a discourse and aesthetic, aimed to standardize blackness in the 1920s. Rather than substantiate the white-marketed staging of blackness, Thurman and Hurston both give the lie to the primitivism and sexual excess of Harlem's cabaret performance and reveal their presentation of blackness as so many bits of stage business.[71]

Emma Lou, who observes performances of blackness from a backstage vantage point, recognizes the stagecraft that goes into these illusions. She is captivated by the performance almost in spite of herself. Echoing Helga Crane, she scolds herself for being so easily seduced and set "aflame" by the rhythms and images of the show. The trance-like effect that the performance exerts over her is only broken when the women spread their legs, leaving her to fear (or perhaps hope) that the fat one's stepins might split. Her view of this sexual display, and thus her spectatorship in this scene more generally, is juxtaposed with the crude appraisal of the white male patron next to her. His drunken verdict, "Dam' good, I'll say," reverberates with but distorts Emma Lou's own reaction (and echoes Hurston's companion who comments obtusely about the "good music they have here"). The technological detail at this moment is significant: focused on the stage show in the dark, Emma Lou allows herself to forget herself and experience the show "like the rest of the audience." It is only when the lights come up that she blinks guiltily and is returned from the position of spectator. She despectacularizes the scene as she gazes upon the white crowd socializing around her, as though a curtain had been pulled back:

> Arline's brother was mixing another highball. All around, people were laughing. There was much more laughter than there was talk, much more gesticulating and ogling than the usual means of expression called for. Everything seemed unrestrained, abandoned. Yet Emma Lou was conscious of a note of artificiality, the same as she felt when she watched Arline and her fellow performers cavorting on the stage in "Cabaret Gal." This entire scene seemed staged, they were in a theatre, only the proscenium arch had been obliterated. At last the audience and the actors were as one.[72]

The obliteration of the proscenium arch that distinguishes the cabaret from theater reveals the whole scene to be a carefully choreographed social performance. This is, we might recall, the very "spirit of the frequenters" that Van Vechten called for to reinvigorate the Broadway stage. But here, the spirit of the frequenters at Small's is exposed as nothing more than a heightened and artificial theatricality, a sociality reduced to the "inane plot and vulgar dialogue" of artificial Broadway constructions like "Cabaret Gal" or *Lulu Belle*.[73] Rather than finding the original scene that inspired the Broadway play, Emma Lou discovers that the play in fact created its own inspiration.

I hope by this point to have demonstrated the importance of seeing and hearing these and other scenes of Harlem cabaret not as individual manifestations of primitivism or faddishness, but within the larger enunciative field of which they are a part. The writers of the Cabaret School were sympathetic to the disruption of black middle-class mores occasioned by *Nigger Heaven* and *Lulu Belle*, but they also found the Negro vogue a limiting possibility. Scenes like those in *Quicksand*, "How It Feels to Be Colored Me," and *The Blacker the Berry* (and in work by Langston Hughes and Claude McKay, as we will see in the next chapters) speak of and to each other, working within and pushing against representational conventions of Harlem's nightlife. By addressing the scene of Harlem cabaret, rather than repudiating it; by contextualizing and historicizing it, rather than romanticizing it; and by challenging primitivism, rather than advancing it, the Cabaret School contributed to the strategies and practices developed by performers like Ellington and Waters, not to mention uncountable everynight subjects, as they labored to create loose spaces within tight structures.

LOOSE ENDS: "GIMME A PIGFOOT (AND A BOTTLE OF BEER)"

I want to end this chapter, and prepare for the next, with one final scene of Harlem cabaret. In November 1933, Bessie Smith recorded Wesley Wilson's "Gimme a Pigfoot (and a Bottle of Beer)" for Okeh Records. By the time she recorded this song, the Negro vogue was not quite over. It would be another two years before the 1935 riot that dramatically punctuated the changed ethos of the neighborhood and shuttered Harlem's remaining white-marketed nightclubs (sending them to reopen in Times Square). Smith's rural working-class background, unabashed sexual expression, and blues sound did not endear her to any uplift crowd. In "Gimme a Pigfoot," she announces her disdain for upscale Harlem clubs like Small's or Connie's Inn. The recording begins with an improvised scene-setting confrontation between Smith and the doorman at one such highbrow nightspot: "Twenty-five cents? Hah? No, no, I wouldn't pay twenty-five cents to go in nowhere, 'cause listen here . . . " Following this rejection of the cover charge that helped to restrict entrance into more upscale clubs, Smith goes on to defiantly declare her preference for loose spaces:

> Up in Harlem every Saturday night
> When the highbrows get together it's just too tight.
>
> They all congregates at an all night strut
> And what they do is tut, tut, tut.[74]

Turning her back on this tut-tutting reproach, Smith refuses to cross the threshold into a realm of moral judgment. She instead issues a female counternarrative about the Saturday Night Function and a woman named Hannah Brown who drinks and dances long into the morning, promising to outlast, so the song goes, even the piano player. Demanding a pig's foot and a bottle of beer, Hannah Brown pays tribute to the vernacular sounds, movements, and foodways of a defiantly unreconstructed urban folk settled in the rent parties and cellar speakeasies of Harlem. Yet by calling attention to the economics and exclusionary practices of middle-class amusement at the beginning—by providing context—Smith keeps the song from slipping into an uncritical celebration of working-class recreation, describing instead what was for many a vital mode of existence. Hannah Brown, in other words, is neither Lasca nor Lulu Belle. "Gimme a Pigfoot" was later recorded by Billie Holiday and Nina Simone, among others, continuing the gender and class critique of this scene of Harlem's cabaret into subsequent generations.

Harlem cabaret after 1926 became more, not less, complex, *Nigger Heaven* and *Lulu Belle* notwithstanding. Smith's performance of "Gimme a Pigfoot"—like the "righteous playing" of Cecil Scott and other musicians at the Capitol Palace, the sounds of Ellington and Waters, and, in a different way, the prose of Larsen, Hurston, and Thurman—not only described or imagined moments of looseness, but actively created such moments in its performance and circulation. Caught in the ever-tightening vise of the spectacularizing demands of the Negro vogue, on the one hand, and the politics of respectability of uplift ideology, on the other, Harlem's performers and writers attempted to evade the representational squeeze of either. As we will continue to see, the Cabaret School developed increasingly inventive ways to preserve, expand, and inhabit Harlem's nightlife under conditions that sought, at every turn, to render it inhospitable or uninhabitable.

CHAPTER THREE

———— ✳ ————

Closing Time

Langston Hughes and the Queer
Poetics of Harlem Nightlife

See
One restless in the exotic time! and ever,
Till the air is cured of its fever.

GWENDOLYN BROOKS, "LANGSTON HUGHES"

RUMOR HAS it Langston Hughes was gay. Such speculation began early in his career—when less ambiguous homosexuals like Alain Locke and Countee Cullen traded clandestine letters about the young poet's potential seducibility—and tiptoed around him throughout his life. The circumstantial evidence is compelling to those eager to reconstruct narratives of African American gay and lesbian history. There is Hughes's knowledge of sexual underworlds—from his description of Harlem's drag balls to his attendance at the parties of close friends Carl Van Vechten and A'Leila Walker, as well as less swanky affairs—which suggests both familiarity and comfort with the codes of modern U.S. sexual subcultures. Then there are his occasional literary explorations of overt homosexuality—such as his poem "Café: 3 a.m." (1951) and his short stories "Blessed Assurance" (1963) and "Seven People Dancing" (unpublished). But with the exception of one opposite-sex relationship early in his life, Hughes himself refused to indicate a sexual identity, preferring to cultivate a sexual ambiguity and doing little to end conjecture about his intimate life.[1]

In the late 1980s, two events propelled such speculation beyond the realm of whispered innuendo and into the public sphere: the publication of Arnold Rampersad's two-volume authorized biography of Hughes (vol. 1,

I, Too, Sing America, 1986, and vol. 2, *I Dream a World,* 1988) and the release of Isaac Julien's film, *Looking for Langston* (1988).[2] Rampersad's biography brought to the question the weight of archival rigor and a plenitude of detail, fact, and context by which to interpret Hughes's inner life. Governed by a fidelity to the archive and the protocols of objective scholarship, Rampersad found the subject of Hughes's sexuality shrouded in "rumor and suspicion."[3] Twenty years after Hughes's death, Rampersad wrote, "no one could recall any concrete evidence for his reputation [as a homosexual]. No one could offer the name of a man who had been involved with Hughes, or recall an incident, even at second hand, involving Langston's presumed homosexuality."[4] Given this lack of eyewitnesses and documentary evidence, Rampersad interpreted the gaps in knowledge around Hughes's sexual desire as an absence of desire. Without verifiable proof of Hughes's homosexuality, he advanced the thesis that Hughes was basically asexual, his sexual desire "not so much sublimated as vaporized."[5] Several critics subsequently accused Rampersad of closeting Hughes through this insistence on Hughes's asexuality and interpretations that resulted in voiding the many queerly rich scenes in Hughes's life and writing of any likelihood of same-sex desire.

Released around the same time as Rampersad's biography, British-based artist Isaac Julien's mythopoetic film about queer Harlem, *Looking for Langston,* offered a very different take on the question of Hughes's sexuality. A montage of text, music, visual images, archival footage, and tableaux, the film established a dialogue between and across black queer culture makers of the twentieth century, including Hughes, Richard Bruce Nugent, James Baldwin, and Essex Hemphill. The film is set in a Harlem nightclub during the Jazz Age, where black and white men in tuxedos drink champagne, socialize, and dance late into the morning. Departing from this scene, the film veers into a number of dreamscapes that imagine various configurations of queer male comings-together in a city street, a park, an open field, a movie house, a bedroom, and under an elevated train. Through the use of literary citation and sonic cues (such as the movement from the classic blues to techno dance music), the past and present bleed into each other as these queer transatlantic contacts seep across temporal boundaries and upset linear narrative history. *Looking for Langston* does less to unearth a gay black past hidden from history than to meditate on the ways in which history—like desire—is dynamic and unfixed.[6]

Unfixed, I should add, for some. The film's release in the United States was famously halted by Hughes's estate, then under the executorship of the late George Bass, which objected to what it perceived as the film's homosexual implications. The Hughes estate filed a legal injunction to prevent the film's distribution, and a number of Hughes's poems were excised from its U.S. premiere at the New York Film Festival. The role of the Hughes estate in attempting to censor Julien's film further cast the interpretations of Hughes's life and work as a struggle over the definitive "truth" of Hughes's life narrative.[7] Rampersad and Julien thus responded to the question of Hughes's sexuality in contrasting ways: while Julien's film dwelt within the speculative, playing with the inconclusive nature of the archive and imagining the multiple ways that archival gaps can signify, Rampersad's biography sought to set the archival record straight.

A new afterward to the 2002 edition of Rampersad's biography gives us occasion to revisit these debates. In it, Rampersad reflects for several pages on how he wrote about the question of Hughes's sexuality, addresses his critics, and defends his methods and conclusions. Loath as he was to speculate on any aspect of Hughes's life without verifiable proof, Rampersad explains that he proceeded under a "strict regard for the rules of evidence."[8] Despite coming to the conclusion that Hughes's sexuality is ultimately unknowable, he nevertheless takes credit—justifiably—for making the circumstantial case for a "gay Langston Hughes" even stronger than it was previously. Taking note of the large volume of scholarship in the wake of his biography that argues for Hughes's queerness, Rampersad charges "virtually all of the critics have been dependent almost entirely on material I myself unearthed and presented in my biography. Virtually none of them, as far as I can tell, has taken the trouble to work in the Hughes papers at Yale or elsewhere, although the papers at Yale have been open to scholars for many years now."[9]

Rampersad's afterward helpfully points to the epistemological assumptions that guide both critical and historical discussions of Hughes's sexuality: it is precisely the terms of the archive itself—how it is defined, read, and lived—that is at issue in Rampersad's rendering and to which his critics object. Even as literary scholars continue to pursue the question of Hughes's sexual identity and his relationship to the history of urban U.S. sexual subcultures, queer readings of his work and his biography—with a few significant exceptions—continue to approach him within a hermeneutics of sexual object choice, concerned with uncovering his "gay voice" and reasserting his contribution to a U.S. gay and lesbian history.[10] Asking after Hughes's sexuality in the way that critics on both sides of this debate have done, however, is to misrecognize the fundamental queerness of

Hughes's life project, not only because this unknowability was something that Hughes cultivated in his life and in his literature, but also because such debates locate the answer of sexuality and desire in the object choice of individuals, rather than posing the question of the constitution and becoming of the sexual subject in the first place. It is this second question that better characterizes Hughes's queer poetics in the 1920s.

I begin this chapter with the complex of rumors, controversy, and contention that swirls around Hughes's sexual identity and its archival traces because it offers important insights into queer history, memory, and performance during the Harlem Renaissance and after. This chapter (and the next) will be concerned with how the Cabaret School recorded and documented queer time and space in ways that both eluded official transcription and cultivated queer narratives and lifeworlds. Langston Hughes will be our entry point into this discussion. Hughes, we will see, offers a way to reformulate this archival predicament made visible by the literary biographer and the avant-garde filmmaker.

The Harlem Renaissance itself, it is useful to remember, was concerned with such questions of historical recovery and archival revision. As a response to white supremacist discourses that located the black body outside of History and effaced the history of slavery, subjugation, and labor in the United States, New Negro historians worked to demonstrate and publicize the achievements of the race within a narrative of civilizational accomplishment and self-determination that had developed prior to and since the Middle Passage. Under the direction of chief librarian Ernestine Rose, the 135th Street branch of the New York Public Library (later the Schomburg Center for Research in Black Culture) began building its collections of Negro literature and history and providing public forums on black history, literature, and politics. The cultivation of the 135th Street branch as a center of black intellectual life complemented other projects of New Negro historical curation like historian Carter G. Woodson's Association for the Study of Negro Life and History (founded in 1915) and the Association's *Journal of Negro History* (begun in 1916).[11] The systematic collection and presentation of evidence was a double project of race pride and black counterpublicity. Historian and bibliophile Arthur Schomburg described this New Negro historiography as the "definite desire and determination to have a history, well documented, widely known at least within race circles, and administered as a stimulating and inspiring tradition for the coming generations."[12]

Hughes had firsthand knowledge of this model of New Negro historiography. In 1925 he worked for a time as an assistant on the compilation of

Woodson's *Free Negro Heads of Families in the United States in 1830,* a massive study based on 1830 census data that compiled a list of over thirty thousand individual names. Among other things, Woodson's project sought to complicate and refine then-current official racial knowledge. In a lengthy and substantive introductory essay, the study outlined the history of the free Negro in the United States and showed how the laws and institutions that had governed enslaved people in the nineteenth century worked to debase the free Negro as well. *Free Negro Heads of Families* was thus an interpretive project embedded within the class logic of uplift ideology: it both documented and publicized the internal differentiation of black populations in the United States, demonstrating the antebellum origins of a black middle class, and argued for the interdependent relationship—and thus mutual fate—of the highest and the lowest of the race. The positivism of the project posed a direct challenge to white supremacist depictions of blackness as an undifferentiated mass and established a historical relationship between those of high and low status. It thus substantiated the developmental narrative of racial progress that informed Progressive Era epistemologies of social organization.

As project assistant, Hughes's task was to alphabetize the names of the free heads of families—all thirty thousand of them. "They were typed on thirty thousand slips of paper," he remembered. "The job took weeks. Then checking the proofs took weeks more. It was like arranging a telephone book, and only myself to do it." Such an introduction to the labor of historical recovery gave Hughes an appreciation for this kind of historical analysis, but also helped him determine that it was not the kind of work for him. "Although I realized what a fine contribution Dr. Woodson was making to the Negro people and to America . . . I personally did not like the work I had to do. Besides, it hurt my eyes."[13] Work that was contributing to helping the nation "see" the race more clearly left Hughes himself with bleary vision.

I invoke this scene here because, in Hughes's gesture of discontent toward the mustering of data, we can hear an implicit call that reverberates throughout the Cabaret School for a work of memory and revision that does not hurt one's eyes. Hughes respectfully yet trenchantly points to the limitations and unintended side effects of such historiographical projects, suggesting that such insistent focus can sometimes obscure the very thing one looks at. The work of ordering and classifying historical data raises other questions. For example: What historical experiences are illegible within developmental narratives and elude the tenets of empiricism and documentation? What alternative histories and historiographic practices might have been developed outside of the established institutions of normative racial uplift? And, further, how might these questions help redirect the dilemma of Hughes's sexual identity and the archival gaps recognized, in very different ways, by Rampersad and Julien? These concerns over evidence and the archive—old and new—can help us rethink our approach to the unsolvable knot of Hughes's sexuality, specifically, and the project of the Cabaret School more generally. Hughes's early verse provides an opportunity to explore how the Cabaret School thought outside of normalizing historiographic conventions and archival practices that were embedded within uplift ideologies and constituted instead an alternative archive of queer practices.

To further explore this last claim I turn to the social performances and intimate spaces Hughes documents in his Harlem Renaissance poetry collections. As scholars at the intersection of queer studies and performance studies have demonstrated, the textual and material logic of the institutional archive often fails to document—and sometimes actively participates in the erasure of—minoritarian histories.[14] Hughes's first two published collections of verse, *The Weary Blues* (1926) and *Fine Clothes to the Jew* (1927), respond to these archival conditions. Both are populated with spaces, figures, values, and social relationships at odds with the normalizing impulses of racial uplift. I argue here that these lyric explorations of Harlem's cabaret performances and sexual nightlife were one strategy by which Hughes evaded the terms of an archival imperative toward empiricism and positivist legibility, while still recording the criminal and sexual spaces of the early twentieth century. In these volumes, we will see, Hughes turns to the lyric form to construct what Ann Cvetkovich calls an "archive of feelings." Supplementing the positivist archival work of New Negro historiography, archives of feeling attend to the textual traces of affect and experience as well as to "the practices that surround their production and reception."[15] They thus direct us toward modes of documentation that sometimes stand in a queer (that is, oblique and askew) relationship to official archives, imagining other ways to preserve and read that which positivist historiography fails to admit (as my mobilization in what follows of newspapers, special collections of libraries, and, yes, Rampersad's biography will attest). At other times, such alternative archives index precisely that which cannot be preserved, those affective states and experiences that both intentionally and unintentionally elude historic inscription.

Hughes's poetry of the 1920s archives spaces and temporalities that seek to escape empirical confirmation and refuse identificatory foreclosure. His poetry thus forces the question: When is the literary not only an object to be historicized, but also itself a repository of historical counterknowledge? My focus here will be on Hughes's lyric archive of the scene of Harlem cabaret and the specific spatio-temporal manipulations that emerge from the sexual and musical underworlds of the early twentieth century: closing time (as a temporal event) and afterhours (as a temporal register). It was in the some-times prohibited, sometimes tolerated time and space of afterhours that the queer rhythms and ethics of Harlem nightlife developed. Hughes's po-ems trace the temporal profile of such spaces, offering an elusive counter-evidence to the city's bureaucratic repositories of knowledge (such as police reports, arrest records, investigative statements, and sensational exposés).[16] *The Weary Blues* and *Fine Clothes to the Jew* demonstrate, against the nor-malizing logic of official archives, Elizabeth Freeman's claim that "various queer social practices, especially those involving enjoyable bodily sensa-tions, produce form(s) of time consciousness, even historical consciousness, that can intervene upon the material damage done in the name of [histori-cal] development."[17] In locating the queer and transient space of the after-hours club within its specific temporal profile—that is, an illegal temporal-ity that is made possible by and exceeds the regulatory administration of the modern city—Hughes poetically inscribes a queer time consciousness that is impossible to archive under the official regimes of documentation and verification. The queer time and space of the afterhours club, in other words, is archived in the line of the poem, if not at the library at Yale.

Before looking more closely at Hughes's lyric archive of queer sociality and his reorganization of respectable time, I first contextualize the practices he documents within the sexual, racial, and juridical matrix of American modernity. After a discussion of the legal and subcultural context of clos-ing time, I turn to Hughes's poetry to demonstrate the formal and thematic strategies by which Hughes records this queer time, offering a different way for us to read the people and desires of the urban underworld and at the same time rethinking some poems that have been either overlooked or underread by Hughes scholars. What I hope to demonstrate is that Hughes uses the formal manipulations of poetic closure to contest the legislated closure of nightclubs, saloons, and cabarets called for by a repressive civic administration. We find in his verse traces of the criminal sociality of after-hours that offer an elusive counterevidence to repositories of official knowl-edge and gesture toward Hughes's larger relationship to the rhythms and temporalities of African American and sexual modernity.[18]

NIGHTLIFE'S QUEER TIME

Hughes's poem "Café: 3 a.m." is set in an afterhours venue marked criminal by the surveilling gaze of the vice squad. Turning the terms of investigation into a guessing game, Hughes undermines the univocal point of view from which the café and its questionable legality becomes legible to the police:

> Detectives from the vice squad
> with weary sadistic eyes
> spotting fairies.
>
> *Degenerates,*
> some folks say.
>
> But God, Nature,
> or somebody
> made them that way.
>
> Police lady or Lesbian
> over there?
> *Where?*[19]

Among other things, this is a poem about surveillance and countersurveillance. The specificity of Hughes's title locates this poem within a fugitive space: an afterhours club operating after the official closing time for bars and restaurants. The poem depicts a struggle between two different modes of underworld knowledge production. In the opening lines, Hughes sets up the official, criminalizing, and pathologizing gaze of the vice squad, which produces juridical and medical discourses of perversion. Such discourses leave behind a record of deviant existence and practices in police reports, arrest records, and sociological analyses. But as the poem continues, Hughes shifts to the unstable, improvisatory, and unofficial discourses of rumor, gossip, and innuendo. Hughes turns to the vernacular—"some folks say"—to cast doubt on the "official" taxonomy of "*Degenerates,*" taking away the authority of the discourse and equalizing it with a vernacular questioning that offers the possibility of other taxonomies—that is, other modes of knowing—for the people in the café.[20] In the final lines, this possibility is realized as Hughes reverses the logic of the poem's opening: the act of spotting and identifying shifts from the vice squad to the "degenerates" themselves, and the undercover detectives now become the objects of surveillance. The lines undermine the notion of a univocal direction for the production of underworld knowledge, offering a counterknowledge and countersurveillance that is posed against the official knowledges and recording practices of the police. It is a scene of criminal intimacies that thrive beyond the threshold of closing time and exist within the temporality of afterhours.

Closing time—the legislated hour by which nightclubs and bars must stop serving and close their doors—is a historical mode of temporality that reorganizes the normative temporal order upon which logics of familial reproduction and capitalist productivity are constituted and maintained. While imagined by the state as an attempt to regulate, contain, and bring to a close the ways certain subjects organize time and space, closing time also inaugurates a queer temporality that extends beyond sanctioned possibilities for sociality.[21] Closing time always reaches beyond itself: rather than marking the termination of social possibilities, it marks a transformation of time and space that operates in the interstices of the law. A bartender's cry of "last call," in addition to announcing a final opportunity to order a drink, is also a declaration of a temporal shift and a call to social reorganization. A harbinger of closing time, the last call marks a decision to lock the doors and continue operation illegally, relocate to a new afterhours location (in 1920s Harlem, often a rent party), or return—alone or not—to the privatized spheres of home and sleep.

Closing time marks the passage to the time and space of afterhours, a temporality that unfolds in defiance of city and moral law to create fugitive spaces like the afterhours club. The afterhours club allows for a heterogeneous assortment of figures and subjective possibilities, especially as it consolidates disparate nightlife populations into its operation. Afterhours sociability brackets the world "out there" and creates a sense of an autonomous time and place where normal social configurations are undone or done differently. Sitting at the interface of racially mixed and sexually deviant social space, such clubs were often important institutional sites of black commercial urban recreation and amusement, as well as part of a network of spaces—bathhouses, city streets, piers and waterfronts, rent parties, YMCAs, "black and tans"—through which semipublic sexual cultures developed. Licensing regulations and curfews circumscribed these spaces within a temporality of deviance and criminality that made certain subjects and desires both possible and legible (to modernity's systems of administration as well as to the subjects themselves). Afterhours time and space shaped the emergence of a modern gay and lesbian community, but its relationship to the urban underworld more broadly created opportunities for momentary contact, public intimacy, and affective exchange.[22] Thus, while afterhours is one condition of possibility for a homosexual subculture, it is not synonymous with it. Instead, afterhours marks a time of subjective possibility that could include but always exceeds the closures of "sexual identity" as such.

Closing time's liminal status has been historically bound up with the city's disciplinary and administrative apparatuses. Until New York City's first ordinances governing closing time were passed in 1907, the closing hour of the city's public drinking establishments was unregulated. The 1907 law allowed for the issuance of all-night licenses at a rate of $25 a week or $10 a day, which could be revoked at will by the mayor. As various regulatory bureaucracies responded to new entertainments and social spaces—the rise of the cabaret in the 1910s, in particular—new policies were adopted, and old laws were newly interpreted on both the state and the city level. The state excise commissioner, for example, introduced "an entirely new construction of the [existing] excise law" in 1912, the *New York Times* reported. Previously, the law required bars to be completely vacated at closing time and public areas to be "exposed to the view of those on the outside of such places." The commissioner expanded the definition of bar to include restaurants, which had previously escaped such regulations, but were increasingly featuring musical performances and floor shows that cultivated a late-night crowd. The campaign thus cast a new type of social establishment under the gaze of state surveillance and multiplied the number of nighttime gathering places to be "closed and exposed"—doors locked and curtains drawn back to confirm legal compliance—at the given hour.[23]

In 1913, Mayor William Gaynor intensified this campaign to illuminate the dark corners of the city's nighttime sociality.[24] The success of Progressive antivice movements—which aligned progressive movements with morals reform movements and produced such illustrious investigative bodies as the Committee of Fifteen (1900) and the Committee of Fourteen (1905)—empowered Gaynor to order raids into nightclubs and limit access to nightlife spaces, revoking every all-night license for cabarets, restaurants, and saloons.[25] In a letter to the police commissioner informing him of the change in policy, the mayor declared, "The people who patronize such places after the closing hour are not as a rule decent people. They are vulgar, roystering, and often openly immodest. They get intoxicated, behave boisterously, and indulge in lascivious dancing in rooms devoted to that use. It is time to put an end to all of these vulgar orgies. I have revoked all of these licenses to take effect April 1 next."[26] One o'clock in the morning became known as "Gaynor Time," and stories of managers and patrons attempting to defy the police and being forcibly removed were common. The mayor even singled out "known subterfuges" for circumventing the law, including "the time honored subterfuge of having guests order a quantity of liquid refreshments just before closing hour and allowing them to sit and drink as late as they please" (cracking down on this practice is the origin of the "last call").[27]

Nightclubs responded to these incursions, adapting their operations to endure for as long into the night as they could. The proliferation of doormen in the early 1910s, for example, was a direct result of these reform campaigns. The doorman, who had previously provided a welcoming presence at the entry point to a bar, now became a sentinel of afterhours space, the underworld's first defense against the policing of nightlife sociality. "The activities of the State Excise Department in this city," noted the *New York Times*, "have revived the almost passing profession of the doorman. In every place where liquor is sold after legal closing hours the 'everybody welcome' has been modified, and to obtain an entrance one must be known to the doorman or prove to his satisfaction that one is not in quest of evidence."[28] As a figure whose primary purpose was to keep out evidence seekers (typically police and investigators, but also, depending on the degree of criminal activity, the unfamiliar in general), the doorman became a guardian of underworld knowledge production who worked in opposition to official attempts to document bars and afterhours clubs. As in-group recognition increasingly became a key means of entrance to much nightlife, "official" knowledge of such places became even more difficult to ascertain; the doorman demonstrates one way that urban underworlds worked to conceal, destroy, and prevent the very traces of such spaces from being recorded by moral or municipal investigators.

Following Gaynor's untimely death, Mayor John Purroy Mitchel eased back on his predecessor's strict enforcement practices, and his administration marked a shift to a more liberal mode of regulation and licensing. Mitchel increased the number of all-night licenses, stating that he was "strongly for personal liberties, yet opposed to a 'wide open town.'"[29] He established a committee known as the Curfew Committee, or the Committee of Seven, to review and revise the licensing policy. Made up of local business and political and religious leaders, its mission was to "devise a policy which would give to the public a reasonable opportunity to get refreshments and diversion in the late hours of the night, yet which would prevent, so far as possible, objectionable conduct." Such a distinction came down to the presence of performance. Cabarets and other spaces featuring music and public dancing would be closed at 2:00 a.m., a slight extension from the previous administration; places without performances would be granted all-night licenses to give late-night workers access to leisure time after work, under the condition that "it has no back room where objectionable conduct might go on."[30]

As these administrative considerations make clear, closing time is a disciplinary technology that produces certain subjects and practices as criminal and deviant. The temporal regulations that limited the hours during which alcohol could be served or establishments could remain open worked in tandem with policies that sought to zone space and control crowds, including regulations that circumscribed the age of participation and consumption, the ability to permit social dancing or live performance, the volume of sound and noise, and the number of patrons permitted to congregate.[31] But these laws and regulations—administered by any number of bureaucratic arms, from state liquor authorities to local fire marshals—were (and are) never consistently or uniformly applied to the businesses and bodies that fall under their purview. Those spaces that are well financed, have the right capital (monetary and cultural), the right patrons, and the right relationships to the civic order find ways around regulations, sometimes under the radar (bribery, understood nonenforcement) and sometimes by having exemptions written directly into the law. Conversely, those spaces that facilitate oppositional publics, develop an antagonistic relationship to the state and the law, or operate subculturally are most at risk from the whims of regulatory dictates and police enforcement.

The arbitrary and contradictory enforcement of such regulations is especially evident in the context of Prohibition and New York City's local reaction to the national alcohol ban. When Hughes first arrived in New York in 1921, Prohibition had been in effect for almost two years. Prohibition and enforcement of the Volstead Act at first dampened nightlife sociality and compelled nightclubs to operate more furtively, encouraging the growth of smaller nightclubs that were more transient than the larger, established cabarets of the previous decade. In 1923, Hughes left New York City for Europe and Africa, settling in Paris for several months and working in a nightclub that featured African American performances late into the dawn. Upon his return to New York, he would have found the timescape of the night greatly changed. After 1924, New York ceased assisting federal enforcement of Prohibition violations, while still maintaining its own more permissive regulations of the city's nightlife. While the federal crime of serving alcohol was selectively ignored, nightclubs and spaces of entertainment were nonetheless required to abide by the local laws governing licensing and closing time. By 1926—the same year that Hughes's *The Weary Blues* was published—New York's police commissioner announced that the 2:00 a.m. curfew would again be enforced against cabarets and nightclubs. As a thriving entertainment district, Harlem was particularly targeted, and the Cotton Club, Connie's Inn, and the Savoy Ballroom all closed their doors at the proper hour in compliance. The following year, nightclub proprietors organized to push the closing ordinance back to 3:00 a.m. and continued to lobby for even later hours of operation.[32] This was one of the many contradictory ways that New York City sought to negotiate federal statutes with local practices.

The gaps between the writing of nightlife regulations and their enforcement created spaces that flourished, but flourished precariously, operating at a low frequency unheard or tuned out, for the moment, by the authorities. The cultivation of these spaces constituted what Foucault called "popular illegalities": the tolerated, even necessary, nonenforcement of laws. "Sometimes," according to Foucault, these popular illegalities "took the form of a massive general non-observance. . . . Sometimes it was a matter of laws gradually falling into abeyance, then suddenly being reactivated; sometimes of silent consent on the part of the authorities, neglect, or quite simply the actual impossibility of imposing the law and apprehending offenders."[33] Though enforcement may be relaxed or unofficially suspended, such laws necessarily remain on the books, able to be activated at any time at the discretion of the state.

While Foucault argues that this nonapplication of certain laws was crucial to the city's smooth political and economic functioning, he also insists that such popular illegalities were no less than the "conditions of existence" of the lowest in society: "The least favored strata of the population did not have, in principle, any privileges: but they benefited, within the margins of what was imposed on them by law and custom, from a space of tolerance, gained by force or obstinacy; and this space was for them so indispensable a condition of their existence that they were often ready to rise up and defend it."[34] Statutes and edicts like those concerning closing time or liquor licenses served a regulatory and repressive function—policing spaces as well as bodies and practices—and allowed the state to exercise its authority through alternating spans of tolerance and repression.[35] Temporary closure could easily turn into a permanent closure with a more fervent application of the law. But within these periodically tolerated zones, afterhours signals—moreover, produces—*forms* of racial and sexual congregation that function against normalizing social relations. What makes these congregations queer is not the teleology of sexual object choice, but the subjects' relations to dominant society. The afterhours club, as sociologists Julian Roebuck and Wolfgang Reese show, constitutes a setting "for deviants to act 'normally' and for 'straights' to act deviantly."[36] In other words, like the epistemological reversal Hughes effects in "Café: 3 a.m.," the afterhours club twists and reverses—queers—the normalizing inscriptions of time and space.

The temporality of afterhours refers, then, to a certain *clock time*, in that it follows—while reorganizing—the twenty-four-hour day and the seven-day week, and a certain *historical time*, in that it allows for the unfolding of modern racial and sexual subcultural formations over the first half of the twentieth century. Afterhours clubs and cabarets, as George Chauncey has shown, were important institutions in the cultivation of sexual subcultures in Harlem, Times Square, and Greenwich Village in the 1920s. Through insider knowledge, word of mouth, and rumor, these public and semipublic spaces fostered a range of sexual and racial subjectivities that included and exceeded lesbian and gay identities, as well as provided material and economic resources for those who rejected or were otherwise unable to function within the emergent middle-class regimes of employment. These institutions depended on parallel or subterranean economies that kept income and flows of money—like the criminal subjects who operated within this economy—"off the books," outside of systems of documentation, excise, and taxation. The laboring subjects who find existence in the afterhours club—the musician, the waiter, the sex worker, the drug dealer, the bartender, the bootlegger—are typically represented as the lumpen excess of the proletariat, but are better seen as occupying a different, rather than a negative, relationship to production and consumption than classical economic theory would imagine.

Operating between the gaps of established nightclubs, afterhours clubs shaped an expressive musical tradition as well as constituted modern subject positions. Such clubs offered many black musicians a crucially supportive environment, both economically and socially. In Harlem's afterhours clubs, musicians could find a place to get a start in a new city, hear about available work, and develop an expressive culture. These networks contributed to a subterranean opportunity for the dissemination of information and the cultivation of social networks. Cotton Club bandleader Cab Calloway described the spread of jazz through the underworld institution of the afterhours club: "Singers, pianists, drummers, horn players, guitarists—we all hustled around the clubs for a drink when we were up against it. That was the way jazz spread in America, not through the big concert halls, not through the big fancy clubs like the Cotton Club and Connie's Inn, but through small cafes and gambling houses and speakeasies, where we could hustle up a drink in exchange for a little of our souls."³⁷ The movement Calloway describes is not simply one of geography, linking large and small cities through musical pathways, but also one of subjective expansion, in which the exchange of musical production for the sociability and recreation offered in semipublic drinking establishments is a negotiation of one's self-hood. Hughes's cabaret poems, as we will see, take up this time and space of afterhours that is central to queer and African American historical and imaginative geographies.

The central role of musicians and performers in the afterhours economy suggests that the queer temporality of such spaces is also a kind of *musical time*. Like the time signature on a piece of sheet music, a distinct tempo governs the social compositions of the afterhours club, even when there is no band in the room. Far from a temporal free-for-all, afterhours structures a countertemporality that unwinds the reified clock of rationalized time and marks time instead by musical sets and the flows of musical time. Pianist Willie "the Lion" Smith calls this tempo of a place its "vibration," the totality of the rhythms, gestures, beats, moods, and movements, the perceptible quiver of the air, that marks the aura of any collectivity or scene.³⁸ These vibrations are produced and managed by sound and performance. Duke Ellington elaborates the ways that these vibrations are felt in, around, and through the body and establish their own autonomous temporal flows. After descending into the Capitol Palace, an afterhours basement speakeasy, to hear Smith play, Ellington described the vibrations of the room: "A square-type fellow might say, 'This joint is jumping,' but to those who had become acclimatized—the tempo was the lope—actually everything and everybody seemed to be doing whatever they were doing in the tempo the Lion's group was laying down. The walls and furniture seemed to lean understandably—one of the strangest and greatest sensations I ever had. The waiters served in that tempo, everybody who had to walk in, out, or around the place walked with a beat."³⁹ The tempo of the performance and the time signature of afterhours establish the beats and values of such spaces, governing the pulse that organizes such (musical, social) improvisations. In Hughes's poetic world, for example, a blues time signature marks the social and historical matrix by which Hughes records the queer relations and subjects in the afterhours club. The time signature of an afterhours club—its *un*common time—is one way that we can understand the confusion, discombobulation, and ineffable ache that subtends what is invariably characterized as a sense of "return" to the rhythms and beats of normal and normalizing time and space.

ARCHIVING AFTERHOURS: "THE CAT AND THE SAXOPHONE (2 A.M.)"

A confession: most of us who do queer Harlem Renaissance studies secretly wish Hughes had written "Café: 3 a.m." for *The Weary Blues*, rather than for his 1951 collection, *Montage of a Dream Deferred*. "Café: 3 a.m" is the only poem in his oeuvre where Hughes explicitly references the terminology of homosexual deviance ("degenerates," "fairies," and "Lesbians"). While the poem suggests the paranoia and surveillance of the early Cold War, its thematic interest in indeterminate and uncertain identity also resonates with the vice policing of the Progressive Era and its precloset sexual epistemologies. In fact, though the poem was published in the 1950s, there is nothing to suggest that it is not set in the 1920s, looking back to a time when sexual group identifications allowed for a greater movement of desire. It is, in many ways, a poem out of time, harkening back, on the eve of a sexually and politically conservative decade, to an earlier moment.

We can find the genealogical traces of "Café: 3 a.m." in Hughes's Harlem Renaissance poetry collections, *The Weary Blues* and *Fine Clothes to the Jew*. Even as his early poems, such as "The Negro Speaks of Rivers" (1921) and "I, Too, Sing America" (1925), earned him recognition and opportunity from uplift guardians of the Harlem Renaissance, Hughes's commitment from the outset of his career to the musical and sexual underworlds of Harlem's nightlife and his valorization of the black folk as something other than a mass to be elevated often made it a challenge to assimilate his work into the cultural uplift endeavors of the black middle class. *The Weary Blues* and *Fine Clothes to the Jew* are commonly noted for Hughes's choice of subject matter, his use of vernacular language, his invocation of the space of performance, and his formal experimentation with the structure and rhythm of the blues. Robert Hale identifies *Fine Clothes to the Jew* in particular as both culturally and aesthetically revolutionary, in that it "embodies a shift in the subject and style of poetry" that constituted the literary norm at the time, and Rampersad suggests that with this volume, Hughes is "deliberately defining poetic tradition according to the standards of a group often seen as subpoetic — the black masses."[40] In poems like "Cabaret Girl," "Red Silk Stockings," "Young Prostitute," "Nude Young Dancer," and "Jazzonia," his revolutionary redefinition of the poetic tradition sketched both the pleasurable possibilities and exploitative relations of the underworld and gave poetic attention to men and, more often, women who stood outside the sexual norms and standards of racial uplift. Black artists and intellectuals of the Harlem Renaissance generally promoted Hughes's poetry, though many critics were wary of his turn to imagery that too easily substantiated dominant racial images of sexual excess and nightlife existence. *Fine Clothes to the Jew*, for that reason, gave rise to some of the most personal and virulent critical denunciations leveled against Hughes and the Cabaret School.[41]

In *The Weary Blues* and *Fine Clothes to the Jew*, Hughes draws from the rhythms, sounds, improvisations, and intimacies of the blues and urban nightlife performance to map the spatio-temporal experience of afterhours. As Stephen Tracy and Brent Edwards have shown, Hughes's use of blues cadence and musical rhythm not only records and documents the scene of black performance but marks and ensures future performances. Tracy's meticulous notation of these blues poems, including diagrams of basic chord changes and time signatures onto Hughes's verse, supports the notion that with them Hughes seeks to perform, rather than simply describe, the time and place of the blues song.[42] Hughes's blues poetry, Edwards argues, not only "suggests a transcription" of the blues, but at the same time also "suggests the graphic particularities of a musical score: a writing that precedes and structures a performance rather than follows and records it."[43]

These blues poems share the page with a number of free-verse poems that similarly evoke the time, space, and performance of Harlem's nightlife. Though these poems have been given less attention, they are a necessary accompaniment to his blues poems, a musical second line that inscribes the space and time of Harlem's performance with a queerness that is both contained within and exceeds blues music as such. Hughes's attention to the temporal profile and time consciousness—the vibrations—of afterhours is one place where we can locate this queerness, not only in his reorganization of respectable time and his critique of the reification of normative temporal orders, but also in his poetry's relationship to history, the archive, and documentation. The specificities of time and place are central to understanding these poems. In titles like "Lenox Avenue: Midnight," "Midnight Dancer," "Harlem Night Song," "To Midnight Nan at Leroy's," and "The Cat and the Saxophone (2 a.m.)," Hughes locates the lyric scene in the spatial and temporal coordinates of Harlem's nightlife and indexes people and events that consciously seek to evade archival legibility.

Among the many poems that mark and extend nightlife sociality past its sanctioned limits in these volumes, "The Cat and the Saxophone (2 a.m.)"

demonstrates the ways in which Hughes's verse both formally and thematically archives queer time and space and frustrates temporal closure. Like
"Midnight Nan at Leroy's," which refers to Leroy Wilkins's nightclub on
135th Street, this poem likely refers to an actually existing nightclub: the
Cat on the Saxophone was a nickname given to an upper Fifth Avenue cabaret by Ethel Ray (Nance), Regina Andrews, and Louella Tucker—probably
Ed Small's Sugar Cane Club, a basement cabaret at 2212 Fifth Avenue that
closed in 1925.[44] Nance, Andrews, and Tucker were flatmates whose parties at 580 St. Nicholas Avenue were legendary among Harlem Renaissance
literati; Hughes was a frequent guest—and once guest of honor—at many
of these parties. The poem itself is thus a piece of poetic evidence, a lyric
remnant that marks the existence of a historically specific time and place.
At the same time, the slight slippage between the club's nickname and the
poem's title locates the poetic scene on a different map than the official grid
of the city, with its recognized names and street addresses. The title points
instead to the practices of everynight life by which city inhabitants negotiate the administration of the city with their own vernacular renamings and
remappings, pursuing an affective cartography of memory, resonance, and
in-group knowledge.

The crowded Cat on the Saxophone, Nance recalled, was the kind of
place where "members of the orchestra would wait on the tables when it
became rushed."[45] Hughes depicts this fragmenting commotion and movement in his poem, making his own emphatic declaration in the noisy scene
through the soundlessness of punctuation:

> EVERYBODY
> Half-pint,—
> Gin?
> No, make it
> LOVES MY BABY
> corn. You like
> liquor,
> don't you honey?
> BUT MY BABY
> Sure. Kiss me,
> DON'T LOVE NOBODY
> daddy.
> BUT ME.
> Say!
> EVERYBODY

Yes?
WANTS MY BABY
I'm your
BUT MY BABY
sweetie, ain't I?
DON'T WANT NOBODY
Sure.
BUT
Then let's
ME,
do it!
SWEET ME.
Charleston,
mamma!
!46

"The Cat and the Saxophone (2 a.m.)" uses a vocal and typographic heteroglossia unusual to lyric poetry to capture the improvisation, sound, and
sociality of the jazz club. The voice of a performer (singing Jack Palmer and
Spencer Williams's Tin Pan Alley standard "Everybody Loves My Baby")
alternates with snippets of conversation between a man and a woman standing at a bar, or perhaps seated at a table.[47] The movement back and forth
between capital and lowercase letters produces an almost drunken unfocus-
ing as the reader works to maintain the sense of two different conversations
simultaneously, as well as the experience of simultaneity itself. This task is
made more complicated as each enjambed line is interrupted and delayed
by a line for its continuation. Following the conversation at the bar, we
overhear the ritual pickup line (a variation of "Can I buy you a drink?") that
inaugurates an exchange of leading questions ("You like Liquor, don't you
Honey?" "I'm your sweetie, ain't I?") and noncommittal answers ("Sure").
This back and forth suggests an improvisation of identity and relationality that culminates in a final coupling as the characters take to the dance
floor. By interweaving this dialogue with the performer's lyrics, the couple
emerges in the literal and typographic spaces made possible by the musical
performance. In this scene, Hughes gives us not specific poetic characters or
voices but generic figures who become legible through a flirtatious linguistic choreography structured by the sounds of performance.

   At the end of the poem, these two alternating conversations—between
the man and the woman and the performer and the audience—merge as the
individuated figures at the bar, now a pair, move onto the dance floor and

become part of the collective audience addressed by the singer. But if there is a thematic convergence between these two lines of dialogue—these two currents that flow into, across, and over each other until they are drawn into the tidal pull of the dance floor—there is also a formal refusal of the apparent poetic culmination of this union. In a poem heavy with terminal punctuation—four question marks, four exclamation points, and six periods in thirty lines—the final exclamation point has always stopped me short. The poem's final line is given over to a visual symbol that cannot be read, per se, but is used to convey that surplus of feeling and emotion that shapes the meaning and interpretation of language before it. Signifying a range of possible affective emphases, from joy to alarm, it designates a heightened sense that locates the scene of the poem outside the register of the simply declarative. How are we to read this last line, the poem's terminal terminal mark, a deferred ending to a poem that seems like it should end in its penultimate line?

In one sense, the final exclamation mark stands as the terminal punctuation, not for any line or sentiment, but for the entire poem, marking the union of the dancing couple and bringing the evening to an end at the 2:00 a.m. closing time. But in another sense, we can understand the final exclamation point as frustrating and refusing poetic closure entirely, leaving the poem an endlessly unfinished project. In this sense, Hughes cannily plays with the end of his poem, marking it emphatically as the formal poetic event that initiates a crisis of poetic identity and declares what philosopher Giorgio Agamben calls a "state of poetic emergency."[48] Agamben defines poetry as a disjunction between sense and sound: instead of meaning at the end of any line, as one expects in prose, the reader gets rhyme; meaning is suspended or delayed by enjambment to the next line. If poetry is defined by this enjambed gap between sense and sound, the end of a poem then constitutes a crisis and "loss of identity" precisely because this gap can no longer be maintained. The impossibility of enjambment of any poem's last line thus radically challenges the poem's unfolding formal identity, leaving it in a "necessary undecidability between prose and poetry."[49]

Hughes makes use of this formal undecidability to leave open not only the poem's last line, but also the scene of the poem itself. This state of poetic emergency is, in the context of the "The Cat and the Saxophone (2 a.m.)," one of both formal and extratextual importance. Hughes exploits this undecidability to defer poetic closure while at the same time opening a space in the legislation of the closing hour where desiring subjects can continue to exist beyond the end of the poem as well as the end of the evening. With the enjambed "!," Hughes avoids closure by extending the poem past its resolution, refusing the coincidence of sound and sense that marks the final line of any poem. In its refusal of confluent sound and sense, the exclamation point insists that the poem itself cannot provide any stable resolution or self-identity. This formal anticlosure thus propels the poem's thematic concerns. The "2 a.m." in the title marks the legal time by which bars and nightclubs should stop serving alcohol and close their doors. The scene in Hughes's poem, however, shows no sign of winding down, with drinks still being ordered, music being performed, and dancing solicited. Deferring conclusion, Hughes gestures toward the radical possibilities of afterhours to extend beyond itself into new configurations of time and space. The emergent relationship between the couple at the bar—and, for that matter, the relationship between the performer and the audience—marks conditions by which certain sexual, racial, and criminal subjects come into existence. Once again, what makes this scene queer is not the sexual object choice of the figures who come together—who seem at least to represent a heterosexual coupling—but their relationship to the queer temporality of afterhours. The union of the couple coming together on the dance floor is not the culmination of the evening, but a moment in a night that will continue. The poem itself refuses their coupling as a teleological moment of social or sexual closure, just as it refuses its own poetic closure and opens into space within the popular illegality of afterhours. "The Cat and the Saxophone (2 a.m.)" thus becomes an afterhours club, one that exceeds the regulatory mechanisms of normal clock time with which Hughes was all too familiar.[50]

MORNING AND MELANCHOLIA: THE LOSS OF NIGHTLIFE

For nightlife subjects like those in "The Cat and the Saxophone (2 a.m.)," the encroaching dawn, rising sun, or sheer exhaustion inevitably brings this fugitive sociality to an end. When there is no afterhours to which to retreat, closing time can mark a radical finality, the death of subjective possibility and possible subjectivity. Even when the space is repeated and reoccupied the next night (assuming that proper payoffs and secrecy are maintained), every closing has something of the eternal in it. For Hughes, this end of the night stands as nothing less than an allegory for death, a transition in which he glimpses a haunting timelessness. In poems like "Suicide," "Suicide's Note," "Saturday Night," "Cabaret," "To a Little Lover-Lass, Dead," "Death of Do Dirty: A Rounder's Song," "Sport," "Closing Time," and "Summer

Night," death waits calmly but firmly on the other side of nightlife's threshold. Unlike "The Cat and the Saxophone (2 a.m.)" and the other poems
referenced above, these poems do not record the possibilities of afterhours
or extend nightlife sociality, but rather mark its ending and trace the effects
of closure by evoking nightlife's loss. Such poems achieve their affective
resonance not by what they describe, but what they do not describe. In
this register, Hughes offers a negative critique that renders nightlife accessible only through memory and other ephemeral remains, further keeping
the popular illegalities of afterhours away from the surveilling gaze of the
vice squad but nonetheless making it available to present and future queer
readers.

While the turn to death that marks so many of the cabaret poems in *The
Weary Blues* and *Fine Clothes to the Jew* can be seen in a lyric tradition of
carpe diem (or, better, *carpe noctem*) poetry, I want to suggest instead that
Hughes's generic concerns with the fragility of joy and pleasure and the
immanence of death take on a specific historical meaning when they are
understood within the context of the legal and administrative struggles over
queer nightlife and the emergence of modern sexual and racial subjectivities.[51] The death that marks the limit of nightlife in Hughes's poems is the
return to that mode of official participation in American life that Lauren
Berlant calls "dead citizenship."[52] Dead citizenship ensures and enforces
a correspondence between act and identity within the space and time of
abstract nationality and privatized heterosexuality. Even as Harlem Renaissance leaders like W. E. B. Du Bois, Alain Locke, and Charles Johnson were
fighting for full participation in American citizenship, many black queer
writers and performers—including Hughes—were challenging the sexual
and class norms on which that citizenship was based. The characters in
Hughes's cabaret poems are not "good" racial or American subjects, nor are
they always proper black proletarian voices. They are criminal and lumpen
subjects who implicitly critique and consciously reject the imperatives of
dead citizenship, racing the clock for as long as they can.

Hughes's poem "Sport," for example, suggests how certain modes of existence are fully dependent on the musical and clock time of the afterhours
club:

> Life
> For him
> Must be
> The shivering of

A great drum
Beaten with swift sticks
Then at the closing hour
The lights go out
And there is no music at all
And death becomes
An empty cabaret
And eternity an unblown saxophone
And yesterday
A glass of gin
Drunk long
Ago.[53]

The "him" in the second line refers to the figure named by the title: a "sport" was a man of the fast set, one who lives the "sporting life" among the gamblers, risk takers, and performers of the underworld, making occasional sorties across the borderland between sanctioned and criminal nightlife practices. The sport of Hughes's poem, however, like the figures in "The Cat and the Saxophone (2 a.m.)," is not a type or a classification of person such as we might find in sociological studies or police reports, but a transient identity that becomes possible only within a certain spatial and temporal existence. The monosyllabic diction and repetition of "And" in the second half of the poem gives the sense of a resistance to the inevitable end of the poem, a delay of poetic and actual closure as the image of the cabaret slips into the past and into memory. The vibrating skin of the jazz drum suggests a pulse and tension that, when silenced, juxtaposes against the unrealized potentiality of the unblown saxophone. The instruments of the jazz band mark the musical conditions and temporal limits by which the sport can, finally, exist at all. Or, as Duke Ellington put it more succinctly, "Night Life seems to have been born with all of its people in it, the people who had never been babies, but were born *grown*, completely independent."[54]

In the deferring liveliness of the "!" in "The Cat and the Saxophone (2 a.m.)," Hughes gives his readers an opportunity to see beyond the "official" end of the night. In "Sport," by contrast, Hughes uses deathly associations to critique what can also be the social suffocation of closing time for certain modes of subjectivity—in this case, the sport. Images and themes of death in Hughes's cabaret poems work as a form of what Barbara Herrenstein Smith calls "closural allusion," the poetic device that draws on a class of words and phrases suggesting ending and finality in order to bring the poem itself to a formal end.[55] Like the halting progression toward "long /

Ago" in "Sport," the syntactic weight of the "drowned girl" at the end of Hughes's "Closing Time" not only demonstrates the poet's formal use of closural allusion but also marks the price of nightlife's closure for the young woman in the poem:

> Starter!
>> Her face is pale
>> In the doorway light.
>> Her lips blood red
>> And her skin blue white.
> Taxi!
>> I'm Tired
> Deep . . . River. . . .
>> O, God, please!
> The river and the moon hold memories.
>> Cornets play,
>> Dancers whirl.
>> Death, be kind.
> What was the cover charge, kid?
>> To a little drowned girl.[56]

Like "The Cat and the Saxophone (2 a.m.)," Hughes uses a counterpoint of voices, but here he juxtaposes the collective joy in the cabaret — the whirling dancers and playing cornets — with the isolated despair of a young woman on the threshold (both literal — the doorway — and temporal, as the title suggests) between the cabaret and the night. The hailing of a cab reflects the material rituals of closing time, as does the existential exhaustion suggested by the line that follows. Hughes's references to the Negro spiritual "Deep River" and to the Harlem River makes a direct connection between histories of black subjectivity and the specific spaces of Harlem's nightlife. As Onwuchekwa Jemie points out about Hughes's jazz poems, the musical and racial history of America was at the center of Harlem's nightlife, rather than, as some bohemians saw it, access to a primitive Africa: "Beneath the glittery surface of the jazz, gin, and jargon of the cabaret flows the silent Deep River of the spirituals, the river of slavery and poverty and frustrated dreams. . . . And after the clang and whir of the syncopation of the night quickly follows the silence wherein the burden of black reality resumes its soul-crushing weight."[57] Whether the "little drowned girl" at the end of "Closing Time" drowns in the actual river to which Hughes alludes or in the "Deep River" of racial frustration and despair is unclear. In either case, we are reminded of the blues singer in one of Hughes's most acclaimed early poems: "The stars went out and so did the moon. / The singer stopped playing and went to bed / While the Weary Blues echoed through his head. / He slept like a rock or a man that's dead."

One final example will suggest the ways that closing time is used in Hughes's poem to mark the conditions of queer existence and the productive time of popular illegalities. In "Summer Night," Hughes archives the ephemerality of loss, absence, and emptiness that marks the departure from the tempo and lope of the cabaret and the return to the structures of dead citizenship that must be withstood:

> The sounds
> Of the Harlem night
> Drop one by one into stillness.
> The last player-piano is closed.
> The last victrola ceases with the
> "Jazz Boy Blues."
> The last crying baby sleeps
> And the night becomes
> Still as a whispering heartbeat.
> I toss
> Without rest in the darkness,
> Weary as the tired night,
> My soul
> Empty as the silence,
> Empty with a vague,
> Aching emptiness,
> Desiring,
> Needing someone,
> Something.
>
> I toss without rest
> In the darkness
> Until the new dawn,
> Wan and pale,
> Descends like a white mist
> Into the court-yard.[58]

This poem appears in the final section of *The Weary Blues,* marking after-hours by its end. Dead citizenship, like the night in the poem, is still and fixed, and does not generate the social fluidity and dynamism of the cabaret. Rampersad, citing the end of the first stanza, characterizes this poem as a "gloomy" and lonely lamentation.[59] But when read in light of historical context, we can see the poem's description of fitfulness not only as a bleak existential complaint (which it surely is) but also in relation to the temporal boundedness of the underworld. The cabaret, finally, closes; afterhours eventually comes to an end. Walking home through the streets of Harlem, past well-kept brownstones where families are sound asleep, and tossing restlessly in bed waiting for the night to end are part of a process of returning to a world that is marked by different rhythms, tempos, and vibrations. In an inversion of the normal understanding of sunrise, dawn in this poem descends rather than rises; rather than offering clarity and enlightenment, it instead obscures with a haze. The courtyard, which we would expect to offer relief from the claustrophobic constraints of urban apartment living, instead provides a confining fog when figured against the subjective possibility of the afterhours club. This fog, like the unblown saxophone and the still waters of the Deep River, hauntingly marks the subjective loss on the other side of queer time. This would, indeed, be a gloomy notion, if the performances, sociality, and sounds of the cabaret did not offer the affective nourishment and comfort that can reform the world and reparatively reinvent the social, even if only fleetingly. "Summer Night" thus indexes the sociality and sounds that the subject just left, leaving an impermanent fossil record in the ringing ears and lingering vibrations that are acutely felt as one readjusts to the tempo of normal life.[60]

IN CLOSING: QUEER LANGSTON HUGHES, AGAIN

In making connections between the historical circumstances of closing time and afterhours and Hughes's strategies of poetic closure, anticlosure, and closural allusions, I have offered another way to read what bell hooks calls the "closeted eroticism" in Hughes's work.[61] While other queer poets of the Harlem Renaissance, such as Claude McKay and Countee Cullen, often adapted the sonnet—a form with strong closural structures—to respond to black aesthetic and historical concerns—Hughes was primarily drawn to the anticlosural impulses of modern, avant-garde, and jazz poetry, forms in which the structural resources of closure are minimal. In contrast to his blues poems in *The Weary Blues* and *Fine Clothes to the Jew*, which invite strong poetic closure by way of the blues conventions of tripartite repetition, the poems that I have referred to here follow the modernist trend toward anticlosure, and in doing so formally reflect their thematic and historical concerns and archive the time consciousness of afterhours in their intimate inscriptions.

This anticlosure and public intimacy is also the place where Hughes's queerness becomes especially relevant. It is not only poetic or commercial closure that is resisted and criticized but also, as I have argued, the closures and foreclosures of sexual subjectivity offered to those who cultivate and are cultivated by the queer time and space of the afterhours club. Reading Hughes's poems in this way suggests something in excess of the narrow winnowing of desire into a binary of sexual object choice. When Carl Van Vechten said that he "never had . . . any indication that [Hughes] was homosexual or heterosexual," he was not suggesting that Hughes was asexual or did not desire.[62] Instead, he was remaining faithful to Hughes himself, who studiously cultivated a suspicion of sexual identity and attended with much more interest to the conditions of queer sociality. Hughes resisted naming and fixing his desire, not out of internalized shame or the logic of the closet, but out of what bell hooks proposes we might think of as his "perverse regard" for desire itself, its mysteries and uncertainties.[63]

It is such a "perverse regard," rather than what Rampersad calls a "strict regard for the rules of evidence," that should guide queer explorations into Hughes's work. The point is neither to devalue the importance of the archival nor to diminish the tremendous accomplishment of Rampersad's biography, which among other things has made conversations about Langston Hughes's sexuality considerably more richly textured. The point is to take note of the limits of the archive, narrowly conceived, for queer knowledge production and to recognize the many forms and unlikely places where residues of queer history and memory might settle. As regulations over closing time and afterhours sociality show, certain practices and experiences are actually designed to elude what counts as the official archive, and instead compel creative and inventive ways to be remembered and preserved. Better than any other Harlem Renaissance author—perhaps better than any author—Hughes captures the special temporality and contact of nightlife in his writing, and captures them in a way that leaves such experiences unclosed and "in solution."[64] His lifework thus compels an approach to intimacy and sexuality that moves us away from his biography and toward the queer poetics of his writing, exploring conditions for queer possibility and experience that resist the "nowhen" of historical documentation and official taxonomic mappings.[65] Yet by inscribing and recording the queer temporalities of the cabaret into his printed books, Hughes's archive nevertheless makes itself available in the library and disseminates the queer, musical counterpublics of Harlem's nightlife—into, for example, the shelves of the Harlem branch of the New York Public Library, just around the corner from "Jungle Alley," as 133rd Street, lined with nightclubs, was known. To this day, within the stacks and manuscript collections, shelved alongside "official" histories, sit pieces of a different community than the one imagined by racial uplift advocates, available to be checked out—underlined, dog-eared, and spine-cracked—by succeeding generations. This, rather than whether or not Hughes might have been "gay," is one reason why his poetic archive continues to be timely to queer history and memory, then and now.

CHAPTER FOUR

Rereading Du Bois Reading McKay

Uplift Sociology and the Problem of Amusement

IN THE June 1928 issue of the *Crisis,* W. E. B. Du Bois published the most infamous book review of the Harlem Renaissance.[1] In his indictment of Claude McKay's novel, *Home to Harlem* (1928), Du Bois accused the author of using primitivist and sexually explicit imagery to appeal to "that prurient demand on the part of white folk for a portrayal in Negroes of that utter licentiousness which conventional civilization holds white folk back from enjoying." McKay, he charged, satisfied this demand by "paint[ing] drunkenness, fighting, lascivious sexual promiscuity and utter absence of restraint in as bold and as bright colors as he can." Frustrated by what he saw as a definite movement in the subject matter of black literature toward the lower classes, the criminal, and the sexually deviant, Du Bois found McKay's book an affront to the politics of literary representation and racial uplift that he advocated. *Home to Harlem,* he lamented, "for the most part nauseates me, and after the dirtier parts of its filth I feel distinctly like taking a bath."[2]

As we saw in the prior discussion of Hughes's *The Weary Blues* and *Fine Clothes to the Jew,* the Cabaret School made use of criminal interruptions into the normative temporal order to imagine an afterhours time that critiques the clocks of bourgeois life narrative, capitalist productivity, and historical teleology. In this chapter we will see how the Cabaret School critiqued the spatial logic of uplift ideology. At the end of his review, Du Bois concludes with regret that such a talented author as McKay had "stooped" to such levels, and "sincerely hope[s] that someday he will rise above it."[3] This language, like the metaphor of uplift itself, is a language of spatialization. The rhetorical approach of mapping—surveying the terrain, delimiting boundaries, spatially cataloguing institutions and practices, and creating a representation of the people, places, and practices being written about—structures narratives of the underworld in genres as varied as sociological studies, journalism, and literature. Cabaret School literature is often interpreted—contemporaneously and contemporarily—as providing maps to guide pleasure-seeking white slummers on their journeys toward greater exoticism and eroticism. Benjamin Brawley, for example, followed Du Bois's lead when he charged that with *Home to Harlem,* McKay adjusted his writing to the fact that "it was not the poem or story of fine touch that the public desired, but metal of a baser hue."[4] Nathan Huggins similarly determined that the novel "pandered to commercial tastes" by providing a tour of Harlem's underworld wherein "the reader is carried into house parties, cabarets, and dives."[5] More recently, Kevin Mumford and Justin Edwards argue that novels like Carl Van Vechten's *Nigger Heaven* (1926) and McKay's *Home to Harlem* functioned as a form of travel literature, "carefully describ[ing] Harlem's institutions and spatial dimensions, employing a kind of sociological realism by layering concrete details of streets, buildings, interiors."[6]

Despite the fact that these novels often provided coordinates to actual locations, I want to suggest that Cabaret School authors in fact critiqued traditional underworld mappings; they offered maps, but not of the terrain that most critics suspected. "To map," writes geographer Dennis Cosgrove, "is in one way or another to take the measure of a world, and more than merely take it, to figure the measure taken in such a way that it may be communicated between people, places or time. The measure of mapping is not restricted to the mathematical; it may equally be spiritual, political, or moral. By the same token, the mapping's record is not confined to the archival; it includes the remembered, the imagined, the contemplated."[7] The encounter staged between McKay and Du Bois in the *Crisis* review serves as an entry point to consider how the Cabaret School could manipulate practices of mapping and movement to critique uplift ideology and offer the underworld as a space of performed political possibility. More precisely, the underworld and the cabaret hold out the possibility for an interclass intimacy between two groups positioned in opposition to each other by uplift sociology: the black working class, on the one hand, and what Du Bois called the "submerged tenth," the morally disgraceful fraction of the race, on the other hand.

Home to Harlem was one of the most sensational novels of the Cabaret

School. It tells the story of Jake and Ray, two itinerant laborers, as they move through the spaces of black recreation and amusement that make up the everynight life of the city. The narrative structure, as Robert Bone characterized it, is "loose and vagrant, tracing Jake's movements from cabaret to 'rent party,' from poolroom to gin mill, from the docks to the dining car." [8] McKay's focus on leisure time and social relationships that develop outside of the spaces of both labor and domesticity put *Home to Harlem* at odds with the normalizing impulses within the Harlem Renaissance, particularly as they congealed around questions of sex and intimacy. The amusements that Jake and Ray frequent are not civic organizations or middle-class recreations, but rather what Howard sociologist William H. Jones called the "pathological forms of entertainment" (*RA* 161). McKay's depiction of these spaces intersects with sociological conversations about the "problem" of African American urban recreation. New Negro sociologists, responding to pseudo-scientific and cultural representations of black social disorder, figured these regions of popular amusement as particularly fraught moral terrain. This underworld was sociologically imagined as an unproductive sphere inhabited by social and sexual deviants—criminals, prostitutes, gamblers, queers, interracial couples, musicians—who threatened to corrupt honest working-class men and, especially, women.

The disciplinary methods of sociology helped produce the sexual, racial, economic, and gender norms by which people and practices could be evaluated.[9] As Kevin Gaines argues, uplift ideology depended on the social scientific identification of a "pathological class" against which to measure a black elite advancement. In this way, "black elites claimed class distinctions, indeed, the very existence of a 'better class' of blacks, as evidence of what they called race progress." [10] Yet during the Harlem Renaissance, Du Bois and others found themselves continually frustrated by the fact that the race's most talented emerging writers occupied a liminal and contingent position between this "Talented Tenth" and the "submerged tenth." These socioeconomic categories, it turned out, were permeable; people rarely remained in their discrete categories. When McKay emerged on the literary scene with his defiant poem "If We Must Die" in the summer of 1919, he demonstrated the characteristics that Du Bois attributed to the cultural leaders of the race: "intelligence, broad sympathy, knowledge of the world that was and is, and of the relation of men to it." [11] But his attraction to and identification with criminals, prostitutes, and other social deviants was in direct opposition to the morally superior and educated tenth Du Bois sought to cultivate. The Cabaret School's easy passage back and forth between these two moral classes threatened the coherence of the entire hierarchy.

Even more than Langston Hughes's poetry, the appearance of *Home to Harlem* confirmed fault lines within Harlem's literary public sphere and revealed the antagonism between the Harlem Renaissance establishment and its queer insurgents. McKay's novel appeared after the controversial publications of not only Hughes's *The Weary Blues* and *Fine Clothes to the Jew*, but also Van Vechten's *Nigger Heaven* (1926) and Wallace Thurman's journal *Fire!!* (1926). *Nigger Heaven*, as we saw in chapter 2, provoked strong dispute over the white author's sensational scenes of Harlem's cabaret and its unfavorable depiction of Harlem's educated classes. *Fire!!* was even more challenging to the Renaissance's Talented Tenth leaders. The journal featured poetry, drama, fiction, and visual art that explored the psychic and sexual experiences of nonnormative black sociality. *Home to Harlem* was immediately seen within this bohemian tradition, one that mapped and detailed the people and spaces of the underworld—its "sweetmen," "sheiks," and "bulldaggers"; its rent parties, cabarets, and buffet flats. To Du Bois and likeminded critics, it opportunistically promoted images of black deviance and social disorganization and gave the false impression that all of Harlem was a cabaret.[12]

Unlike Van Vechten's novel of black middle-class manners or *Fire!!*'s patchwork of bohemian decadence, however, McKay characterized *Home to Harlem* as a "real proletarian novel."[13] It presents a stunning example of what Gary Holcomb calls McKay's "queer black proletarianism," a politics and aesthetics that depends on the mutual constitution of class, sexual, and racial positions.[14] In exploring a subterranean landscape of recreation and pleasure, McKay charged that the politics of his novel would never be understood by "nice radicals" who wanted their "own fake, soft-headed and wine-watered notions of the proletariat" as a figure ennobled by his oppression and full of revolutionary authenticity.[15] Rather than focusing explicitly on the workday and the conditions of labor, McKay instead foregrounded a landscape of deviance and pleasure as he impressionistically sketched the leisure and contact between the black working classes and the black underworld's submerged tenth. For McKay, the cabaret and other places of amusement are places for the cultivation of nonnormative intimacies that ultimately imagine a world of interclass solidarity between the working class and a criminal and sexually deviant underclass. In this way, *Home to Harlem*'s depictions complicate uplift epistemologies that would quantify and organize the types of people who make up the "underworld" and the "working class" as discrete, even opposed, populations, thus uprooting the moral hedges that uplift sociologies plant. As sensory alternatives to the totalizing and invasive gaze of sociological-realist interpretations, McKay instead foregrounds touch, sound, and smell—a revolutionary intimacy called for by social theorists Alexander Negt and Oskar Kluge in their desire for a proletarian solidarity "that can be grasped with the senses." [16]

In what follows, I read *Home to Harlem* to show not only that the Cabaret School is very consciously opposed to the interpretive imperatives of sociological realism—the hermeneutic most critics apply to these works—but also to demonstrate how performance can undermine sociological assumptions and practices. Uplift sociology's primary projects were to differentiate intraracial class distinctions and to quantify and spatialize urban moral regions. This spatialization worked, as we will see, to fix and arrest social practice through processes of sociological representation. *Home to Harlem* resists these efforts of uplift ideology by rhetorically reanimating these arrested underworld performances. When I do propose mimetic readings of the novel in this chapter, it is not in the service of a mimetic realism, but what we could call an affective mimesis—the ways in which McKay uses certain rhetorical and literary strategies not to represent the types of people or the scene of performance, but to disseminate the feelings, intimacies, and qualities such spaces produce and foster. McKay gestures toward public intimacies and nightlife practices that are not chained to a politics of representation but make possible a politics of transfiguration: a politics which "emphasizes the emergence of qualitatively new desires, social relations, and modes of association within the racial community of interpretation and resistance *and* between that group and its erstwhile oppressors." [17] Such a politics of transfiguration as enacted in the literary is, to paraphrase performance theorist Elin Diamond, an attempt to "unmake mimesis." Challenging the very premises of cultural uplift, McKay strategically stages the failure of realist representation to depict Harlem's everynight life, offering instead an anticartography that works not by accurate representation but by affective resonance.

Though Du Bois stands in this argument as an example of larger sociological and normalizing trends, he is not the bad guy of this chapter. The critical encounter between McKay and Du Bois in the *Crisis* review, I contend, is incompletely read when it is taken simply as a bourgeois affront to bohemian or primitivist tendencies. Instead, I will read Du Bois's review against its grain to restore the ambiguities of his denunciation. Reading *Home to Harlem* through Du Bois's review anew, we can see that McKay does not fix and map the people and practices of Harlem's underworld, as sociological and realist readings lead us to believe, but rather shows how everynight life performances produce their own possibilities of social transformation across class borders. Unlikely as it would seem, Du Bois affirmatively points to the aspects of *Home to Harlem* that most incisively shape its contribution to both a black and queer literature—a literature that sees beyond narrow conceptions of race and sex toward a greater horizon of racial and sexual becoming.

To substantiate this interpretation, I first provide a discussion of the sociological practices of mapping that spatialize and produce "official knowledge" of the black underworld. I show how Du Bois and other New Negro social scientists helped establish the link between economic and sexual normativity by yoking questions of recreation, leisure, and expenditure to moral disposition under the objective imprimatur of sociology. Here, I also consider aesthetic strategies that seek to confuse and rewrite these linkages. These early sociological investigations into black moral character and social dance provide a larger context for understanding the rhetorical project of the Cabaret School generally, as well as McKay's novel and Du Bois's ambivalent response to it. While reading Du Bois alongside McKay highlights the enormous gap between how each approaches the event of black performance, it nonetheless reveals the dance floor as a place where both writers locate the production of black intimacy and modernity. As both authors ultimately agree, the practices, performances, and labor of the cabaret produce a surplus intimacy that was neither simple primitive excess nor antisocial pathology.

THE CARTOGRAPHY OF UPLIFT

The impulse to read *Home to Harlem* sociologically, or as a sociological-realist novel, haunts its reception (as it does the reception of most Harlem Renaissance literature; as it does the reception of most African American literature).[18] Although, as James de Jongh observes, McKay's language is highly stylized and figurative, his descriptions of the people, ethics, and relationships of the black underworld have either been interpreted as realist documentations depicting the "truth" of Harlem's working-class spaces or denounced for luridly exaggerating its excesses.[19] At the center of Du Bois's review of McKay's novel, for example, is the problem of representation and normalizing distribution around a statistical mean. The novel is "untrue," Du Bois writes, "not so much on account of its facts, but on account of its emphasis." The question of truth and emphasis echoes Du Bois's earlier response to Van Vechten's *Nigger Heaven*, in which he concedes that "probably some time and somewhere in Harlem every incident of the book has happened," but argues that the prominence given to barbaric and drunken nightlife scenes leaves the reader with an image of Harlem that is "ridiculously out of focus and undeniably misleading." The truth, which, according to Du Bois, statistical fact will bear out, is that "the overwhelming majority of black folk there never go to cabarets."[20] By focusing on social outliers instead of averages, Du Bois concludes, both McKay and Van Vechten offer a skewed representation of Harlem's population.

Such reviews point toward the larger sociological vision that informs uplift critiques of black cultural production in the 1920s. Indeed, perhaps no American literary movement has been so closely tied to the sociological as the Harlem Renaissance. While sociological hermeneutics have organized the reception of African American literature for three centuries, the Harlem Renaissance is unique in its close institutional relationship to social scientists and their disciplines. *The New Negro*, Alain Locke's anthology often characterized as inaugurating the Harlem Renaissance, was an expanded version of a special issue of the sociological journal *Survey Graphic*. The two periodicals sponsoring cash prizes for emergent poetry and prose — *Crisis* and *Opportunity* — were edited by sociologists (Du Bois and Charles S. Johnson). Du Bois himself first emerged on the national scene as director of the sociological laboratory and the Atlanta University Conferences from 1897 to 1910, when he led a number of inquiries into the social conditions of black life in the generations after Emancipation. It was at this time, too, that Du Bois theorized his concept of the Talented Tenth, a key ideological underpinning of the literary movement in Harlem that he sought to guide. Though by the 1920s he had relocated himself from institutions of sociology to institutions of political advocacy and print culture, his earlier social scientific approach continued to shape his response to black arts and letters.

As a project of a black modernity, early uplift sociology existed in an uneasy and often antagonistic relationship to canonical American sociology. Uplift sociology took on the double task of both correcting canonical (pseudo)scientific studies "proving" innate racial inferiority and also diagnosing problems that stood in the way of social progress and civic development, often prescribing programs for racial uplift and advancement. In this, uplift sociology complemented other black institutions in the early twentieth century: preachers and professors, editorialists and labor organizers worked together to constitute a normalizing discourse of moral standards, gender conformity, sexual hygiene, and capitalist productivity in order to manage the organization of black communities and families as they entered a post-Emancipation America.

Two prominent black sociological studies that advanced this project in the early twentieth century were Du Bois's 1899 study *The Philadelphia Negro* and Howard sociologist William H. Jones's 1927 study *Recreation and Amusement among Negroes in Washington, D.C.* Rather than undertake a sustained examination of either of these texts here, however, I will look to the practices of moral and geographical spatialization in these studies, turning to the paratextual—maps, tables, and footnotes—as one location of the normalizing technologies that linked moral value to city space. Our attention to these practices of sociological mapping will point us in a useful direction for reading the spatial practices of *Home to Harlem,* specifically, and the literature of the Cabaret School, more generally. Jones and Du Bois show the methods and strategies of mapping by which sociology attempts—and fails—to fix a racial and criminal underworld.

As director of the Atlanta Conferences, part of Du Bois's early academic project was to use the institutional and methodological weight of social science to counter racist narratives of black idleness and shiftlessness, on the one hand, and narratives of excess black sexuality and criminality on the other. Du Bois's methodological synthesis of statistical analysis, historical contextualization, and participant observation is fully elaborated in *The Philadelphia Negro,* his first major sociological work.[21] This study presented an exhaustive sociological survey of the history and then-current makeup of Philadelphia's Seventh Ward, the city's African American district. One of its many goals was to assert, document, and publicize the internal differentiation of Philadelphia's urban black community against a dominant racist logic that worked at the time to undifferentiate the black community by "bind[ing] even the most talented Negro citizen to the most abject black criminal."[22] Du Bois's statistical data and historical context produced both an economic norm—the black middle class—and a moral (sexual and gender) norm. Such quantification and distribution around a fictive statistical mean constituted a normalizing judgment that, as Foucault has shown, perpetually "compares, differentiates, hierarchizes, homogenizes, excludes."[23]

The Philadelphia Negro opens with a totalizing map of the Seventh Ward that, block by block, identifies streets and houses by the moral quality of its inhabitants from an "objective" perspective that takes in the entire landscape (fig. 7). In the original edition of the study, this map appears as a four-color, seven-page accordion fold inserted before page 1; as the reader unfurls the diagram, the Seventh Ward literally unfolds in her hands, allowing her to explore the social makeup of its various streets and alleys.

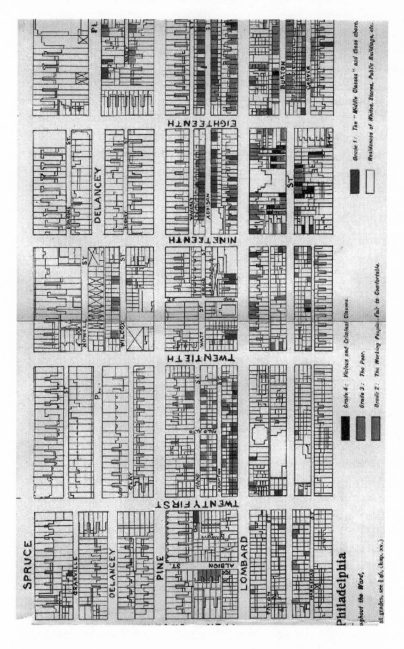

FIGURE 7 Portion of "The Seventh Ward of Philadelphia, the Distribution of Negro Inhabitants throughout the Ward, and Their Social Conditions." From W. E. B. Du Bois, *The Philadelphia Negro.* 1899.

Providing a moral panopticon of population distribution and "social conditions," Du Bois differentiates four social classes, or "gradations," of urban African Americans and charts their location in the Seventh Ward, ranging from the "'middle classes' and those above" to the "fair to comfortable" to the "vicious and criminal classes." By placing this map so prominently and spectacularly in his study, Du Bois links street life and spatial practice to the moral disposition of the city's population, functioning, as Marlon Ross suggests, as an attempt to contain and quarantine undesirable characters from contaminating the more respectable members of the race.[24]

A parenthetical note at the bottom of the map refers readers to chapter fifteen "for a more detailed explanation of the meaning of the different grades." Grade 1 is composed of families of "undoubted respectability," where the wife is "engaged in no other occupation save that of housewife" and the children are all in school; grade 2 is the "respectable" working class; the poor, "people not earning enough to keep them at all times above want," make up grade 3; and grade 4 is the "lowest class of criminals, prostitutes, and loafers; the 'submerged tenth.'"[25] In a telling footnote to the explanation of these grades, Du Bois momentarily refuses the rigorous empiricism that characterizes much of his study, substituting for it an avowed moralism:

It will be noted that this classification differs materially from the economic division in Chapter XI. In that case grade four and a part of three appear as the "poor;" grade two and the rest of grade three as the "fair to comfortable;" and a few of grade two and grade one as the well-to-do. The basis of division there was almost entirely according to income; *this division brings in moral considerations and questions of expenditure, and consequently reflects more largely the personal judgment of the investigator.*[26]

This footnote establishes a connection between economic and moral class at the same time it differentiates them as two different modes of classification. In creating the submerged tenth as a sociologico-moral category, Du Bois sought to do what Marx did when delimiting the category of the lumpenproletariat: to rinse the proletariat clean of the elements that do not fit neatly into the movement toward a productive class or racial consciousness. This discursive strategy relied on endlessly proliferating taxonomies of social differentiation and deviance in order to identify the outliers and simultaneously construct a homogenous, normalized bourgeois subject.[27] The submerged tenth cannot be characterized strictly in terms of economic class, as members of various economic backgrounds make up its numbers.

It exists, rather, as a stratum of moral failure, nonproductivity, and irresponsible expenditure. In this sense, the submerged tenth and its perceived antisocial (dis)organization—as well as the spatial domains it appropriates, labeled as slums, red-light, and vice districts—represents a threat to the respectable and the "fair to comfortable" working classes, especially to the young men and women of those families who may be led astray by the temptation of vice. Notably, "undoubted respectability" is in part defined by an intact heterosexual family with traditional gender roles.[28] This characterization inversely imagines the submerged tenth as a realm structured and reproduced through improvisational kinship relations and nontraditional gender roles.

Du Bois's *The Philadelphia Negro* map links the taxonomic classification of moral character to the geographic grid of the city's streets. As opposed to the private lives of the fair-to-comfortable and the well-to-do, the submerged fraction of the race is associated with publicness and street life. One other example will illustrate the ways in which *The Philadelphia Negro* maps moral value onto the everynight life of the city. In a chapter entitled "The Environment of the Negro," Du Bois includes a scientific table that shifts from the macro gaze of the earlier map to a micro surveillance of specific "slum" blocks in the Seventh Ward (fig. 8).[29] Titled "Some Alleys Where Negroes Live," this table mirrors the grid organization of the cityscape that Du Bois exploits in his larger map. Along the top of the table, Du Bois names specific streets (e.g., Allen's Court, Lombard Row, Alley off Carver Street). Along the left side, Du Bois lists a number of categories that describe the material and environmental aspects of the block (its "general character," the width of the alley, the material with which it is paved, the number of stories in each house, the ethnic makeup of the street, its cleanliness, the width of its sidewalk, the number of streetlights that illuminate it, and whether bathrooms are private or common). A final row of cells at the bottom of the grid provides Du Bois's own comments on the population of each street: for example, "poor and doubtful characters," "poor people and some questionable," "respectable homes mingled with gamblers and prostitutes." Each column typographically resembles a long, narrow alley, entered through the general character and descending deeper into the alley through more and more specific and revealing details, culminating with the state of toilet plumbing and Du Bois's own assessment of the street. Like the city grid and social gradations mapped in figure 7, this table provides an easy way to cross-reference physical property with the moral properties of those who inhabit it. Du Bois transforms his visual map—with its color-coded moral

SOME ALLEYS WHERE NEGROES LIVE.

	Govett's Court.	Hines' Court.	Allen's Court.	Horstman's Court.	Lombard Row.	Turner's Court.	Alley off Carver Street.	McCann's Court.	Cross Alley.
General Character	Poor.	Poor.	Very Poor.	Squalid.	Fair.	Wretched.	Fair.	Poor.	Bad.
Width, in feet	3	3-6.	6	12	9	3-12	6	12	12
Paved with	Bricks.	Bricks.	Bricks.	Bricks.	Bricks.	Bricks.	Bricks.	Bricks.	Asphalt.
Character of Dwelling	Poor.	Back Yard Tenements	Back Yard Tenements	Back Yard Tenements	Fair.	Old Wooden Houses.	Old Brick Tenements	Old Brick Tenements	Wood and Brick.
Number of Stories in Houses	3	3	3	2 and 3.	3	1 to 3.	3	2 to 3.	2 to 3.
Inhabitants	All Negroes.	All Negroes.	All Negroes.	All Negroes.	Negroes and Jews.	All Negroes.	Jews and Negroes.	All Negroes.	Jews and Negroes.
Cleanliness, etc.	Fair.	Fair.	Dirty.	Dirty.	Fair.	Fair.	Fair.	Fair.	Dirty.
Width of Sidewalk . . feet	4	5	6	None.	None.	None.	None.	None.	None.
Lighted by	No Lights.	No Lights.	No Lights.	1 Gas Lamp.	1 Gas Lamp.	1 Gas Lamp.	1 Gas Lamp.	1 Gas Lamp.	No Lights.
Privies in Common or Private	Common.	2 for whole Alley.	½ for each House.	5 in open Court.	Private.	Common.	Common.	Common.	Common.
Remarks		Emigrants from 5th Ward slums.	Poor and Doubtful Characters.	Very Poor People.	Respectable Homes mingled with Gamblers and Prostitutes.	Many Empty Houses; Poor and Doubtful People.	"Blind" Alley; Fairly Respectable.	Poor People and some Questionable.	Some Bad Characters.

FIGURE 8 "Some Alleys Where Negroes Live." From W. E. B. Du Bois, *The Philadelphia Negro*. 1899.

key and row after row of blocks and houses—into a representational language of social disorganization.

Gaines credits *The Philadelphia Negro* as setting "the standard for a sociological version of racial uplift ideology." [30] We can see traces of its influence in William H. Jones's *Recreation and Amusement among Negroes in Washington, D.C.*, published in 1927. With its focus on spaces and practices of urban leisure, Jones's study is at once more narrowly conceived and more specifically prescriptive than *The Philadelphia Negro*. Commissioned by the Juvenile Protective Association of Washington, D.C., Jones's study was begun with the assistance of students in a class on "social pathology" that he offered at Howard University in 1925 (*RA* xi). As a visual resource to his study of commercial and noncommercial recreation in the nation's capital (including playgrounds, sports, summer camps, country clubs, and community organizations along with cabarets and dance halls), Jones includes a city map that, like Du Bois's, makes use of the organizational grid of the city to isolate and identify the location and distribution of recreational and amusement centers (fig. 9). Jones's map charts constellation-like patterns of geometric symbols that appear over the city's grid when the sun goes down. He labels pool halls, dance halls, cabarets, and theaters, noting dense clusters on Florida Avenue between Eleventh and Thirteenth Streets and along the length of Seventh Street.[31] Lest these identifiable sites not generate enough moral panic, Jones promises that there is an entire "hidden night life" that practices in secret and encourages hidden forms of association (*RA* 177). These areas, the legible and the illegible, constitute the "moral region" and "disorganized community" of the everynight, which offer a "museum of types" for the understanding of antisocial behavior, degeneracy, and "human nature" (*RA* 161, 121).

Jones's and Du Bois's paratextual renderings illustrate how sociological representations of the underworld enforce intraracial class distinctions and spatially link moral value to discrete people, places, and practices. Yet these attempts to map the underworld also demonstrate the paradoxes of uplift cartography. As Jones concedes, such mappings cannot represent the hidden nightlife, a mobile and transitory realm that only becomes known through word of mouth, rumor, and "occasional night raids by the police," which "bring to light bits of evidence of what is going on under cover" (*RA* 179). The moral regions of urban recreation develop unchecked by social mores or community discipline, Jones finds, because of the "transient and unstable character of the population. This mobility results in a lack of permanency or fixity of life" (*RA* 161). Thus not only does uplift sociology seek to halt

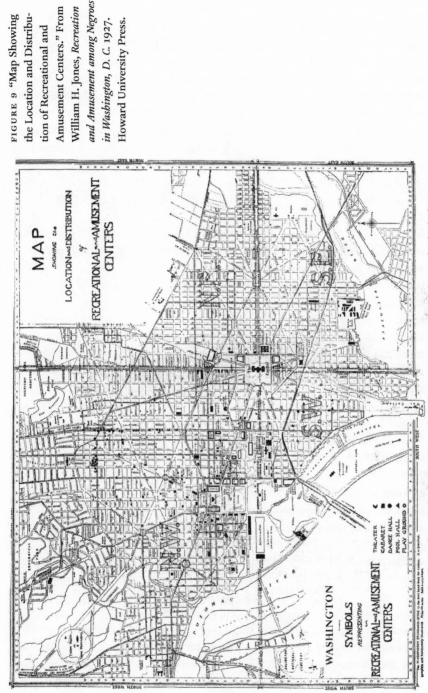

FIGURE 9 "Map Showing the Location and Distribution of Recreational and Amusement Centers." From William H. Jones, *Recreation and Amusement among Negroes in Washington, D. C.* 1927. Howard University Press.

A map showing the location and distribution of recreation and amusement centers in relation to other institutions the flows of modern life in its representational practices, but it calls for such motionlessness in its policy prescriptions as well: "Where a population is transient, it is virtually impossible to develop anything like public opinion and normative social attitudes" (*RA* 162). This totalizing sociological vision seeks to fix and stabilize an underworld that is dynamic and adaptable. In other words, these cartographic strategies of uplift sociology try to keep the underworld silent and still in order to pin down and paralyze precisely what makes the underworld function as such: bodies in motion that disorganize the official arrangement of the city and the family.

SOME NOCTURNAL WANDERINGS

Ray was not happy. The sudden upset of affairs in his own country had landed him into the quivering heart of a naked world whose reality was hitherto unimaginable. It was what they called in print and polite conversation "the underworld." The compound word baffled him, as some English words did sometimes. Why underworld he could never understand. It was very much upon the surface as were the other divisions of human life. Having its heights and middle and depths and secret places even as they. And the people of this world—waiters, cooks, chauffeurs, sailors, porters, guides, ushers, hod-carriers, factory hands— all touched in a thousand ways the people of the other divisions. They worked over there and slept over here, divided by a street.

MCKAY, HOME TO HARLEM

Jones dedicated *Recreation and Amusement among Negroes* to "all movements designed to improve the social life of the Negro city-dweller." Jones of course refers to racial uplift and progressive movements organized to address and redress African American social conditions and moral lassitude. But what if we intentionally misread Jones's dedication—his commitment—against itself, within a different context, one both narrower and broader at the same time: not "movement" as a collective of people coming together toward a common goal, making up a unified and homogenous body, but "movement" understood as the individual gestures and isolated comportments— the countless acts of changing locations and positions within social configurations—that rearrange and realign disparate bodies as they come together and break apart? This slight shift in connotation points to what is lost and obscured by these sociological mappings: the actual embodied practices that bring something like an underworld into existence. By attending to these movements, it becomes apparent that what appears to sociologists as a dissolute and immoral mass, a "chorus of idle footsteps," is revealed to be, in Michel de Certeau's words, an "innumerable collection of singularities." [32]

With this notion of movement in mind, I want to juxtapose these sociological mappings of urban moral and recreational districts with practices that unmap and remap official depictions of the city. This is important not only for conceptualizing what sociologists call the underworld, but also for better understanding the aesthetic responses to the Cabaret School. Official maps, which fix words and images and offer totalizing knowledge, obscure the temporal aspect of bodies moving through space. This mode of documentation transforms "action into legibility," as de Certeau tells us, but in doing so, it causes "a way of being in the world to be forgotten." [33] The Cabaret School sought to retain this way of being in the world, both formally and thematically. Yet if the underworld is constituted by embodied practices and performances, what kinds of literature can develop from these practices? How can literature perform or enact such practices? If walking writes the city, as de Certeau suggests, can writing walk the city? And can it do so in ways that do not provide totalizing, disciplinary representations but work to elude such surveillance?

Black cartoonist E. Simms Campbell's remarkable 1932 drawing, "A Night-Club Map of Harlem," suggests one answer to these questions (fig. 10). Campbell studied at the Art Institute of Chicago, worked successfully as an illustrator for popular magazines (including, for many years, *Esquire*), and had his work exhibited at the 1935 Harmon Exhibition. In "A Night-Club Map," Campbell caricatures the sociological mapping of moral and recreational regions of black neighborhoods. This drawing shows Harlem at night, mapping not just spaces but temporalities as well: the moon is marked in the top right corner; Campbell notes that the Radium Club hosts a "big breakfast dance every Sunday morning at 4 or 5 a.m.," and that "Nothing happens before 2 a.m." at Club Hot-Cha; clubs that are open all night are denoted by a star; and the halo of the street lamps on the corner of each block cast the neighborhood in an artificial glow. Campbell also visually catalogues the characters and types of the underworld. Actual figures are represented in their clubs — Cab Calloway sings at the Cotton Club, Bill Robinson taps at the Lafayette Theatre, Earl Tucker dances at the Savoy Ballroom, Gladys Bentley delivers her dirty song renditions at Gladys's Clam House, the "headman" at the Radium Club is identified as Jeff Blount, Garland Wilson plays a grand piano at the Theatrical Grill — as are archetypal characters — chorus girls form kick lines at Connie's Inn and the Cotton Club, a "sheik" (a dandified hustler) surrounded by fur-coated admirers

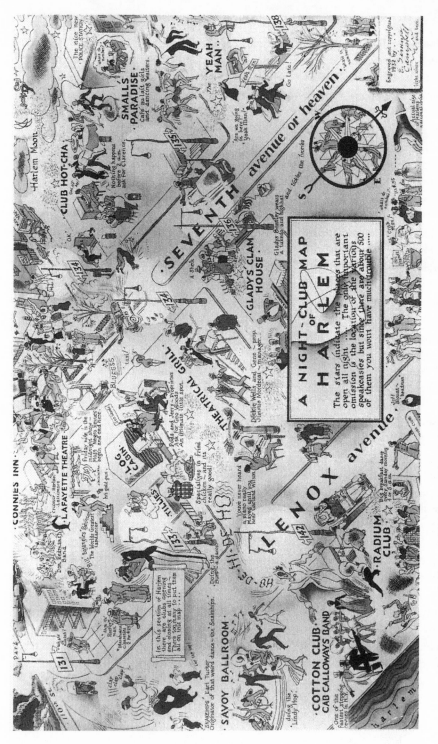

FIGURE 10 E. Simms Campbell, "A Night-Club Map of Harlem." 1932. Courtesy of Elizabeth Campbell-Moskowitz.

stands at the corner of 134th Street and Seventh Avenue, dancing waiters perform and serve at Small's Paradise, the "reefer man" sells "marahuana cigarettes 2 for $.25" along Lenox Avenue while police officers play cards in the "nice new police station," white flappers hail taxis while limousines pile up at Connie's Inn, and musicians fill the landscape: pianists, tuba players, saxophonists, and whole orchestras.

Yet Campbell is not only signifying on scientific and popular discourses of the underworld in his art; there is also an affective dimension to his map. Cotton Club bandleader Cab Calloway claimed in his autobiography that Campbell's map provided "a better idea of what Harlem was like in those days than I can give you with all these words." [34] This map of black performance and black publicity not only represents an "expressive geography" (Houston Baker's term) of African American modernism, but also illustrates how such geographies palimpsestically appear over the neighborhood's streets; an underworld located very much, as Ray suggests in the epigraph to this section, on the surface of the city.

Campbell's map reminds us that the everynight performances of 1920s Harlem cannot be accessed through the realism or literal language of sociological uplift. One legend on the left side announces the map's contingency: "In this section of Harlem there are clubs opening and closing at all times — there are too many to put them all on this map." A disclaimer under the title reads, "The only important omission is the location of the various speakeasies but since there are about 500 of them you won't have much trouble . . . " This indefiniteness stands in stark contrast to Jones's attempt to mark the locations of dance halls and cabarets; one can be sure that by the time Jones's study was published, his map was already out of date. Campbell's map, on the other hand, depends on its own inaccuracy to be accurate. Moreover, in the style of caricature, the scale is exaggerated and not to be taken literally. For example, 133rd Street runs into 142nd, and cramped Tillie's Crab Shack is larger than a three-story apartment building. As if to suggest the dizziness and blurriness of the representation, the compass rose in the right corner — the sign of direction and bearing — is draped with various passed-out revelers. One could ask: What good is a map if it cannot show you where and what things are? Rather than charting a realistic representation of Harlem's nightlife, Campbell's map diagrams affective points of reference. In place of the view of social science, which would fix the terrain and the population of the underworld in a normalizing gaze, Campbell pictorially presents the underworld by a logic of performance, contingency, and relationality.

Campbell remaps the underworld, that is to say, by the logic of the stroll. Strolling, as an African American aesthetic and social practice, had a long tradition in rural southern street life before northward migration transformed it into a modern remapping of the metropolis (and a necessary escape from the heat of stifling tenement apartments in the summer). When strolling in Harlem, James Weldon Johnson writes,

> One puts on one's best clothes and fares forth to pass the time pleasantly with the friends and acquaintances and, most important of all, the strangers he is sure of meeting. One saunters along, he hails this one, exchanges a word or two with that one, stops for a short chat with the other one. He comes up to a laughing, chattering group, in which he may have only one friend or acquaintance, but that gives him the privilege of joining in. He does join in and takes part in joking, the small talk and gossip, and makes new acquaintances. . . . This is not simply going out for a walk; it is more like going out for an adventure.[35]

Akin to modernist practices of flâneurie, strolling is shaped not only by the commodity culture of nineteenth-century European metropolises (as Baudelaire and Benjamin argue), but also by the performances of fugitivity, mobility, and self-fashioning embedded within a stance toward life after Emancipation.[36] Unlike the anonymity and disappearance promised by European models of flâneurie as one loses oneself in the flows, rhythms, and movements of the throng, strolling is a practice of relationality. The evening promenade or Sunday afternoon stroll has its own patterns, sights, and sounds that write over the "official" organization of the city: laughter and joking, greetings and goodbyes, cat calls and whistles, whispered gossip, hushing, the faint sound of radios from apartment windows, and the sounds that drift through the streets from storefronts, saloons, and other commercial establishments. People enter and exit the flows of the stroll at innumerable points, grouping, ungrouping, and regrouping along the way. Strolling is a walk without aim, yet it is not aimless.[37]

This is the relationship to the city that inaugurates *Home to Harlem* in its first few chapters and emerges not only as a theme throughout the novel, but could be said to formally structure it as well. Strolling—as a social practice and a posture toward the city—provides McKay with an idiom through which to write the sociality, contact, and self-fashioning of the everynight in a way that both evades and critiques the realism and "objectivity" of sociology. Returning to the epigraph that began this section, we can see this critique of sociological mapping made in *Home to Harlem*. As Ray reflects on the urban world that Jake inhabits, he reveals it in a different light. Rather than the shadowy alleys and dark corners Du Bois illuminates or the "hidden night-life" Jones exposes, Ray sees the "underworld" not as a recessed depth but "very much on the surface." The "compound word" *underworld* in particular confuses him; with connotations of assemblage and unification, it suggests a self-contained world. But rather than feeling separated off, Ray observes how those people who inhabit the underworld are continually brought into contact with each other, "touch[ing] in a thousand different ways" those in other social divisions. This touching (closely following the word "hands") crosses over the boundaries and divisions that are discursively enforced by the quantification of sociological mapping. As Ray notes, while the city streets may separate the areas of the city, they also connect them, providing routes to and from. This movement challenges sociology's clear distinction between moral regions and regions of proper socialization.

Ray's rhetoric of touch refracts the fear of contamination and contact that informs a New Negro "sociology of surveillance." [38] When Du Bois declaimed that he needed to take a bath after reading *Home to Harlem*, he invoked a long-established trope in urban representation that links dirt and cleanliness to social and physical notions of contamination and purity. The gaze of the submerged tenth, as Peter Stallybrass and Allon White argue about the English lumpenproletariat, was experienced by the black bourgeoisie as an "aggressive and humiliating act of physical contact," a touching that contaminated the normalizing look of the reformer. The avoidance of contact is necessary to retain the purity and hygiene of the middle-class observer. [39] Like the perspective of the balcony in nineteenth-century British literature, which symbolically represents the desire of the bourgeoisie to look upon but avoid contamination from the lumpen below, the views of the city mapped in figures 7–9 can be understood in a tradition that desires to look in upon the submerged tenth, and at the same time act as a "sanitary regime" that would quarantine the literal and moral filth they represent. [40]

If Du Bois looks upon the submerged tenth from a sociological balcony, McKay thrusts his reader into the underworld's streets and cabarets. The transformation of visual signs into linguistic signs that Du Bois effects from figure 7 to figure 8 mirrors literary and journalistic constructions of the underworld. While such rhetorical mappings were common in slumming novels and journalistic exposés, *Home to Harlem* undermines such efforts to spatially fix the underworld by remapping the city with the subjective, affective, and relational practice of strolling. Strolling in *Home to Harlem* can be understood as a variation on the pedestrian negotiations that de Certeau calls "walking in the city," the everyday use of city space that reappropriates it from its official disciplinary functions.[41] As soon as Jake arrives in Harlem, he "went for a promenade on Seventh Avenue between One-Hundred and Thirty-fifth and One-Hundred and Fortieth Streets." He then "turned off on Lenox Avenue. He stopped before an ice-cream parlor to admire girls sipping ice-cream sodas through straws. He went into a cabaret. . . . "[42] McKay allows the sentence to trail off, with an ellipsis of footsteps for the reader to follow. Later in the novel, when Jake returns to Harlem after train work, he immerses himself in Harlem's streetlife: "Lenox Avenue was vivid. The saloons were bright, crowded with drinking men jammed tight around bars. . . . The pavement was a dim warm bustle" (*HH* 204). Jake "loitered along Seventh Avenue. Crossing to Lenox, he lazied northward and over the One-Hundred and Forty-ninth Street bridge into the near neighborhood of the Bronx" (*HH* 279). An afternoon stroll reveals that "the broad pavements of Seventh Avenue were colorful with promenaders. Brown babies in white carriages pushed by little black brothers wearing nice sailor suits.[. . .] Charming brown matrons, proud yellow matrons, dark nursemaids pulled a zigzag course by their restive little charges. . . . " (*HH* 289-90). By following the routes walked in *Home to Harlem,* we can see more clearly the way in which McKay palimpsestically remaps the sociological-realist mappings of the underworld. Guided by a compass of social contact that crosses a zigzag course over the carefully organized official grid of the city, he traces the way Harlem's population uses its streets.

A brief look at the details of the novel's well-known opening scene will demonstrate the way that McKay uses strolling to disorganize uplift sociology's official mappings of space and morality in *Home to Harlem.* The episodic structure of the novel is loosely organized by Jake's search for Felice, a woman he meets, and loses, during the course of his first night back in Harlem. After first meeting and sharing drinks in a cabaret, Jake and Felice stroll down a street while they negotiate a price for her company. They dance at a buffet flat, where Jake pays Felice an agreed-upon $50, and then they retire to Felice's room. Back on the street alone the next morning, Jake absently reaches into his pocket and finds that Felice has returned his money, a common literary trope — and male fantasy — signifying an emotional connection that transcends the commercial.[43] This stroll unfolds, however, not along a carefully charted path, but in fragments and lacunae, blank spaces of unknown terrain. Every time Jake and Felice move to each destination in their stroll, the narrative is interrupted by a hard break between paragraphs, a gap that leaves blank the routes taken and the spaces produced through their walk. Rather than depicting a path that could be taken up in the city's systems of surveillance—like many slumming narratives, sociological studies, and sensationalistic journalism—McKay writes in a way that does not trap the everynight and its people in a fixed transcription. The transitoriness of Jake's path is reflected in the unfolding narrative of his relationship. This is, to paraphrase de Certeau, walking as a space of queer enunciation. In place of the social realism of which McKay's critics accused him, McKay offers an affective mapping that writes over the city's administrative systems. McKay leaves the map incomplete, offering instead metaphoric and typographic spaces to be filled by his readers' own memory and imagination.

After Jake discovers the money returned to his pocket the next morning, McKay makes explicit the failure of Jake's path to be fixed by the conventions of sociological realism. Finding the money in his pocket, Jake "stopped in his tracks . . . went on . . . stopped again . . . retraced his steps . . . checked himself" (HH 17). When he finally attempts to retrace his route to Felice's apartment from the previous night, he finds that, in the daytime, he is lost: "'Street and Streets! One Hundred and Thirty-Second, Thirty-third, Thirty-fourth. It wasn't One Hundred and Thirty-Fifth and it wasn't beyond theah . . . O Lawd! How did I fohgit to remember the street and number [. . .] Thirty-fourth, Thirty-second, Thirty-third. . . . Only difference in the name. All the streets am just the same and all the houses 'like as peas. I could try this one heah or that one there, but—" (HH 26). The path Jake walked the night before has been erased, replaced by the ordered and numbered grid of the city, as if covered by shifting urban sand dunes. And like Campbell's drawing, the streets themselves are incoherently arranged, the numbers recorded out of order. The same streets the next morning have none of their affective resonance or identity. McKay's asyndetonic use of ellipses and dashes, here and throughout the novel, work to insert such space into the wanderings and feelings of his characters.[44] As this juxtaposition between nighttime Harlem and daytime Harlem demonstrates, strolling produces a geography not of space but of relations; the landmarks of the underworld, as Ray suggests, are not street signs and buildings but social interactions. As such, they are transitory, contingent, and ephemeral.

We can add to this discussion one last example of remapping city space by way of the stroll: McKay's own biographical wanderings and pedestrian explorations of New York City. McKay's biographer, Wayne F. Cooper, describes one such investigation undertaken with Adolf Dehn, an artist for the radical monthly *Liberator* and friend of McKay's. Their walk began innocently enough, but Dehn recounts his growing alarm near the end of their nighttime stroll:

> I was startled and disturbed to realize that [McKay] was indubitably making homosexual overtures to me. They were fairly delicate but became quite insistent. It took me a long time to get him to leave. This all took place on the waterfront so at least I was not in the position of getting him out of my small apartment where we had been earlier. He did not want to accept the simple fact that I was not interested in such activities. This all was done in a most friendly if a somewhat embarrassed manner on my part. My notion of him is that he was a most lecherous fellow with considerable charm and that it did not matter whether he took on man or woman.[45]

McKay describes this same stroll in his autobiography, though he leaves out his failed overtures, simply describing it as "some nocturnal wanderings with Adolf Dehn, the artist, spanning blocks upon blocks along the East River and the vast space-filling feeling of the gigantic gas tanks."[46]

Cooper cites this scene as evidence for McKay's bisexuality, though I find it more interesting for what it tells us about McKay's understanding of public space, walking at night, and the remapping of New York's sexual landscape. It is possible to speculate about the route of Dehn and McKay's "nocturnal wanderings." The *WPA Guide to New York City*, published in 1933 (about a decade after this scene), describes "bulky gas tanks" uptown near the river: "brown, massive, ugly, yet no more ugly than the houses huddled in their shadow."[47] This one-dimensional image of urban crowding and alienation is rewritten by McKay's description of the "vast space-filling feeling" of the gigantic tanks, evoking a fullness and an openness that echoes for "blocks upon blocks" along the river. To Dehn's ostensible relief, McKay refrained from making his advance in the private realm of Dehn's apartment, choosing instead to pursue his desires in the semipublic strip by the East River. We can only speculate as to why McKay waited until they were on the waterfront to make a pass at Dehn. Most likely the public venue itself was one factor in McKay's attraction. Perhaps the intoxicating effects of alcohol played a part. Regardless of the reasons, it is not gratuitous to suppose that after Dehn extracted himself from this awkward situation, McKay continued wandering along the waterfront.

In tracing McKay's route through the *WPA Guide*, I am not attempting to historically verify or precisely place the events of that evening (it is unclear that Dehn and McKay, who both lived downtown at the time, would have been so far north in the city, or how far south the gas tanks extended), but rather to point out the rhetorical ways in which the city was written and rewritten by the queer wanderings of its nocturnal pedestrians. In much the same way as McKay leaves spaces in *Home to Harlem,* he transforms the massive, ugly gas tanks of his walk with Dehn into a "vast space-filling feeling" in his autobiography. For readers who know the paths by which desire produces the city, McKay provides a space to be filled by their own memory and imagination. McKay and other men cruising the waterfront make use of space that is not legible to the disciplinary grids of urban regulation and industrial construction; as de Certeau says, these walkers make use "of spaces that cannot be seen; their knowledge of them is as blind as that of lovers in each other's arms." [48]

The streets and alleys that uplift sociologists use to partition the moral regions of the city are appropriated by the practices of everynight life to facilitate contact, intimacy, and touch. The official and sociological maps of the city—with their institutional imprimatur, scientific objectivity, and totalizing view—attempt, but ultimately fail, to freeze the people and practices of the city in visual representations that have no room for movement. Uplift sociology's paratextual strategies of charting the streets of the urban underworld with its maps and tables inverts the quotidian inscriptions written by the underworld's strolling bodies. The Cabaret School remaps these practices and restores the dynamism and desire that propels everynight life. As we will see, McKay turns to the scene of Harlem cabaret and the dance floor in *Home to Harlem* to stage this affective choreography of the underworld, ultimately insisting on the underworld not as a fixed terrain but as a world in motion.

THE PROBLEM OF AMUSEMENT

For those looking for a map to Harlem's underworld, McKay's novel appeared to provide exact coordinates of its people and places. McKay's rhetorical strategy of strolling, however, which produces the underworld through the spatial practices that reappropriate the official organization of the city, reorients sociology's moral and representational compass. Here I want to move from the sociological construction of the underworld as a region of the city to one of its central institutions: the cabaret. Harlem's cabaret remained an important institution for McKay long after the 1920s vogue receded. Looking back in his autobiography, *A Long Way from Home,* he remembers how "the cabarets of Harlem in those days enthralled me more than any theatre downtown. They were so intimate. . . . There, coming off the road like homing birds, we trainmen came to rest awhile and fraternize with our friends in the city—elevator runners and porters—and snatch from saloon and cabaret and home a few brief moments of pleasure, of friendship and of love." [49] The emphasis here is on the social experience of masculine contact and intimacy, a Whitmanesque "adhesiveness" that we see in the cabaret literature of Langston Hughes and other queer Harlem Renaissance writers.[50] In the crowded cabaret, McKay describes an elaboration of shared affect that is organized by the architecture and sociality of a performance space. We see in this description, also, his characterization of an instinctive migration toward the cabaret, and by extension a criminal sociality and sexual excess, that resonated within primitivist discourse and was the basis of much of the criticism levied against McKay.

McKay's use of actual street numbers and cabaret names in *Home to Harlem* only buttresses the realist interpretation of his novel and the charge of racial opportunism made against him. Immediately upon his return from Europe, Jake's strolls take him through Harlem's nightlife districts. He catalogues a number of Harlem's more famous nightclubs for his reader: Barron's Exclusive Club, Goldgraben's, Edmond's, Connor's, Leroy's. But with these real cabarets as reference points, McKay moves off the map to fictional spaces like the Baltimore and, most prominently and luridly, the Congo. With a name invoking the primitive modernism of Vachel Lindsey's "Congo" and Joseph Conrad's *Heart of Darkness,* McKay offered his readers access to a cabaret space imagined as uncontaminated by the presence of white spectators and white capital. The Congo is depicted as a place of "authentic" blackness of the darkest hues: no white people were permitted, and even light-skinned black patrons are scarce. When Jake enters, a band is performing a number that was rumored to be banned by the police because of its "pornographic" lyrics. A variation of Bessie Smith's "Foolish Man Blues," the song was one of many that explicitly acknowledged the possibility of homosexual contact.[51] As we saw in the previous chapter's discussion of Hughes—and will explore in more depth in the next chapter's discussion of Lena Horne—such performances aurally marked public spaces as locations of sexual permissiveness and deviance and forged a discursive and ethical space from which a feminist blues tradition might be constructed. This blurring of reality and fiction in his pages fueled the criticism against McKay.

The sociological assumptions that underlie Du Bois's review point us toward a better understanding of McKay's rhetorical deployment of the cabaret. As a commercial space of recreation and leisure, sociology approached the cabaret as the primary institution of the underworld, the *locus classicus* of social disorganization, demoralization, and sexual deviance; William H. Jones's study, as we saw above, contributed to the sociological linkage that inscribes moral value on black bodies through everynight practices of gesture, comportment, and dance. In his exploration of the dance hall, Jones found that "many of the modern dances are sexual pantomimes." After undertaking "careful investigation," he assured readers with certainty that "the originators of these extreme forms of behavior have clearly in view of sexual end" (*RA* 122). Like other uplift sociologists and proponents of representational politics, Jones understood social dance as mimesis, a pantomime of sex with a teleological end whose direction is "clearly" mapped, rather than as an undetermined horizon of possible configurations of intimacy and sociality. As with Du Bois, Jones characterizes institutions of social dance as a fork in the road toward proper social behavior; the dance hall, he writes, affords "an opportunity for young people of every class to cultivate quickly an intimacy which may either lead them into finer forms of association, or further still on the downward path to crime" (*RA* 121). The cabaret, on the other hand, offers little toward the development of proper social behavior. "Cabaret behavior is dance hall behavior intensified. . . . Excesses in dancing, jungle music, and semi-alcoholic beverages are characteristic features of their life," he concludes (*RA* 122, 133).

In framing this dance, music, and underworld sociality as expenditure, New Negro sociology focuses its gaze on play and recreation, marks the cabaret as a location of social disorganization, and makes distinctions between the "honest poor" and the "submerged tenth." A sociological paper by Du Bois (1897), published just prior to *The Philadelphia Negro*, gives us an even more prescriptive—and personal—look at what Du Bois called "the problem of amusement." Concerned with the question of leisure and recreation in a modernizing American south, this paper offered the first black sociological response to American nightlife. Originally a public address, "The Problem of Amusement" appeared in the *Southern Workman*, one of the key print sources for the dissemination of nineteenth-century uplift ideology. This journal was launched to develop and publicize the educational philosophies and aims of the Hampton Institute, an agricultural and normal school founded in 1868 for the education, uplift, and modernization of newly emancipated slaves and Native Americans. This essay, then, should be understood as a prescriptive intervention into the moral and social education of southern black youths, addressed to educators, administrators, preachers, and parents; in other words, this essay is one of the first attempts of uplift sociology to wrestle with the problem of amusement.

In "The Problem of Amusement," Du Bois sought to counter scientific and popular imagery of black idleness by foregrounding black subjects as laboring subjects, insisting on leisure as the honest counterpart to respectable work, and making the case for popular amusements as a potential space for moral instruction and social organization. Popular amusements, in Du Bois's characterization, include such arenas of recreation as dancing, theater, billiards, cards, sports, drinking, and "kissing games."[52] According to Du Bois's diagnosis, the historical relationship between southern black social organization and the church had led to an untenable contradiction between the church's role in sociality and community, on the one hand, and its negative attitude toward secular recreation, on the other. Pulpit prohibitions of popular amusements had only encouraged young men and women to flee to urban centers and give themselves over to depravity, creating that "distinct class of Negro libertines, criminals, and prostitutes which is growing among us day by day."[53] He instead calls for a relaxing of rural attitudes and religious proscriptions, offering a defense of amusements as a "necessary, legitimate pursuit" and the natural complement to honest work.[54]

But Du Bois does more than refigure recreation as a natural and necessary practice in this paper; he appropriates popular amusements for the role of moral instruction through his formulation of "proper amusements." Proper amusements, he writes, "must always be a matter of careful reasoning and ceaseless investigation, of nice adjustment between repression and excess."[55] In such a formulation, amusement is proposed as a disciplinary technology used to produce "good" racialized subjects whose sexual and criminal distance from the urban underworld is maintained through sanctioned, modest expression and external surveillance. To exemplify "proper amusements," Du Bois offers an autobiographical anecdote from his youth that illustrates the productive and socializing uses to which social dance can be put. While in Germany as a graduate student, he attended a dance whose organization was wholly novel to him:

> Contrary to my very elaborate expectation the young men did not accompany the girls to the dance; the girls went with their fathers and mothers; the boys went alone. In the pretty, airy hall the mothers seated themselves in a circle about the sides of the room and drew up their daughters beside them; fathers and elder brothers looked on from the doorway. Then we danced under the eyes of mothers and fathers, and we got permission to dance from those parents; we felt ourselves to be trusted guests in the bosom of families; three hours glided by in pure joyousness until, finally, long tables were brought in; we sat down and cooled off and drank coffee and sang. Then the mothers took their daughters home, and the young men took themselves.[56]

Du Bois juxtaposes this closely chaperoned social interaction—with women's freedom circumscribed by ever-widening circles of familial vigilance: from mothers on the inner circle to fathers and elder brothers on the outer, conveniently monitoring the exits and entrances as well as their daughters and wives—with American amusements, where daughters "unattended and unwatched" pair disgracefully with unknown escorts in country districts and city streets.[57] There is an implicit connection between amusement and sexual expression in Du Bois's conceptualization. The dance floor emerges here as a choreo-graphic space, a placing of bodies and a writing of sexual subjectivity within the Oedipal narrative of prohibition and the family. Amusements serve as a place for instruction of what Du Bois calls "monogamic sex *mores*," the cultivation of internalized chaste and normative sexual values and the exclusion of deviant, nonprocreative, or commercial sexual behavior.[58]

Loosely obscured in this description of the dance in Germany—suggested only by the pronoun "we"—is a more personal, affective experience underlying Du Bois's essay that exists in excess of his moral prescriptions. This dance held great significance for Du Bois. According to biographer David Levering Lewis, it was "an epiphany of liberation" for the twenty-four-year-old Du Bois as he was welcomed among the German families with none of the race prejudice to which he was accustomed in the United States.[59] Du Bois was further struck by the fact that racial difference was not an issue in his romance with Dora Marbach, the daughter of his German host family. The romanticism that shapes Du Bois's memory of this German dance calls for us to see his dance floor as a space not only of moral purity and innocence, but also of an interracial or even aracial utopia where the sexually sheltered Du Bois, by his own account, fell in love for the first time. Dancing with the town's white daughters without the stigma and prohibitions of race consciousness allowed Du Bois to imagine "something of the possible beauty and elegance of life"; of that night he wrote, "I have had many good times in life, but not one to which I look back with more genuine pleasure and satisfaction."[60] Though Du Bois is concerned about the potential for social disorganization posed by the dance floor, he also recognized it as a choreographic space of intimacy, modernity, and futurity. At the end of "The Problem of Amusement," Du Bois asks, not rhetorically, "Is it not possible for us to rescue from its evil associations and conditions, so pleasant, innocent, and natural an amusement as dancing?"[61]

QUEER CRISIS

"Ain't nobody evah lonely in Harlem that don't wanta be," retorted Billy. "Even yours truly lone Wolf ain't nevah lonesome."

"But I want something as mahvelous as mah feelings."

Billy laughed and fingered his kinks: "Harlem has got the right stuff, boh, for all feelings."   MCKAY, HOME TO HARLEM

As McKay's autobiographical wandering with Adolf Dehn points toward the rhetorical use of strolling in his fiction, so too does Du Bois's autobiographical turn with Dora Morbach tell us something about his published review of McKay's *Home to Harlem*. Tucked inconspicuously between the scathing and personal denunciations in his *Crisis* review is Du Bois's reluctant acknowledgement that McKay is "too great a poet to make any complete failure in writing." In one fleeting sentence, he singles out "bits" of the novel that struck him as "beautiful and fascinating," including "the continued changes upon the theme of the beauty of colored skins" and "the portrayal of the fascination of their new yearnings for each other which Negroes are developing." [62] Given his early experience with social dance as a student in Germany and his subsequent study of Negro amusements, perhaps it is not simply ironic that Du Bois, despite his denunciations, views *Home to Harlem* as most valuable for its portrayal of public intimacies and black sociality. While scholars of McKay and of the Harlem Renaissance rarely hesitate to cite the rhetorical extremes of Du Bois's *Crisis* review, discussions of the review usually fail to note those things that Du Bois liked about *Home to Harlem* and that he felt it contributed to black literature. The gossip-value of Du Bois's negative critique too often overshadows these observations, which in fact characterize the importance of McKay's novel. In *Home to Harlem*, the cabaret and its larger underworld milieu are refigured not as unproductive spheres but as spaces productive of new desires and allegiances across classes. It is Du Bois, of all people, who recognizes the intimacy and relationships in McKay's novels not as antisocial pathologies, but as enactments of emergent alternative sociality.

The first thing Du Bois notes is McKay's play with "the continued changes upon the theme of the beauty of colored skins." The pages of *Home to Harlem* are populated with a spectrum of skin tones. Cabaret patrons are "coffee-colored" (*HH* 31), "chocolate, chestnut, coffee, ebony, cream, yellow" (32), "potato yellow and dull black" (33), "cocoa-brown" (50), and "crust-yellow" (55). A crowd in a cabaret is described as "dark-colorful" (36). In reference to the skin tones created through racial mixing, McKay catalogues "fascinating new layers of brown, low-brown, high-brown, nut-brown, lemon, maroon, olive, mauve, gold. Yellow balancing between black and white. Black reaching out beyond yellow. Almost white on the brink of a change" (57). Others are "lemon-colored or paper-brown" (58), "light-brown" (73), "straw-colored" (91), "rich-browns and yellow creams" (105), and "ravishing maroon" (320). All of this occasions a strategic flattening and devaluation of whiteness. White patrons in Harlem cabarets appear "like faded carnations among those burning orchids of a tropical race" (106). This, however, is a rare mention of white people, who have little presence in the novel at all.

Mark Helbling proposes that color in *Home to Harlem* "is not only a chromatic spectacle delightful to the eye, but a highly charged scale of emotion calibrated to measure one's own and another's self worth."[63] He draws attention to the ways that McKay uses color to describe intraracial hierarchies of racial value, such as the character Gin-Head Susy, who "lived with a yellow complex at the core of her heart" and subsequently made her parties "as yellow as she could make them." McKay's own well-documented ambivalence toward light-complexioned black men and, especially, women, supports Helbling's interpretation. But McKay's play with color is also, as Du Bois suggests, an aestheticization. McKay racializes the underworld by aestheticizing and multiplying the phenomenology of race—fragmenting the force of what Frantz Fanon, influenced by McKay, called "epidermalization," the process by which racial inferiority is inscribed on skin color and internalized.[64] "There is no human sight so rich," Jake observes as he enters Harlem's newest cabaret at the end of the novel, "as an assembly of Negroes ranging from lacquer black through brown to cream, decked out in their ceremonial finery" (*HH* 320). McKay revalues blackness and black sociality as beautiful and multiple, with as many gradations and shadings as feelings and desires.

In his review of *Home to Harlem*, Du Bois also refers positively to McKay's "portrayal of the fascination of their new yearnings for each other which Negroes are developing." In this assessment, Du Bois poignantly marks the self-consciousness that McKay's novel depicts: it is not simply the "new yearnings" that Du Bois finds beautiful, but the characters' own awareness of and fascination with those yearnings. The characters in *Home to Harlem* recognize that they are enacting and exploring new desires; the novel portrays desires in the process of being articulated and elaborated. Du Bois is able to see this as important social activity and is even, in his reading of *Home to Harlem,* moved by it (and here we cannot help but to recall Du Bois's own new yearnings as a young man in Germany, imagining an aracial utopia and intimacy with Dora Marbach on the dance floor). But he could not reconcile the portrayal of these "new yearnings" with the conditions for their emergence and his commitment to normative uplift. Du Bois, in this review, frames the novel in two different registers: for some white readers, Du Bois fears, *Home to Harlem* will provide a literary affirmation of their fantasy of Harlem and blackness more generally, sexualizing and objectifying its black protagonists for a white gaze. But Du Bois perceives a second register in which the black protagonists are not the objects of a white reader's desire, but subjects of desire for each other.

This "fascination of their new yearnings for each other" that Du Bois discerns is explicitly rendered by McKay in the cabaret and dance hall. Consider this description of the Sheba Palace, for example, when Jake first enters: "On the green benches couples lounged, sprawled, and, with the juicy love of spring and the liquid of Bacchus mingled in fascinating white eyes curious in their dark frames, apparently oblivious of everything outside of themselves, were loving in every way but . . . " (*HH* 295). The ellipses, again, are McKay's; his unfinished sentence, like the lacunae in his strolls, implies that it cannot be completed—that the ways of loving are only limited by the possibilities the lovers can imagine. While lovers entangle, McKay catches in their eyes a curiosity that marks their own self-conscious awareness of their desire, a shared inwardness that renders to oblivion "everything outside of themselves."

McKay continues:

> The orchestra was tuning up. . . . The first notes fell out like a general clapping for merrymaking and chased the dancers running, sliding, shuffling, trotting to the floor. Little girls energetically chewing Spearmint and showing all their teeth dashed out on the floor and started shivering amorously, itching for their partners to come. Some lads were quickly on their feet, grinning gayly and improvising new steps with snapping of fingers while their gals were sucking up the last of the crème de menthe. The floor was large and smooth enough for anything. (*HH* 296)

The language of possibility is built into a dance floor "large and smooth enough for anything." The bodies that make use of it, and the musical call that organizes them, appropriate the polished surface of the dance floor to improvise new choreographic arrangements. Like the bodies that stroll through *Home to Harlem*'s streets, these movements are not easily sedimented, nor are they policed, like Du Bois's German dance floor, by the imperatives of familial reproduction and generational descent. And yet within this elaboration of desire, the figures on the dance floor are not only caught in the immanent flows of desire, but also self-consciously reflect on the invention and expansion of new intimate social relations. This self-reflexive consciousness is queer in the sense delimited by Lauren Berlant and Michael Warner: it represents "the critical practical knowledge that allows such relations to count as intimate, to be not empty release or transgression but a common language of self-cultivation, shared knowledge, and the exchange of inwardness." [65] Or, as Houston Baker Jr. says about blues performance, the scenes and relations McKay depicts "offer interpretations of the experiencing of experience." [66] They are queer, they are blues, not only because they invent and elaborate new ways of relating to self and other, but also because of the knowledge and self-conscious intention of such inventions.

The aestheticization of skin color and the "new yearnings" produced and contemplated in the cabaret are closely connected to each other in that they both gesture toward the futurity and possibility of sexual and racial transgression. To further explain this connection, I want to turn to an earlier piece of writing by McKay. In a 1920 review of the all-black Broadway musical *Shuffle Along*, McKay meditates on what he dubs Harlem's "color nomenclature," the performance and multiplication of blackness in Harlem's everynight life. Commenting on the famous near-white conformity of *Shuffle Along*'s black chorus girls, McKay extols the beauty of color diversity, suggesting that the prettiness of the chorines is a pale shadow of the rich, colorfully varied beauty of the women of Harlem's streets. But despite his call for an aesthetic appreciation of darker hues, McKay refrains from judging those black men who prefer lighter-complexioned women. Instead, he proposes that they are part of an irreversible tide that promises to wash over the color line. Those—black and white—who protest against miscegenation are "but foam on the great, natural, barrier-breaking current of interracial contact." [67]

By 1928, a number of Harlem Renaissance novels and stories had explored this long history of interracial contact, primarily through the social performance of passing. The ability of some light-skinned characters to "disappear" from their race on the other side of the color line was taken as the privileged location of this history and has subsequently been used to deconstruct the very notion of "race." But McKay's multiplication of skin color in *Home to Harlem* turns forcefully away from this literary tradition and its obligatory pathos and tragedy. The pageant of skin colors in the cabarets and buffet flats of Harlem's everynight life is a sign of the sexual cultures and contacts that maintain racial identity while expanding and complicating the sociology of race. "The Negroes of the western world," McKay wrote, "are producing and fostering new types." [68] Here, as he later will in *Home to Harlem,* McKay counters Jones's sociological imperative to seek in the cabaret or theater a "museum of types" through which to elaborate a theory of social pathology. McKay reframes this will-to-typology, offering instead a "color nomenclature," an antitaxonomic catalogue that is not concerned with identifying and categorizing the interiority of the types in the nightclub but with the surface connections and the processes of relationality that foster new types.[69] Against a project like the passing narrative, which deconstructs the fiction of race, McKay seeks to extend the social construction of race into the future, imagining new racial permutations and social configurations. The segregated and fixed grids of uplift sociology's maps and taxonomies collapse under the music and motion of the dance floor, a surface "large and smooth enough for anything."

Home to Harlem thus presents an experience of Harlem's nightlife that explicitly references McKay's own affective experiences of the cabaret, described in his autobiography, as a place where black laborers and other marginalized subjects could "snatch . . . a few brief moments of pleasure, of friendship and of love." [70] In a final, extended cabaret sequence at the end of *Home to Harlem,* McKay writes: "Negroes, like all good Americans, love a bar. I should have said, Negroes under Anglo-Saxon civilization. A bar has a charm all of its own that makes drinking there pleasanter. We like to lean up against it, with a foot on the rail. We will leave our women companions and choice wines at the table to snatch a moment of exclusive sex solidarity over a thimble of gin at the bar" (*HH* 324). In a further queer formal disruption of mimetic realism, McKay here writes himself into *Home to Harlem,* stepping into the story and addressing the reader directly. As in Du Bois's own authorial insertion in his footnote to *The Philadelphia Negro,* McKay offers up himself and his position to evaluate the production and consumption that occurs in the cabaret. There is an inexplicable shift of voice in this passage from third person to first person: it is not a character who utters these thoughts, but McKay himself erupting into the narrative of his story.[71] And McKay appears in his own novel not only in the first person, but in first-person *plural,* as a part of the black sociality he depicts. He indexes himself when imagining the intimate world and relations that are made possible in the nightclub.[72] Like the queer cartography of Campbell's "A Night-Club Map of Harlem," *Home to Harlem*'s narrator affectively expands the horizon of Harlem's everynight life through queer formal corruption and antirealist representation.

This passage is the second time that McKay has characterized the homosocial intimacy of the cabaret—produced through bodily comportment and the materiality of the bar ("we like to lean up against it, with a foot on the rail"), the consumption of strong alcohol, and the exclusion of women—as something "snatched," as though it was withheld from a class whose efficiency is better exploited without such intimate relations. In writing the relationships that are possible in the cabaret, McKay not only messes up the easy taxonomy of sociological uplift, but he positions the cabaret as a central, not ephemeral, location for social consciousness and contact. We can see here the queer black proletarian consciousness McKay brings to the intimacy of the cabaret. As McKay well knew, Marxism, in the end, offers a theory of how to transform social relationships in order to have meaningful and happy lives. McKay directs our attention to the way that modern institutions of knowledge production obscure intimacies between the working class and a lumpen criminal class. *Home to Harlem* thus refigures the everynight moments and movements that are pathologized and excluded by normalizing pressures—movements without aim but not aimless. For early Du Bois, amusement is seen as a bourgeois disciplinary technology (through which, nonetheless, we can catch glimpses of interracial or aracial potentiality); for McKay, amusement emerges as a place of racial multiplication and radical desire, rearranging—or, better, anarranging—bodies ordered otherwise by the knowledge of sociological uplift.

McKay's romantic vision would almost lead us to forget that the historical cabaret was also itself a place of social regulation. While rarely as explicit as Du Bois's German countryside dance, the social codes and spatial arrangements of some cabarets often gave the illusion of greater intimacy while maintaining a carefully hierarchized system of behavior, especially enforcing strict racial and gender roles. Many of New York City's more upscale cabarets, for example, required women to have escorts, served them in rooms separate from male patrons, or used waiters to deliver drinks, which often consigned women to their tables with their parties. And even when cabarets did not officially police women's behavior, normalizing discourses and class codes helped manage social behavior.[73] As I have done throughout this chapter, I want to argue against a mimetic reading that would find in McKay's cabarets a similarly normalizing and policing discourse. McKay's romantic scenes of the cabaret were not designed to obscure the disciplinary practices of Harlem's nightlife, but, for better or worse, to propose ways in which the everynight life of Harlem could rewrite these larger social constraints. The aesthetic—whether in the form of a novel, a cartoon, a dance, or a nightclub performance—offers moments of memory, imagination, and possibility that exceed even these constraints. As we saw in Langston Hughes's afterhours poetry and the writings of Nella Larsen, Zora Neale Hurston, and Wallace Thurman, McKay writes not what was, but what could be, in the spaces that sidestep the logics of normative social organization.

In this way, it is worth noting that McKay tempers the utopian potential of his cabaret with the awareness that such intimacies are dialectically shaped by alienation and hostility. We will see in the next chapter another negotiation of this dialectic in the performance practices of Lena Horne, and how it could be manipulated in order to refuse sexual subordination. Like other literature of the cabaret school, *Home to Harlem* does not ignore the violence, self-hatred, addiction, hunger, and desperation that pervade the facts and fictions of black underworld life. Like Ray at the end of the novel, McKay left New York for Europe in the early 1920s, in part, he wrote, to "escape from the pit of sex and poverty, from domestic death, from the cul-de-sac of self pity, from the hot syncopated fascination of Harlem, from the suffocating ghetto of color-consciousness" (although when he got to Europe, he immediately sought out the nightlife of Weimar Berlin).[74] McKay depicts the "new yearnings" that develop in the cabaret in spite of, because of, and within those more stark and desolate experiences. He does not identify and tag the heterogeneity of the underworld, but articulates its practices and configurations; in other words, he does not write the everynight life of the underworld as a class or a fixed space, but as a process and a potentiality.[75] By attending to the everynight practices of the underworld, something that sociological and realist mappings refused to do, McKay undoes uplift by offering an alternative conceptualization of space and movement. His strolling words reveal the submerged aggregate not as an unruly mass or another endless litany of types, but as a collection of carefully choreographed practices yet to come.

CHAPTER FIVE

Lena Horne's Impersona

"THERE ARE certain women singers," wrote Ralph Ellison, "who possess, beyond all the boundaries of our admiration for their art, an uncanny power to evoke our love. We warm with pleasure at the mere mention of their names; their simplest songs sing in our hearts like the remembered voices of old dear friends, and when we are lost within the listening anonymity of darkened concert halls, they seem to seek us out unerringly. Standing regal within the bright isolation of the stage, their subtlest effects seem meant for us and us alone: privately, as across the intimate space of our own living rooms. And when we encounter the simple dignity of their immediate presence, we suddenly ponder the mystery of human greatness."[1]

Lena Horne was not one of these women.

As a performer for over six decades on nightclub stages and on screen, Horne reflected in her style, repertoire, and public image the complex and often contradictory negotiation of changing racial politics and popular performance practices throughout the twentieth century. In this chapter, I examine the impersonal persona cultivated by Lena Horne on the cabaret stage in the first half of her career. Horne sang in a different affective key than the women Ellison describes, hitting a very different note. She offered not love but hostility, not warmth but aloofness, not presence but absence, not immediacy but hesitation, not touch but distance, not an old friend but a stranger. She did not seek her listener out in the anonymity of the concert hall, but compelled her audience to come after her. This aloofness characterizing her early career could be understood within the theatrical and gendered discourse of the diva. The diva is often exemplified by the un-

FIGURE 11 Lena Horne performing without a microphone in Savoy-Plaza Hotel's
Café Lounge, 1942. Photo by George Karger. Courtesy Pix Inc./Time Life Pictures/
Getty Images.

attainability and self-involvement that Horne cultivated. The musical diva,
though, from her origins in opera, functions as a figure of grandiosity and
surplus. While the musical diva may be difficult to reach offstage, onstage
she offers everything in her performances; she elaborates a social, corpo-
real, and affective excess that marks the pure presence to which Ellison

refers.[2] Yet Horne withheld herself in performance and contradicted the expectation of the cabaret stage as a place of performed plenitude. The diva makes her listeners think they are being given something; Horne worked instead by subtraction. Rather than seeing this carefully developed and repeated relationship to her audience as a reflection of the demanding and narcissistic personality of the prima donna or as a "mastery of form" that would find in her flawless performance of the American songbook an act of radical masquerade, I argue that it is a withholding of any persona at all. I am interested, that is, not in dismissing Horne's negative affect or looking past it to her true self beneath, but in recognizing her aloofness as a strategic mode of black performance developed and inhabited in different ways by a number of women nightclub performers in the twentieth century, including Florence Jones, Hazel Scott, Dorothy Dandridge, Eartha Kitt, and Diahann Carroll.[3]

Lena Horne might seem at first glance to be an unlikely figure to include in the Cabaret School. Born to one of Brooklyn's most respected families, she came from a lineage firmly ensconced in traditions of racial uplift. Despite ever-present financial insecurity throughout her childhood, Horne was inculcated with values of middle-class respectability and normative racial uplift. Her mother and grandmother were active members of the Urban League, the NAACP, and other reform organizations. And Horne's baby picture was featured on the October 1919 cover of the NAACP's *Branch Bulletin* newsletter as part of the Talented Tenth "family album" that the organization sought to catalogue and publicize.[4] Later, as a young girl, Horne joined the Peter Pan Club and the Junior Debutantes, and as an adult she contributed to racial advancement through organizations like the National Council of Negro Women, the Delta Sigma Theta Sorority, and the Urban League—social organizations that sought racial improvement through moral and social reform. One of the first black female movie stars, Horne was promoted by the NAACP, then under the direction of author and activist Walter White, as a symbol of refinement and respectability that could push against the color line and expand the parts available for black women beyond the stereotypical roles of maid or mammy. Further, as a nightclub singer, Horne benefited from the privilege and access that her middle-class status accorded her as she developed a career in respectable— and white—spaces of performance that were not accessible to most black women performers of the time. Horne thus embodied the politics of racial respectability that would displace attention from structural forms of oppression and work to marginalize black-working class and queer sexual subjectivities. This relationship to racial uplift and respectability, however, is precisely what makes Horne a crucial figure to our consideration of the Cabaret School. Horne's performances offer a middle-class autocritique of the racial, sexual, and gender norms of uplift ideology from the position of the middle-class performer. Though she approached the scene of Harlem cabaret from a different perspective than that of Langston Hughes's closing time or Claude McKay's underworlds, she nevertheless presents important insights into the snares of racial and sexual normativity.

Horne's contribution to the Cabaret School is related to but highly distinct from the racial and sexual critique enacted by the classic blues tradition of the 1910s and 1920s. Precipitated by the passage of folk and country blues into tents, theaters, vaudeville halls, and cabarets, and culminating in the mass commodification of blues music by radio and race records, the classic blues era marks what Amiri Baraka called the "movement toward performance" of black music as it was professionalized and formalized in the early twentieth century.[5] This tradition of black women's performance has been excavated by scholars such as Hazel Carby, Angela Davis, and Daphne Duval Harrison, each of whom have examined the sexual and racial politics of the blues lyric and sound.[6] The woman blues singer is positioned by these scholars as a figure and agent of an African American modernism and feminism, one who tells a tale of emancipation, self-formation, migration, desire, and loss through the use of a fragmented, repetitive blues lyric that reorganizes narrative itself.

The performative address of singers such as Gertrude "Ma" Rainey, Bessie Smith, Alberta Hunter, Ida Cox, and Mamie Smith created a counterpublic sphere that articulated a working-class feminist critique to a working-class audience. The classic blues was an always implicit, often explicit critique of normative uplift ideology. Lyrics often explicitly addressed sexual self-determination, extramarital relationships, homosexuality, workingclass experience, and women's social oppression. Such antibourgeois sexual politics inscribed the blues and the cabaret within the same domain as the queer politics that inspired the work of the Cabaret School we have seen in previous chapters. As Davis notes, "because women like Bessie Smith and Ida Cox presented and embodied sexualities associated with working class black life—which, fatally, was seen by some Renaissance strategists as antithetical to the aims of their cultural movement—their music was designated as 'low' culture, in contrast, for example, to endeavors such as sculpture, painting, literature, and classical music."[7] The sexual self-determination and independence articulated—and often enacted—by these blues singers challenged the representational politics of the Harlem Renaissance and located racial and sexual knowledge production in the time, space, and experience of nightlife.

Horne, however, did not sing the blues. As she put it, "You could say that I had never really heard the blues before; I had only overheard them" (*Lena* 114). Nor was she given to improvisation in her acts. Indeed, she spent most of her early career withholding those creative impulses from her audiences. Horne's performance style (sophisticated, reserved, and refined), musical repertoire (drawn from popular standards, nightclub revues, and Tin Pan Alley compositions), and her performance venues (upscale white nightspots, hotels, and cabarets), all distance her from a feminist blues tradition. And yet, despite her more standardized mode of vocal performance, I will suggest here that Horne has something to contribute to our understanding of blues legacies and black feminisms. In doing so, I follow the direction of Hortense Spillers, who advises that when looking to the black female vocalist as a figure of sexual self-knowledge, song lyrics are not necessarily the primary location in which to find alternative narratives of race and sex. "The singer," Spillers writes, "is likely closer to the poetry of black female sexual experience than we might think, not so much, interestingly enough, in the words of her music, but in the sense of dramatic confrontation between ego and world that the vocalist herself embodies." It is not the singer's discursive intervention that makes such performances central for Spillers, but her phenomenological unfolding through space and time as she interfaces with a public, masculine, and economic world. The singer on stage, through her "motor behavior, the changes of countenance, the vocal dynamics, the calibration of gesture and nuance in relation to a formal object—the song itself—is a precise demonstration of the subject turning in fully conscious knowledge of her own resources toward her object. In this instance of being-for-itself, it does not matter that the vocalist is 'entertaining' under American skies because the woman, in her particular and vivid thereness, is an unalterable and discrete moment of self-knowledge." Spillers describes the black woman vocalist as a historical position available to the articulation and embodiment of a sexual ethics, one whose phenomenological situation may approach "the poetry of black female sexual experience."[8] This is a very different image of the woman singer than the one described by Ellison, whose presence, rather than an act of self-knowledge for the performer, "seems meant for us"—the audience—"and us alone."

Spillers's formulation offers a way to reconceive the political force behind Horne's resistant and resisting cabaret performances. While the performances of the classic blues singers offer moments of self-knowledge and social critique, so, too, do the performances of popular singers like Lena Horne. While her public image was presented as a proper alternative to the sexual subjectivity of the working-class blues singers who helped make a mass audience for black music, Horne in fact developed a performance impersona that sought to elude the politics of racial representation that shaped the Harlem Renaissance and uplift ideology. Looking to Horne's vocal production in the scene of her performance—segregated cabarets in the first half of the twentieth century—I seek to build on and extend the work of scholars such as Lindon Barrett, Farah Jasmine Griffin, and Fred Moten, who explore the historical and phenomenological effect of the black woman's voice in performance as one that has the capacity to disrupt and dislocate dominant fictions of self, narrative, and race. As Barrett argues, the black woman's voice emerges historically and formally as "a site of the active production of meaning."[9] Horne's aloofness, however, shows us what happens when this production of meaning is frustrated and refused by the performer. By examining how Horne's performance shaped and manipulated the dynamics of segregated cabaret performance, we can similarly plumb the consequences of Griffin's proposition that the black woman's voice "is like a hinge, a place where things can both come together and break apart."[10]

Horne's aloofness is a product of a specific historical conjunction, emerging from the milieu of segregated urban nightlife performance in the early twentieth century, and reflects her decades-long refusal to be a symbol within any structure of meaning. Her reputation as a diva has its origins in this stubborn insistence early in her career to transcend the expectations of racial representation—imposed by both white audiences and black uplift elites—even as she actively fought for civil rights. Horne began her career at the age of sixteen as a chorus girl at Harlem's Cotton Club in 1933. From that entry point she quickly achieved access to national concert tours (first with Noble Sissle's orchestra, then with Charlie Barnet's), Broadway, and Hollywood. She never completely abandoned the cabaret circuit, however, and continued playing in upscale clubs and hotels throughout her career—what she exhaustedly referred to as the "plushed-carpeted" treadmill (*Lena* 227).

Her 1942 engagement at New York's Savoy-Plaza Hotel showcases the reserve of her performance style. Horne was the first African American to perform in the hotel's intimate Café Lounge (fig. 11). The engagement attracted national publicity. She was described by *Time* magazine as radiating a "seductive reserve" with "the air of a bashful volcano." The review went on to note that, "unlike most Negro chanteuses, Lena Horne eschews the barrel house manner."[11] Horne, singing without a microphone, instead performed standard love songs and ballads written by white and Jewish popular songwriters, which she delivered with a straightforward and detached stylization. Isolating Horne in a frame-by-frame sequence that captured her rendition at the Savoy-Plaza of Cole Porter's "Let's Do It (Let's Fall in Love)," a *Life* magazine photo spread illustrated her repertoire of reticence: the controlled gestures, precise phrasings, deflecting glances, and restrained physicality that were easily contained within the narrow frames of each photograph (figs. 12 and 13).[12] As Horne put it later in her career, "It was a self-absorbed kind of performance. I was there to be had, but not too much."[13] None of the reviews of the Savoy-Plaza engagement, of course, reported the fact that Horne was not permitted to stay overnight as a guest at the whites-only hotel; after each night's performance, she commuted uptown to the Hotel Theresa in Harlem.

Horne's restraint on the cabaret stage found its cinematic counterpart in her film career. She appeared in over a dozen Hollywood musicals, but primarily as what she called a "pillar singer." In films like *Panama Hattie* (1942), *I Dood It* (1943), *Thousands Cheer* (1943), and *Boogie-Woogie Dream* (1944), Horne was featured, usually propped against a marble column or pillar, in a musical number that was supplemental to the narrative of the film. This isolation from the story allowed her number to be easily deleted before distribution to southern theaters. "I looked good and I stood up against a wall and sang and sang. But I had no relationship with anybody else," Horne recalled in 1957. "Mississippi wanted its movies without me. It was an accepted fact that any scene I did was going to be cut when the movie played the South. So no one bothered to put me in a movie where I talked to anybody, where some thread of the story might be broken if I were cut. I had no communication with anybody."[14] This filmic isolation contributed to Horne's reputation for affective distance. In the three films in which she had starring roles—*The Duke Is Tops* (1938), *Stormy Weather* (1943), and *Cabin in the Sky* (1943)—her reserve and her refusal to inhabit the images available to her still rendered her detached from the narrative.[15] As James Haskins notes about her performance as the seductive vixen Georgia Brown in *Cabin in the Sky*, "Undoubtedly she infused the role with as much dignity as she could muster and managed to be the most aloof 'bad girl' ever seen in a film to date. She was not believable as a slut, and as such she was an enigmatic character who invited puzzled contemplation as much as sexual desire in the male members of the audience."[16]

FIGURE 12 Lena Horne singing Cole Porter's "Let's Do It" in Savoy-Plaza Hotel's Café Lounge, 1942. Photo by George Karger. Pix Inc. / Time Life Pictures / Getty Images.

FIGURE 13 Lena Horne singing Cole Porter's "Let's Do It" in Savoy-Plaza Hotel's Café Lounge, 1942. Photo by George Karger. Pix Inc./Time Life Pictures/Getty Images.

This aloofness, communicated and enacted both on film and in live performance, was a response to the interracial intimacy produced by performing across the color line. The stance toward her audience and the model of intersubjectivity Horne describes when speaking about her cabaret performances suggests that the scene of segregated nightlife performance organizes an aesthetics of interracial intimacy. The intimacy of the segregated cabaret was predicated on the promised display and exposure of black female interiority, an expectation that informed the different but related racial discourses of primitivism and exoticism shaping black representation in the 1930s and 1940s. In framing it in such terms, Horne's own accounts of her performances reorients and demystifies notions of intimacy as a private phenomenon, casting it as a public and contradictory affect and exploring both its potential for individual and collective transformation as well as its deployment in environments of hostility, alienation, violation, and surveillance.

Lena Horne's reflections on her career, especially in her 1965 autobiography, *Lena*, suggest that the segregated cabaret stage offers us a place to turn for exploring the concessions, perils, and promises of such interracial intimacy. In turning to Horne's autobiographical recollections of her early career, I take to heart Thomas Postlewait's admonition against uncritically using performer autobiography as theater history. Postlewait cautions theater historians drawn to the rich record offered by such sources to attend to the generic conventions, rhetorical acts, and historiographical traps of these first-person accounts.[17] I propose that, rather than view it as a document of performance history, we read *Lena* instead as an instance of performance theory, an attempt by Horne to make sense of her by then more than three decades of performing before white audiences. For Horne-as-theorist, the formal conventions of cabaret performance and its ethos of intimacy offer a mode of performance by which black women could resist the circumscribed roles available on the Jim Crow stage. Horne's carefully cultivated impersonality refuses her incorporation into any of the images or subject positions available to her, opening up within ethical and psychic space what Spillers envisions as "a free-floating realm of self-didactic possibility that might decentralize and disperse the knowing one."[18] I will return to Spiller's formulation and its possibilities for understanding the sphere of performance at the end of this essay. First, I outline an approach to performance autobiography that will allow us to take Horne's life story as an attempt to theorize her performances. Then, I elaborate how Horne's performance of aloofness renegotiated the fraught intimacies of the segregated cabaret stage. In her autobiographical account of these nightclub performances, Horne describes a process of unperforming the self through the cultivation of an impersonal intimacy that defers a fixed subjectivity. She develops this impersona through three tactics she describes in her autobiography: a disarticulation of self and song, a reversal of the psychic positions of audience and performer, and what we can consider—borrowing from the performance theories of Bertolt Brecht—as "third person singing." This impersona was developed in response to the psychic, material, and theatrical conventions of performing across the color line. As the civil rights movement increasingly challenged the logics of Jim Crow, we will see that Horne reinhabited this impersona and employed it toward different and more reparative effects in the political and musical public spheres of the 1950s and 1960s.

LISTENING TO LENA

Lena Horne's impersona—her psychic distance and aloofness from her audience—was a strategy developed throughout her long career as a black woman performing in cabarets before white audiences. Early in her autobiography, Horne describes the realization that her nightclub performances sparked a short-circuiting of narrative that, as we will see, was made possible by the conventions of the cabaret circuit itself. As her reputation grew, her celebrity depended on a public image around which her performances could be promoted. Presenting one of the first mass-produced images of a woman from the black middle class, Horne was difficult to place within existing structures of racial intelligibility. "I came to realize," she writes, "that nobody (and certainly not yet myself) had any sound image to give a woman who stood between the two conventional ideas of Negro womanhood: the 'good,' quiet Negro woman who scrubbed and cooked and was a respectable servant—and the whore" (Lena 2-3). Horne's frustration about the sexual Manicheanism of the subject positions available to black women in the public sphere was shaped by her experience in Hollywood as much as by those on the popular stage. The figures she identifies as the respectable servant and the whore were developed, as Donald Bogle suggests, by way of literary and cinematic stereotypes of the sexless mammy, on the one hand, and the hypersexualized mulatta, on the other.[19]

Horne's "star image"—Richard Dyer's phrase to describe the ideological construction of celebrity through filmic performances, promotion, publicity, and commentary—was shaped by this narrow racial discourse that was in many respects unable to accommodate her.[20] Reacting to seeing herself on film years later, Horne described her failure to fit the various shapes Hollywood provided her. "It's like looking at someone else," she told the New York Times. "MGM didn't want blackness in those days, except in the role of being some native in the jungle or a loving, confidential maid. So, I was made into a kind of neuter."[21] Theater critic Walter Kerr even more directly confirmed that "the films she made had nothing to do with her."[22] Her inability to fit into the racial discourse of Hollywood and the mass media effectively halted her film career; after *Stormy Weather* and *Cabin in the Sky*, MGM kept her under contract but refused to cast her in any more starring roles, and she famously lost key "mulatta" roles to white actresses in *Pinky* (1949) (to Jeanne Crain) and *Showboat* (1951) (to Ava Gardner). In suggesting that all available images of black women were ultimately readable in one of two frameworks of sexual interpretation, Horne identified the representational trap faced by black women performers. Her response to this forced legibility was to position herself outside any formal plot by which her audience — or even, she notes, she herself at the time — could narrate her. As a racialized body performing against representational entrapment, Horne sought a way to elude this policing of the black woman's body, even while standing center stage.[23]

As she makes clear in her autobiography, her mastery of the conventions of segregated cabaret performance provided a way out of these representational confines. Black autobiography in the United States, as Stephen Butterfield, William Andrews, and others show, is shaped by its initial emergence as a slave narrative and carries with it into the twentieth century the burdens of racial, as opposed to strictly individual, representation.[24] *Lena* progresses, in the tradition of mid-twentieth-century African American autobiography, as a black bourgeoisie *Bildung*, moving from a crisis of individuality and alienated identity to an existential reunion with the totality of the race. Horne was born to a respectable family in Brooklyn, and much of *Lena* follows the narrative conventions that Butterfield describes as the dominant storyline of black autobiography until the civil rights era: "As the individual author succeeds in the white world by virtue of his outstanding abilities, he is more and more removed from the black masses; the gulf increases between himself and his own people, and at the same time he can never wholly enter the white American mainstream because of his color."[25] The charge of Horne's distance and aloofness as a performer was often made in association with her background as a middle-class, light-skinned black woman who, removed from stereotypical images of blackness, confounded the expectations of white audiences. By shaping her autobiography as a journey of racial awakening that culminates with her accumulated outrage at white supremacy and her commitment to the civil rights movement, Horne's autobiography rhetorically ameliorates what she characterizes as the double alienation of the black middle class.

This autobiographical tradition of teleological race consciousness is, however, complicated and rerouted by the conventions of performer autobiography, another autobiographical tradition that shapes Horne's narrative. The autobiography is the literary form of interiority par excellence, and performer autobiography is the one most self-consciously engaged with the performative act of fashioning a life and creating a persona that structures all autobiography.[26] The trope of the stage in performer autobiography allows an author to approach the writing and ordering of a life narrative as a relational process, done in collaboration with directors (or amanuenses and editors), an audience (or readers, including, as Postlewait notes, both "the members of one's intimate circle, including those of family and profession, and the general public"), and a large supporting cast.[27] Performer autobiography does not constitute a position outside of performance, in which the writer withdraws from the stage to take stock and reflect on her or his career, but constitutes a location inside and forming part of her or his performance. Thus, black performer autobiography constitutes a position from which to simultaneously enact and denaturalize the teleological narrativity of twentieth-century black autobiography. Seen within these intersecting traditions, Horne's autobiography proposes a different journey of self-knowledge that produces, albeit provisionally, the possibility for her to think herself outside the intersubjective field of Jim Crow—even while remaining under its blinding spotlight—and to multiply the possibilities of racial subjectivity.

Given its location at the intersection of these two autobiographical traditions, Horne's autobiography can be seen as an attempt to recuperate her reputation as a "difficult" and demanding star—a diva—and to reinvent her performance persona. Alternately, it can be seen as a response to the perception that she was, in her white repertoire and middle-class privilege, too far removed from the experiences of the majority of the race to have anything to say to them. While both these interpretations are available, I want to suggest another way of understanding the cultural work that her autobiography does, taking seriously Horne's own rhetorical configuration of her performances. That is, I do not necessarily assume that she is only writing out of self-interest or self-promotion, but that she offers in her performances some insight into sexual and racial subject formations in modern American culture. This is certainly no less than what critics allow for blues performers Ma Rainey or Bessie Smith. The question is not whether or not Horne should be included in a feminist blues tradition, but rather what constitutes her relationship to that tradition. How do her performances intersect with and diverge from that tradition? And how do they elaborate other ways of understanding the production and counterproduction of black women's sexual subjectivity?

With these questions in mind, I want to return for a moment to Horne's notion of an as-yet-unrealized "sound image" of black womanhood, which she poses as the dominant theme and governing conflict of her performer autobiography. While Horne might mean this as an adjective-noun construction, it also resonates provocatively as a compound word—*sound image* as a representation formed by and through sonic production. Horne cultivated and perfected a sound image that worked against and displaced Hollywood's and the culture industry's ideological and racially organized star image. Sound-image is, of course, also the word Ferdinand de Saussure used to define the signifier, that linguistic entity that conjures a corresponding concept, or signified. Within a language, the connection between a sound-image and the concept that it designates shapes our comprehension and understanding of the world before us. Saussure writes that "only the associations sanctioned by [a] language appear to us to conform to reality, and we disregard whatever others might be imagined."[28] This notion of a sound-image of black female sexuality invoked by Horne is, for Hazel Carby as well as Angela Davis, that which shapes the political and aesthetic tradition of a blues feminism, by which black women performers forcefully, as Carby puts it, "constructed themselves as sexual subjects through song."[29] Carby and Davis both demonstrate the ways in which performers like Ma Rainey and Bessie Smith were able to forge new associations between the concept of black womanhood and the language used to articulate it. These new associations, contra Saussure, remained unsanctioned by the dominant language and not only imagined new realities but brought them into existence.

As I have intimated, Horne complicates this feminist blues tradition. Because of her repertoire and performance tradition—that of popular music rather than blues—we cannot always rely on Horne's lyrical performance to understand her relationship to racial and sexual discourse. Unlike Rainey or Smith, Horne did not express or present a sexual subjectivity in performance, even if her audience insisted on discovering one. Rather, her performance worked to unperform the sexual subjectivity that her audience expected of her. She did not counter the representational constraints for women performers by articulating, through her song and voice, a counterdiscourse of women's sexual subjectivity. Instead, as I will demonstrate, Horne offered sound *in place of* subjectivity, displacing the intersubjective field of the segregated cabaret that would limit the possibilities of selfhood and adopting a psychic stance that withholds, rather than makes accessible, a sexualized and racialized subjectivity.

The color line is always a sexual borderland, an erotically informed boundary that produces—on both sides—both threat and fantasy. From Horne's perspective, the sexual field organized by segregated performance was more perilous and uncertain on the nightclub stage than in a theater. When white audiences attended a black play, she wrote, "the plots and even the love duets kept sex carefully segregated behind the color line and where the white audience was invited merely to observe, not to entertain the possibility of involving themselves imaginatively in miscegenation" (*Lena* 127). This gap between audience observation (theater) and participation (cabaret) is, as we have seen, one of the defining features of the cabaret's distinct mode of performance. Intimacy is not here a simple exchange of inwardness but a structural aspect of the nightclub. Horne points to the structural differences between theater and cabaret in both architecture and performance conventions. A love duet, delivered by one actor to another, created affective distance between the audience and the performer. This distance had to be traversed in the cabaret, where one's success "depends on establishing a certain intimacy with the audience," rather than with other dramatic characters (*Lena* 127). The cabaret performer, unlike the stage actor, addresses the audience directly, as her- or himself.

This structure and style of cabaret performance compelled Horne to invent different strategies by which to negotiate her audience's expectations. To counter the violence of intimacy that organizes cabaret performance— the demand to make herself affectively available—Horne in turn created a psychic fourth wall that served as a substitute for the theatrical fourth wall missing from the nightclub:

> I felt unconsciously that if I created an atmosphere of reserve, a wall between me and the audience, I would not be hurt or angered by anything that might happen. But this introverted quality in my work was also a response to something much simpler than race—the atmosphere of a cabaret. In a play, the story and the characters you play and the costumes, scenery, and lights all create a framework for the performer. But cabaret work gives you no framework at all. You must create your own, without any outside help. (*Lena* 197)

The hurt and anger that Horne knows as a fact of segregated performance is compounded by the style and structure of the cabaret. When Horne suggests that the cabaret deprives a performer of any kind of scaffolding on which to build a character who interacts with the audience, she points to one of the immanent aspects of cabaret's intimacy. The performer's self is exposed, without footlights or fourth wall—that is, both physically and psychically—to keep the audience at a distance.

Given her distance and aloofness, it should come as no surprise that Horne's resistance to this exposure often left her audiences disappointed: "I confused a lot of people," she wrote, "especially those who liked to think in terms of images" (*Lena* 126). Socialite and professional hostess Elsa Maxwell, for example, criticized Horne's performance for its racial impersonality. Maxwell lamented Horne's inability to "project herself beyond herself" in performance, and compared her unflatteringly to Ethel Waters, who, unlike Horne, in Maxwell's estimation, offered in her performances "the great, warm, human quality which takes in all feeling."[30] Horne's resistance to this "warm, human quality" in her performance (which, to be clear, reveals more about Maxwell's expectations of racial openness than about Waters's performances) should be understood as a resistance first on the local level to the psychically and physically demanding effects of performing on the cabaret circuit, and second on the more abstract level to the psychically and physically demanding effects of an individual burdened with the demand to perform her race. It is worth noting, as well, that this complaint from Maxwell was one that Horne was highly conscious of at this point in her career. She was particularly concerned in the 1940s and 1950s by the possibility that her popular song repertoire, affective distance, light complexion, and middle-class privilege (which often led to charges that her success was unearned) would generate a reaction of indifference or disdain from black music critics and black audiences.[31]

To more fully understand Horne's refusal to "project herself beyond herself," and by extension the failed attempts by audiences—black and white—to give Horne what she could recognize as a sound image of herself, we do best to look more closely at how Horne's impersonality functioned in performance from her perspective. When she stepped onto the stage, the audience was unable to possess her, unable to incorporate her self into their spectatorial psyche, even as the cabaret proffered her as imaginative material for intimate and sexual fantasy. The sound image that Horne offered her audience—produced through repertoire, repetition, and quotation—was one that offered song *in place* of self. Horne thus carried Maxwell's critique a step further: "The image I gave them was the exact one Miss Maxwell saw, that of a woman they could not reach. I rarely spoke on stage. I was too proud to let them think they could have any personal contact with me. They got the singer, but not the woman" (*Lena* 197). By keeping herself just out of psychic reach of her audience, Horne displaced racial and sexual structures from her self and her performing body to her song, giving the audience the singer, but not the woman. Unlike current understandings of Rainey or Smith, Horne's song was not an expression of her inner self, nor did it offer an explicit critique of her external condition. Instead, by "focusing insistently on the notes and lyrics of a song, she was able to shut out the people who were staring at her."[32] Through the studied precision of firmly fixed notes, precise diction, averted eyes, and controlled gestures, Horne crafted her song as an aural surface that displaced the access to interiority her audiences expected. This self-displacement was further produced through bodily comportment. A description of her stage presence in the *New Yorker* noted, "She never addresses her listeners directly, and her eyes are closed, or nearly closed, a good part of the time. In acknowledging applause, she tilts her head, eyes cast down, and bends and turns with . . . self-effacement."[33] In turning inward bodily and producing her song instead of herself—not, that is to say, a song *of* herself—Horne exploited the dialectic of intimacy and alienation that shaped the cabaret as modernist performance.

Perversely, Horne's theorization of her cabaret performances aligns her with another theorist of intimacy, alienation, and theatricality: Bertolt Brecht. This alignment of Brecht and Horne appears less unlikely, perhaps, when seen in the venue of Café Society, the integrated leftist nightclub in New York's Greenwich Village. Horne began performing at Café Society in 1941, an experience she credits as having a profound effect on her emergent politicization. Café Society represented a dramaturgical exchange between two different cabaret performance traditions, offering a "remarkable synthesis of the radical political cabarets of Berlin and Paris with the African American jazz clubs and revues of Harlem."[34] This synthesis helps us to recognize some of the structural similarities between American and European cabaret. Brecht's theatrical theories of the alienation effect and of the quotable actor were informed by his experiences in Berlin's dance halls and nightclubs. Specifically, he argued that the "so-called 'cheap' music, particularly that of the cabaret . . . has for some time been a sort of gestic music."[35] By "gestic," Brecht means to describe a stance or attitude in performance that refused simple identifications, interrupted spectatorial common sense, and commented on the social and historical conditions of any choice, action, or situation. In finding Horne's performance strategy resonant with Brecht's theatrical theories, I mean to suggest that there is something in the intimate structure of the nightclub and cabaret—something noted by Brecht and exploited by Horne—that makes itself available to such affective and identificatory manipulation.

In his explication of Brecht, Fredric Jameson argues that such gestic strategies as third-person acting—that is, the actor's quotation of a character's feelings and emotions, rather than the becoming of that character—offers "a way of outflanking the situation [of identification], with its evident impossibilities, and ratifying the 'imaginary' nature of the self by holding it at a distance on the stage and allowing ventriloquism to designate itself." [36] In her segregated performances, Horne assumed this relationship of distance toward her song, interrupting her own identification with the self imposed on her by segregated spectatorship and producing the sense of aloofness. The image of black womanhood that Horne gave her audience, "that of a woman they could not reach," is paradoxical—it is an image they cannot imagine, a sound image without a corresponding signified. By disarticulating her self from her song, Horne created, despite the cabaret's insistent intimacy, a distance between herself and her audience. She interrupted and refused the bonds and binds of intimacy that her audience expected by performing in the third person instead of in the first.

By separating self from song, or, to put it another way, by refusing her vocal performance's identical alignment with her self, Horne achieved a reversal of the psychic positions of audience and performer. This voice throwing has important repercussions for our understanding of racial and gender identifications in the modern cabaret. "In a funny way," Horne wrote, "the audience and I reversed roles. Usually performers seek the audience's approval, but in my appearances they, in a sense, had to seek mine. In effect I challenged them to break through the wall I create, challenging them to interrupt what seems to be my self-absorption. I believe, anyway, that is where the tension, and therefore the excitement, is in my work" (*Lena* 197). In defining the performer as one who seeks recognition and the audience as that which recognizes, Horne's autobiography then inverts these roles and compels her audience to seek recognition from her—a recognition she ultimately withholds.

To take the Brechtian analogy of performing in the third person a step further, we can understand Horne's performance as a kind of impersonal verb in the grammatical sense of a verbal form that expresses the action of an unspecified subject. This subjectless grammar of the cabaret stage is the condition of possibility of the impersonal intimacy that marks the emergence of cabaret performance in modernity (as opposed to its precursors in folk or popular entertainment). Horne, in a sense, conjugates the cabaret stage in her performance, offering the third person instead of the first, exteriority instead of interiority, distance instead of closeness, song instead of self, all in order to forge a position within Jim Crow from which she can remain outside of any forced structure of representation or discursive formation, outside of any images that would fail to fully depict her self to herself.

Horne thus historicizes her aloofness—in both her written and her performance work—as a product of specific performance conventions under the regime of Jim Crow. Alongside the story Horne relates in her published autobiography, I want to place Horne's performance of her autobiography in her 1981 one-woman show *Lena Horne: The Lady and Her Music,* in which Horne brought the performance conventions of the cabaret to the Broadway stage and vividly sounded the aloof impersona she cultivated in her early career.[37] David Román suggests that contemporary cabaret performance—as a place where women singers narrate their musical histories through story and song—can constitute an "embodied archive of American cultural history."[38] Horne's Broadway show took up this cabaret tradition of life writing and theater history on the nightclub stage to voice a critical counterhistory of twentieth-century black popular performance. The program was organized by representative songs from key moments in Horne's musical career. Early in the show, three singer-dancers recreate nightclub routines from the 1933 and 1934 *Cotton Club Parades* as Horne comments on her experiences as a chorus girl and the conditions under which black performers labored. She then performs a Hollywood sequence, scored to Richard Rodgers and Lorenz Hart's "Where or When," in which she performs the ordeal of having various directors and producers manipulate her image, voice, and body in fashioning her for the screen. (A disembodied director's voice instructs her midsong: "Now Miss Horne, try not to open your mouth so wide when you sing. Remember the screen is different than the stage. Try to sing with a pretty mouth. You know, like Jeanette MacDonald.") In numbers like this and throughout *The Lady and Her Music,* Horne not only articulates an account of her own musical career, but also contextualizes it within the historic shifts in black performance and civil rights over the previous fifty years. Rather than just telling contemporary audiences about Jim Crow conventions, Horne performs them; she makes us hear history and historical revolution.

This is most clearly demonstrable in *The Lady and Her Music* in her renditions of "Stormy Weather," Horne's signature song since her starring role in the film of the same name. In *The Lady and Her Music*, Horne sings "Stormy Weather" twice: once near the end of act 1 and again near the end of act 2. In the first rendition, in the context of revisiting her musical history on the segregated stage and in 1940s Hollywood, Horne delivers a competent, compelling, but somewhat remote and dispassionate version of "Stormy Weather." This number resembles her earlier recordings of the song and fits—chronologically and affectively—into the historical narrative she has been describing in her show (and that I have been describing in this chapter). When Horne unexpectedly sings "Stormy Weather" again at the end of the program, she sings it differently. She begins by saying quietly to herself, "I'm still finding things to think about when I sing this. It's taken me a lot of years to grow into it." And then, as the *New York Times* described the performance, "Before she even hits the first lyric, she lets loose with a gospel cry that erupts from her gut with almost primeval force. Then she bobs gently up and down, staring into her hand mike, letting the words pour out. By the time she tells us 'it's raining all the time'—packing about a dozen torrential notes into the word 'raining'—she is blind with sweat and tears." [39] The second version of the song stages the contrast between Horne's aloof persona of the Jim Crow era and the affectively open, outspoken, and aggressively exposed performer she became later in her career. She lets her voice roam freely and intensely over the song, rather than seeking refuge behind it and offering it in place of herself. This repetition of "Stormy Weather"—this musical repeating of history, but with a difference—does more than track Horne's own transformations as a performer and a vocalist. The two versions of "Stormy Weather" mark a historical as well as a personal revision, and locate her aloof impersona as a product of and response to historical forces and Jim Crow spectatorial relations.

Horne's cultivation of her performance impersona in the 1930s and 1940s thus approaches the history of black performance and double consciousness under Jim Crow within a problematic that seeks to sidestep the politics of sexual and racial representation. It would be easy to read her performance simply as a *persona* of aloofness or coldness (in the terms of her more benign critics) or snobbishness or haughtiness (in the terms of her more violent critics). In other words, it would be easy to read her performance as another variation of "mastery of form" or of "wearing the mask" that has been the dominant trope for understanding segregated performance. The practice of wearing the mask was a way to circumvent and manipulate racial stereotypes by inhabiting them from within and deploying them toward different ends. Performers like Bert Williams and George Walker in the early twentieth century, for example, and Horne's costar in *Stormy Weather*, Bill Robinson, mastered the form of the minstrel mask and exploited white audiences' expectations to shape a black expressive culture.[40] Yet as the histories of these performers attest, the psychic toll such performances often took made them an ambivalent option, to say the least, for psychic and material survival. To see Horne in this tradition of wearing the mask—in this case, performing the role of the mulatta figure offered by American racial discourse—would thus be to sink into the very representational quicksand that she sought to avoid in her performances. This approach merely generates a new sexualized image of the black woman on stage that allows the audience yet another way to access her interiority within the intimate conventions of the cabaret.

Against this interpretation, I have suggested here that Horne offers a different way of understanding her performance: not one of performing a false self, but one of unperforming the self, undoing any representational notion on stage and creating a space of confusion, uncertainty, and failed expectations for her audience and a space of provisional subjective agency for herself. Of the myriad options, personas, and masks available to her, Horne chose none. "I might have chosen," she writes, "to let my protective covering be more 'colored'—I could have sung spirituals and blues; or I might have gone the other way—and developed the Spanish accent. But by that time I had a lot more ego, and maybe not the right kind, but enough to make damn sure that nobody but *me* was going to pick my 'image.'"[41] Wearing the mask depends on taking up the images dominant popular culture offers and reinhabiting them from within, pushing against their boundaries and exceeding their constraints. But Horne insisted on her right to refuse these images and hold open a subjective space in which to select her own. Dyer signals toward this right of refusal when he characterizes Horne's image in the Jim Crow era as notable for "its presentation of itself *as* surface, its refusal to corroborate, by any hint of the person giving herself, the image of black sexuality that was being wished upon her."[42] She did not give her audience the image it wanted or expected, but gave it instead an image out of reach.

Rather than see Horne's impersona as an aspect of her personality—as either authentic or performed content—she insisted that we see her performance in terms of its form, making us look to what Jameson calls the "impersonal gesture itself."[43] Responding to her audience's voyeuristic hostility with her own hostility toward her audience, Horne describes nothing less than a method, a particular *"way* of isolating myself from the audience" (*Lena* 42, emphasis added). The crowd at the cabaret, she claimed, was "so busy comparing me to their preconceived images of what a Negro woman should be like, and so busy being surprised that I did not seem to fit it, that they never seem to notice they are not getting me—someone they can touch and hurt—but just a singer" (*Lena* 42). By withholding her self, Horne circumvented—even as she acknowledged—the fraught politics of representation that have so overdetermined African American cultural reception by white audiences and created the possibility for a future refiguring of her sexual subjectivity outside existing structures of intelligibility. Horne's canny manipulation of cabaret's intimacy and her performance of aloofness thus invite us to expand the formation and strategies of something identified and reconstructed as a feminist blues tradition and aligns her with the work of the Cabaret School. Her thrown voice does not articulate sexual subjectivity but withholds it, does not critique her material conditions but rearranges and eludes them. Sometimes song is a shield: when we listen to Lena, we might not hear anything at all.

FROM UPLIFT TO UPRISING:
BEYOND THE POLITICS OF EXCEPTIONALISM

Lena stands at the threshold of both a personal and a historic transformation. Between 1954 and 1963, the logic of Jim Crow that upheld Horne's segregated cabaret space was unable to resist the pressure of a mass civil rights movement. As we saw in *The Lady and Her Music*, Horne responded to the historical events of this era by redefining her performance impersona. One biographer, James Haskins, wrote of this transformation that Horne "had virtually offered her former cold self on the pyre of the civil rights movement." [44] And it is here that we might want to reintroduce the notion of Horne as a musical and political diva. Lauren Berlant, for example, rethinks the figure of the diva as the agent of an aural irruption into the gendered and racial fictions of the nation that asserts itself forcefully into the public sphere. [45] Horne enacted this "diva citizenship" in a striking moment in 1960, which she described as "the famous unscheduled, but not unexpected, performance I gave in a Hollywood nightclub." [46] This performance did not take place on stage, but while she was having a drink with a friend at Beverly Hills's Luau Club. After decades of quotidian violences and spectacular hostilities, Horne reacted furiously to a white patron who had drunkenly demanded to be served before her, muttering angrily, "She's just another nigger. Where is she?" By Horne's account, she held the table lamp to her face and shouted across the dimly lit club, "Here I am, you bastard, I'm the nigger you couldn't see." Horne punctuated this speech-act by throwing first the lamp, then her drinks and an ashtray, across the room at him, striking him in the head and cutting him over his eye.[47]

The event attracted some media attention, which Horne expected. What she did not expect were the letters, telegrams, and telephone calls of support from African Americans who were both surprised and pleased that Horne acted on her outrage. In her telling, this event and the black support she received inaugurated the transformation of her aloof impersona and her commitment to the mass protest of the civil rights movement. One of the projects Horne undertook in this period was her autobiographical collaboration with Richard Schickel to reintroduce herself to black America and to properly historicize her aloofness. (Horne's performance in *The Lady and Her Music,* with its subaltern narrative of the history of segregated performance, can similarly be seen as an act of diva citizenship that redefines the sound of Horne's repertoire and the shape of black musical history.)

Horne's transformation further suggests that her aloof impersona was not only a performance strategy that enabled her to create a psychic space in which she could resist the spectatorial violences of the Jim Crow cabaret, but also a product of normative uplift ideology's political program. As we have seen throughout this book, elite uplift ideology insisted on positive and exemplary representations of blackness and black public figures as a strategy to secure citizenship rights. Horne's middle-class background and welcome reception by Hollywood made her an important early symbol of black accomplishment, refinement, and respectability. But confronted with the limitations of such accommodationist politics, Horne articulates her frustration with the failures of uplift's politics of representation and positive images: "All of us who had been symbols for Negro aspirations for the past couple of decades, had minded our manners, been the responsible, reasonable people we were supposed to be, and nothing had come of it" (*Lena* 271).

The civil rights movement, in relocating political agency from the Talented Tenth to the black majority, marked a decisive repudiation of the politics of respectability and racial symbolism. This generation of activists, Horne noted, "knew the symbol was obsolete—before I did" (*Lena* 272). To underscore the connection between these personal and historical transformations, Horne's autobiography culminates with her 1963 performance at a civil rights rally in Jackson, Mississippi, days before the assassination of

Medgar Evers. This performance marked what Horne called her "personal reawakening" and stands rhetorically as an existential reunion with and acceptance by the black masses (*Lena* 293). It also signaled a rhetorical break from her segregated performances of the first half of the twentieth century as she turned her address from a sophisticated white audience to the southern black majority. In her description of performing for this rally, Horne articulates an important critique of uplift ideology's political program and its model of black leadership. Writing against the conservative nostalgia that identifies exceptional leaders and isolates them from their organic relationship to the black majority, Horne resisted the pressure to allow her celebrity to take the place of political leadership. After performing, she declared, "the Southern Negroes don't need 'celebrities' to come down and 'talk' to them. To use an old-fashioned phrase, there is a People's Revolution, and they have their leaders. Although it took his murder for it to happen, the whole world now knows one of them in Medgar Evers." [48] Relegating the politics of symbolism and normative uplift to a different historical consciousness, Horne concludes her autobiography with this turn to self-knowledge and the politics of transfiguration.

Not content to end her autobiography with this scene however, Horne extended *Lena* with an epilogue and offers us one final performance. She wrote,

> Not so long ago I found myself at three o'clock on a Sunday afternoon climbing on to a revolving stage about to be transported by it before a matinee audience in a theatre-in-the-round. There was nothing terribly glamorous about that huge, coldly modern place and the atmosphere was not really right, I thought, for my kind of performance. But I went on and entertained that audience. I worked and felt a great pride that I had rarely felt in my professional ability. There was nothing special about this crowd—no chi-chi. They were just people. And I was just doing my job. But I did it well. I did not feel the contempt for the medium that I have so often felt in show business. Neither did I feel they had come to see a freak—the Negro who doesn't sing like a Negro. They had come to see Lena Horne, who may not be the world's greatest entertainer, but who sure gives you your money's worth. Lena Horne, the professional. How I used to hate the critics who reluctantly praised me with that term. Now I could feel what they meant and I could accept it. (*Lena* 297)

This concluding passage of *Lena* offers an ethopoetics of performance, an encore that reimagines the relations of self to other in the light of the history of segregated performance and in the midst of the social uprisings in the United States in the 1960s. Horne uses this moment to conjure a performance space in which she would seem, at first glance, to transcend the markers of race and exist outside sexist and racist discourse. Her transportation to this revolving theatre-in-the-round has a dreamlike uncanniness to it, where the audience is "just people" and she is no longer a Negro—a mark of discursive production—but a singular Lena Horne. In one sense, this passage evokes a historical moment of immediacy and potentiality that from today's perspective—when the civil rights gained in the mid-twentieth century continue to be systematically eroded and undermined—seems to have been an unlikely, even naïve, fantasy. But Horne rhetorically defers this fantasy through a narrative fissure that rescues these final moments of her autobiography from being simply a mark of historical nostalgia. The temporality that governs this passage is indeterminate: "Not so long ago" is a temporal deictic that performatively enacts its referent, always referring to the recent past of whenever it is read. Read in 2008, for example, the scene that Horne described in 1965 had not yet occurred (framed in her autobiography as an epilogue, moreover, it is a paratextual passage outside the story proper). We can, in other words, read this performance as a future performance for her—one that is always working to produce and materialize the phantasmatic space it describes. She concludes with this final utopian impulse that seeks to bring the future into being and imagines a relationship to her audience not marked with the hostility and alienation that shaped her earlier performances.

In characterizing Horne's aloofness throughout this chapter as a studied performance impersona, I am not suggesting that her performance was a simple negation of herself. This would be cold comfort indeed, and self-defeating as any kind of minoritarian survival strategy in a majoritarian public sphere. Beyond withholding herself from her audience and unperforming dominant racial images, Horne's impersona claimed the psychic space to elaborate a self within the constraints of Jim Crow spectatorial relations, under terms that she was better able to manage. By displacing her self from discursive and representational systems, even while appearing within them, she was able to maintain a subjective space for herself that allowed her to bracket the damage such systems effect. As I stated earlier, Horne's segregated cabaret performances and the performative acts of her autobiography present themselves as "a free-floating realm of self-didactic possibility that might decentralize and disperse the knowing one" called for by Hortense Spillers.[49] The concept of "the one" is a psychic position that Spillers differentiates from the position of "the individual" constructed by discourses of bourgeois individualism, on the one hand, in which the individual is figured in relation to private property, and discourses of American racial logic, on the other, in which the individual is understood as a "synec-

FIGURE 14 Lena Horne performing at a nightclub, 1947. Photo by Yale Joel. Time Life Pictures/Getty Images.

dochic representation" of the race as a whole: "Every Black Man/Woman *is* the 'race'—as the logic of slave narratives amply demonstrates—and the elements of the formula are reversible and commensurate."[50] The figure of "the one" allows for a bracketing of "the individual" to approach the particularities of an interior intersubjectivity. Like Horne's future performance, "the one" is, for Spillers, a temporal structure: it is "the small integrity of the now that accumulates the tense of the presents as proofs of the past, and as experience that would warrant, might earn, the future."[51] Horne's autobiography, not least in its epilogue, puts her past in relationship to the future by way of the here and now of performance. Such performances are, like Horne's Luau Club "engagement," often unscheduled, but rarely unexpected.

I find Spillers's conception of "the knowing one" useful for understanding the theoretical work accomplished by Horne's performance of aloofness, though I stress here that neither Spillers (in her invocation of "the one") nor Horne (in her invocation of the "professional Lena Horne") ignores the historical or social position of the racialized subject. Instead they both seek to gain perspective within the historical, the discursive, and the social. The idea that Horne could elude the discursive confines that limited her sense of self, and the strategies by which she made that possible, happen for her in performance. The aloofness Horne cultivated on the Jim Crow stage enabled her survival and in some ways accounts for the longevity of her career. It gave her insight into the ethical spaces constituted through performance, and recognition of the political and social possibilities of interior intersubjectivity, of a self-knowing that enables a knowing of the other. After the transformations of the civil rights movement, Horne's coldness toward her audience thawed and her aloofness took on a different timbre: "When I exposed myself to the person in the audience, I felt something different. . . . It was an acknowledgement—we're not really alike, but maybe you can understand. Whereas the song used to be a selfish piece of property, it became a way of reaching out."[52] The song as a formal object is transformed and redirected toward a different notion of intersubjectivity and a different notion of politics—a politics of transfiguration rather than one of representation. The performance of aloofness Horne developed in the segregated cabaret was one way in which she sought to invent and inhabit a self that was not symbolic. Such a performance allowed Horne to survive the psychic damage and physical danger of segregated cabaret performance while imagining and enacting a future that contained the possibility of understanding.

———— ✳ ————

Irrealizing the Queer Harlem Renaissance

IN 2002, drag impressaria Vaginal Davis, who has been making queer culture through her music, zines, films, and performances for over two decades, added a new character to her repertoire of performance personas. That year she launched Bricktops, a queer club in Los Angeles that she hosted as Ada "Bricktop" Smith.[1] The historical Bricktop was responsible for the most influential club of the Parisian *tumulte noir,* the period between the wars when African American and Afro-Caribbean performance were in international vogue. Though she was skilled at both singing and dancing, Bricktop described herself primarily as a "hostess-entertainer" whose foremost accomplishment was establishing an atmosphere of intimacy, familiarity, and pleasure in her clubs.[2] She became a fixture of Montmartre nightlife at Le Grand Duc (Langston Hughes's description of which I discussed in chapter 1) after making a name for herself at prominent cabarets in Chicago and Harlem. Bricktop quickly transformed Le Grand Duc from an afterhours club for black musicians and entertainers into the center of American society in Paris. Her success there allowed her to open her own club, Bricktop's, in 1927. For the rest of her career, Bricktop would use her name as a point of reference as she opened clubs elsewhere in Paris as well as in Rome and Mexico City. In this way, Bricktop offers a particular confluence of persona and place that marks the spatial and geographical routes of Harlem cabaret and black performance around and beyond the black Atlantic. Her name invoked an atmosphere of public intimacy and belonging that resonated with the legacy of black Montmartre nightlife. "When hard times hit in the Forties and I had to move from place to place," she writes, "I carried the name, and people knew how to find me."[3]

When hard times hit in the first years of the twenty-first century, a time of reactionary U.S. politics and imperialist expansion energized by homophobic, xenophobic, and racist policies and demagoguery, Davis's Los Angeles club gave contemporary queer audiences a new opportunity to find — or discover — Bricktop. On most Friday nights between November 2002 and August 2005, adorned with a short strawberry-blond bob with a peacock feather in the part, Davis transformed West Hollywood's Parlour Club into Bricktop's Montmartre nightclub. Circulating among a motley audience made up of a mix of genders, sexualities, ethnicities, ages, races, and styles, Davis embodied Bricktop as hostess-entertainer. While she performed a couple of numbers each night (accompanied by her house piano player, Mr. Uncertain, a "male ingénue" who resembled a punk Cole Porter), the stage was primarily given over to guest performers from Los Angeles music and performance subcultures, with special guests often appearing from around the country. After the Parlour Club closed in 2005, Davis traveled with Bricktops, transiently staging the event in locations such as New York and Berlin. By way of music, costumes, and performance, Davis returned to the scene of Harlem cabaret as a historical resource to counter the stultifying homogeneity of a de-politicized and corporate-sponsored national gay and lesbian culture.

I have argued throughout this book that black writers and performers of the Harlem Renaissance turned to the scene of Harlem cabaret to critique the racial and sexual norms of uplift ideology and to articulate alternative narratives of race and sex. I have described this project as the work of Harlem's Cabaret School, a loose and fissured tradition that offered a rich revaluation of nightlife's ethics and performances. In conclusion, I turn to what could be thought of as the Cabaret School's legacy and further realization. Taking up the persona of Bricktop, Davis both drew from and continued the queer work of the Cabaret School that I have traced through these pages, updating it for contemporary critique. Her re-creation of Bricktop's cabaret was one of several queer cultural works produced in the past decade and a half that return to the scene of Harlem cabaret and its queer habitus in order to imagine possibilities for their current moment. Prefigured by Isaac Julien's pioneering film *Looking for Langston* (1989; discussed in chapter 3), other such works include Rodney Evans's film *Brother to Brother* (2004), which imagines an intergenerational black male friendship between Perry, a young artist and college student, and a fictionalized Richard Bruce

Nugent, now homeless, who haunts contemporary New York's landscape; Ben Neihart's novel *Rough Amusement: The True Story of A'Leila Walker, Patroness of the Harlem Renaissance's Down-Low Culture* (2003), which follows over the course of one night familiar queer characters such as A'Leila Walker, Langston Hughes, Carl Van Vechten, Nancy Cunard, and Ralph Werther (also known as "Jennie June") as they circulate around the boxes, back hallways, and stage of Harlem's largest drag ball; and Michael Dinwiddie's full-length play *Hannibal of the Alps* (2005), which stages Hughes's 1924 sojourn to Paris and his attempts to resist the subjective foreclosures of either a hetero or homo identity.[4] To this catalogue I would also add Cheryl Dunye's film *The Watermelon Woman* (1996), which though not located in Harlem, indexes the queer-of-color performance history and productions of intimacy that we have seen throughout this book as it imagines the difficulties of documenting the life and world of "lost" 1930s nightclub singer and movie actress Fae Richards (who is in fact a fictional invention of the filmmaker).

While some of these artists engage more directly with the scene of Harlem cabaret than others (and while they achieve varying levels of artistic accomplishment), they all draw on the history of black nightlife performance and evoke the critique of the Cabaret School. Deeply and carefully researched, each of these cultural productions begins from the open and contingent archive constituted at the intersection of the expressive nightlife culture and African American literature of the Harlem Renaissance. They approach this archive—these remains of Harlem's everynight life—as a collaborative practice of reviewing the past and imagining a history that can address and serve the needs of various queer communities in the present. These creative works treat the queer Harlem Renaissance as an ongoing and unfinished project, one neither past nor fully knowable. In doing so, they not only intervene in African American literary history by marking the Harlem Renaissance as a site of queerness; they also intervene in contemporary gay and lesbian cultural, political, and critical spheres by using that history to speak to the transfigurative possibilities of queer intimacy.

As queer/of color projects, moreover, they are not interested in spectacularizing and exposing Harlem's sexual practices and nightlife spaces so that we can better incorporate them into our current sexual and racial epistemologies, but in despectacularizing such scenes and imagining feelings and experiences that might disrupt our current politics, histories, and epistemologies of race and sex. In this commitment to queer-of-color imagination and critique, they are indebted to earlier projects of cultural reflection and collection such as Joseph Beam's *In the Life: A Black Gay Anthology* (1986) and Essex Hemphill's *Brother to Brother: New Writings by Gay Black Men* (1991), as well as earlier black feminist and queer work like Alice Walker's "In Search of Our Mothers' Gardens" (1974) and "In Search of Zora Neale Hurston [Looking for Zora]" (1975) and Audre Lorde's biomythographical *Zami: A New Spelling of My Name* (1982).[5] Like these prior projects, this contemporary Cabaret School uses imaginative performances of the past to expand the possibilities of queer associational life in the present and future.

Davis, for example, in a description of Bricktops as a nightlife project, explains her investment in the queer legacy of Harlem's cabaret:

> Bricktops faithfully re-creates the splendour of Jazz Age Cafe Society Paris, Weimar Berlin, and Greenwich Village bohemian intelligentsia. For literate clubgoers sick of the corporate careerist vulturism and youth culture myopia that plagues the tired and stagnant L. A. club scene, Bricktops provides the only satisfying true alternative. The style and allure of the 1920s has created a "flaming" youth movement and sub-culture, that exercise in camp and kitsch, but something more demanding that explores our not so distant past in an environment ripe to promote the creation of new political, artistic and cultural movements. Appropriate lost generation attire requested.[6]

Bricktops further narrated its performances by way of different themes each week that drew from the artistic and social histories of the transatlantic and cosmopolitan culture of the early twentieth century. Nights at Bricktops were organized around themes such as "Drinking with Carl Van Vechten Buffet Flat Soiree," "Brechtian Modalities," "Bessie Smith Tributata," "Django Reinhardt—King of the Gypsies," "Loves of Isadora Duncan Nite," "The Savage Genius of Baroness Elsa," and "Anna May Wong Salute." Davis's themes functioned pedagogically as well as artistically to create continuities between cultural producers of the 1920s and 1930s and contemporary queer subcultures of Los Angeles. They invited clubgoers to consciously inhabit history in ways foreclosed by corporate media and gay conservative nostalgia, actively shaping and embodying historical memory.[7]

In returning to the scene of the cabaret, Bricktops, like the other recent cultural productions mentioned above, responded not only to a standardizing and normalizing gay and lesbian present but also to a standardizing and normalizing gay and lesbian past. These are all, in other words, historical projects that mark the limits of positivist historical investigation. They return to the nightlife of Harlem in the 1920s not simply to catalogue same-sex relationships; nor to fix gay and lesbian identities on the practices, people, and spaces of the Harlem Renaissance; nor to establish canons of African American gay and lesbian literature. They instead take the past as inventive and imaginative material to intervene in current notions of queer politics, performance, and history at the turn of the twenty-first century. Elaborating on this notion of imagination in a discussion of his film, *Looking for Langston*, Isaac Julien explained that "If one wanted to try and look in an archive to find specific images of black gay dance halls one would be undertaking a journey that would have no beginning because such places didn't exist then. . . . One can only view that world [the Harlem Renaissance] or review it from an imaginary position. Once one accepts that there are a number of historical moments that one can grapple with and debate over, the rest is imaginary. I want to exploit that." [8]

It is Julien's investment—his critical exploitation—in the imaginative faculties that I am most interested in here. In these final pages, I want to suggest that Julien, Davis, and other contemporary queer culture makers who return to the scene of Harlem cabaret practice a queer critical imagination in order to irrealize a queer Harlem Renaissance. I take the notion of the "irreal" from Jean-Paul Sartre's phenomenological theory of art and imagination. Unlike perceptual consciousness, which apprehends objects in the "real" world (and is thus limited by discernible realities, perspectival constraints, and the laws of physics), for Sartre the imagination is a mode of consciousness activated by an "irreal" object, one that exists elsewhere, or perhaps nowhere. The imagination allows for a freedom of possibility and engagement beyond the perceptual confines of the present and bounded world. Performance, literature, and film have a particularly unique valence in Sartre's phenomenology as objects of both perception (that is, real objects before us) and imagination (that is, irreal objects that exist beyond their physical properties only in and as consciousness). The force of these aesthetic objects inspires the activity of the imagination, casting the spectator into an imaging-consciousness that can work as a negation of the real to accommodate new configurations of social possibility. Seen within this framework, we can see how artists like Julien, Davis, Dunye, Evans, Dinwiddie, and Neihart turn to the history of Harlem Renaissance–era nightlife as a resource for contemporary queer imaginations. These literary, cinematic, and nightlife performances approach the Harlem Renaissance not as a perceptual object—one we can know—but as an imaginative object—one we can conjure. These irrealizing practices ultimately point us toward a more meaningful engagement with the past and refigure our understanding of what a queer Harlem Renaissance was and can be.

Sartre illustrates his understanding of the irreal with a strikingly queer example that resonates provocatively with Vaginal Davis's performance of Bricktop. Consider, Sartre offers, a performance by the French actress Claire Franconay doing a music-hall impersonation of café singer and Folies Bergère star, Maurice Chevalier.[9] How is it, Sartre asks, that the audience comes to see through the perceptual reality of Franconay, a short, dark-haired woman, to imagine on the stage Chevalier, a tall, thin man? In this quasi–drag king performance, the audience first takes account of the references and signs of Chevalier—the trademark tilt of a straw hat, the jut of the bottom lip, a familiar song, the announcement that advertised such an impersonation. These, however, are still only referential aspects of the impersonation that belong to the realm of perception. While Franconay may suggest Chevalier, the audience still sees the woman presenting these signs. As the performance goes on, Sartre writes, Franconay begins to disappear. These signs of Chevalier become images, no longer referring to the absent actor but bringing him present to our imagination. Franconay thus makes her audience feel the way they would feel if Chevalier were present. These images—the hat, the lip, the voice—activate the emotional response that we have when we see Chevalier. This "affective impression" created by the impersonation makes the absent or imagined person present, transforming Franconay into Chevalier.[10] It is this affective imprint, for Sartre, "that realizes the synthetic union of the different signs, it is this that animates their fixed dryness, that gives them life and a certain depth."[11] This affective animation of the stuff of perception initiates an imaging-consciousness: it is not that we now see an imagined object in our perception, but that in imagining we have activated our imaging-consciousness. In the words of Sartre scholar Thomas Flynn, the imagined object "is not a thing but an act" that enables us to regain the affective experience of that which is absent, elsewhere, or nowhere.[12]

These gestures, costumes, movements, and sounds that Franconay uses to activate the affective impression of Chevalier are what Sartre termed *analogons*, the "equivalents of perception" that serve as the material for the imaginative act.[13] Davis, too, becomes an analogon for Bricktop, though unlike Franconay's audience, it is likely that most in Davis's audience had never seen Bricktop perform or even knew who she was prior to Davis's introduction. Davis provides images, signs, and analogons of the past to create an affective impression of prior queer histories, asking her audience to perform connections between their own feelings and knowledge and the feelings and knowledge of the past.

Toni Morrison helpfully elaborates on this relationship between imagi-nation, memory, and history. Describing the relationship between history and fiction as they came together in the writing of her novel *Beloved* (1987), Morrison suggests that "on the basis of some information and a little bit of guesswork you journey to a site to see what remains were left behind and to reconstruct the world that these remains imply. What makes it fiction is the nature of the imaginative act: my reliance on the image—on the remains—in addition to recollection, to yield up a kind of truth." [14] Davis, Julien, and others animate the remains of the Cabaret School and of the queer Harlem Renaissance more generally. They take bits of images, sounds, and move-ments as analogons to conjure and make available the affective impressions of history. When Davis claims that Bricktops is a "faithful recreation" of Jazz Age Café Society, for example, it is this kind of recreation, one that performs a fidelity to a kind of truth not reducible to facts, a fidelity to what could be alongside what was, or what Morrison calls "the possible" along-side "the actual." [15]

This is history in the subjunctive, rather than the indicative, mood. In irrealizing the queer Harlem Renaissance—rather than offering a docu-mentary account—these contemporary queer culture makers supplement and expand the possibilities of historical memory and knowledge offered by the protocols of positivist gay and lesbian history. In making *Looking for Langston*, for example, Julien insists that "the choice I made *not to make a documentary* was important. I did think of constructing a series of inter-views with different people who knew Hughes or were around during the Harlem Renaissance, but that became too constricting because the idea was to have desire exist in the construction of images and for the storytelling to actually construct a narrative that would enable audiences to meditate and think, rather than be told." [16] Julien's film marshals description, images, and sounds of the past less to construct a historical narrative than to activate an affective impression of queer historical possibility. Thus we can see Julien's film, Davis's nightclub, and these other cultural works not only as issuing a critique of contemporary gay and lesbian political thought, but also as deeply committed and ethical practices of history that aim toward a fidelity to the possibilities of Harlem's queer everynight life.

These works offer, in other words, resources for queer historical knowl-edge that exceed the limits of positivist gay and lesbian history. They do so by privileging what critic Carolyn Dinshaw has called a "queer historical impulse" that supplements a reliance on knowable facts and evidence with the affective impressions and connections that history's remains can produce. This is, as Dinshaw puts it, an "impulse toward making connections across time between, on the one hand, lives, texts, and other cultural phenomena left out of current sexual categories back then and, on the other, those left out of current sexual categories now." [17] This impulse appears in the work of Davis, Julien, and the others as an effort to expand the queer Harlem Renaissance as something other than a stop on a teleological narrative of gay and lesbian identity and community formation. In remaining faithful to the truth of Harlem's everynight life, they aim not to expose, explain, fix, or demonstrate but to conjure, perform, and continue. The affective impression of these works is produced less in the service of constituting a black gay and lesbian past or a contemporary connection to a gay and lesbian community than in conjuring the cabaret's criminal intimacies and fugitive socialities that allowed for, and continue to allow for, subjectivities, feelings, and experiences that do not always neatly align with easy sexual or racial identifications—the queer remainders of the gay and lesbian Harlem Renaissance.

Importantly, this critical queer imagination is not an alternative to politics or political organization but an indissoluble and essential component of it. These acts of queer critical imagination, these queer "freedom dreams," aspire to reinvent the perceptual realm by enacting transformations in their audiences that may have an existence beyond their immediate occasion. When creative work inspires such participatory consumption, the effect is the irrealization not only of the objects or worlds imagined but also of the imagining subject her- or himself. When we conjure an image, Sartre writes, "without doubt it is present but, at the same time, it is out of reach. I cannot touch it, change its place: or rather I can indeed do so, but on the condition that I do it in an irreal way, renouncing being served by my own hands, resorting to phantom hands that will deliver irreal blows to this face: to act on these irreal objects, I must duplicate myself, *irrealize myself.*" [18] To irrealize yourself is to put yourself in a different affective relationship to the communities, relations, and identities of our perceptual world. Such self-reflexivity in the imaginative act is what can allow such irreal possibilities to have effects in the perceptual world, multiplying and broadening the affective horizons of the real.

The return of contemporary queer culture to the scene of Harlem cabaret—from Bricktops's tribute to Carl Van Vechten and Julien's tribute to Langston Hughes to Dunye's reconstruction of lost queer women's worlds and Evans's cross-generational, cross-historical friendship—invites this self-reflexive irrealization. These works reanimate the remains of Harlem's everynight performances through practices of critical queer imagination to expand our understanding and experience of the queer Harlem Renaissance. The Cabaret School of the Harlem Renaissance, in other words, consists as much of Julien, Davis, and the like as it does Langston Hughes, Claude McKay, Lena Horne, Duke Ellington, Ethel Waters, and the others we have seen throughout this book. Collaborating across time and space, these contemporary culture makers draw from the queer reservoir of the Harlem Renaissance to revise previous histories, critique their current political moments, and imagine other possibilities of racial and sexual subjectivity. Their respective engagements irrealize the queer Harlem Renaissance, leaving it open, unfinished, and ongoing. In this respect, these last pages of *The Scene of Harlem Cabaret* serve less as a conclusion than as an open ending; less as an afterword than as an afterward. These contemporary queer culture makers continue the project of the Cabaret School of the Harlem Renaissance. They conjure the cabaret as a space for new possibilities. They extend the history of queer nightlife into its afterhours. They insist that queer nightlife will continue to endure. They perform its perpetual unending.

Notes

INTRODUCTION

1. Hasse, *Beyond Category*, 133, 112.
2. Ibid., 166–67.
3. Sonny Greer, interview by Stanley Crouch, New York City, January 23, 1979, Jazz Oral History Project, Institute of Jazz Studies, Rutgers University, Newark, New Jersey; quoted in Hasse, *Beyond Category*, 112.
4. Quoted in Hasse, *Beyond Category*, 112
5. Benjamin, "The Work of Art," 221.
6. "Black Belt's Nite Life," *Variety*, October 6, 1929, 12.
7. Hutchinson, introd., 3.
8. Shaw, *What a Woman Ought to Be and Do*, 74.
9. Gaines, *Uplifting the Race*, 2.
10. Ibid., 17; emphasis in original.
11. Johnson, preface, 9.
12. Davis, "Our Negro 'Intellectuals,'" 268.
13. Harrison, "Cabaret School of Negro Writers," 3.
14. For discussions of queer-of-color critique and analysis, see Ferguson, *Aberrations in Black*; Johnson and Henderson, *Black Queer Studies*; Muñoz, *Disidentifications*; Reid-Pharr, *Black Gay Man*; and Somerville, *Queering the Color Line*.
15. For more on the role of the working-class immigrant opera house in American culture, see Levine, *Highbrow/Lowbrow*, 85–168.
16. "Operas and Cabarets," 71.
17. Gaines, *Uplifting the Race*, xv.
18. In addition to Gaines, *Uplifting the Race*, see Baker, *Turning South Again*; Carby, *Race Men* and "Policing"; English, *Unnatural Selections*, 35–64; Foley, "Jean Toomer's Washington"; Higginbotham, *Righteous Discontent*; Mitchell, *Righteous Propagation*; Moore, *Booker T. Washington* and *Leading the Race*; Moten, "Uplift and Criminality"; Murdy, *Teach the Nation*; Shaw, *What a Woman Ought to Be and Do*; and Wolcott, *Remaking Respectability*.
19. Griffin, *In Search of Billie Holiday*, 72.
20. Gaines, *Uplifting the Race*, 69.
21. Du Bois, *The Philadelphia Negro*, 311.
22. Du Bois, "The Talented Tenth," 842.

23. Gaines, *Uplifting the Race*, 69.

24. Duggan, *Sapphic Slashers*, 157.

25. For more on the interarticulation of racial and sexual knowledge production in the late nineteenth and early twentieth century, see Duggan, *Sapphic Slashers;* Somerville, *Queering the Color Line;* and Terry, *An American Obsession.* American sex researchers' focus on problems of basic heterosexuality is in contrast to European sexologists' focus on problems of sexual deviance and homosexuality. See Bullough, "The Development of Sexology in the USA."

26. For more on antivice and social reform movements see Chauncey, *Gay New York;* Donovan, *White Slave Crusades;* Erenberg, *Steppin' Out;* Gilfoyle, *City of Eros,* 179–306; Mackey, *Pursuing Johns;* and Peiss, *Cheap Amusements.*

27. Carby, "Policing"; Ferguson, *Aberrations in Black,* 56–58; Mumford, *Interzones,* 18–49; Ross, *Manning the Race,* 145–99. See also Bulmer, *The Chicago School of Sociology;* Coser, "American Trends"; and Gaines, *Uplifting the Race,* 152–78.

28. Ross, *Manning the Race,* 167.

29. Indeed, Charles S. Johnson became national director of the Urban League after completing his doctorate in sociology at the University of Chicago. Both the Urban League and its journal, *Opportunity,* of which Johnson was the founding editor, were central to the cultural politics of the Harlem Renaissance. For more on Johnson's and other black sociologists' relationship to the Chicago School, see Robbins, *Sidelines Activist;* Lewis, *When Harlem Was in Vogue,* 46–49; and Ross, *Manning the Race,* 166–91.

30. Jones, *Recreation and Amusement,* 121; hereafter cited in text as *RA*.

31. Stallybrass, "Marx and Heterogeneity," 82.

32. Foucault, *Discipline and Punish,* 182–83.

33. Ibid., 183.

34. Uplift elites, of course, were not above attending the cabaret themselves. In the double standard that characterized much class-based outreach in the Progressive Era, such elites believed they had the discipline and constitution to practice in moderation and, above all, to not publicize. See Lewis, *When Harlem Was in Vogue,* 105–106.

35. For a thorough analysis of performance in the first half of the New Negro movement, including pageantry, dance, theater, parade, and sport, see Krasner, *A Beautiful Pageant.* For a discussion of concert dance and the Harlem Renaissance, see Perpener, *African American Concert Dance.* For a discussion of symphonic music, see Floyd, *Black Music in the Harlem Renaissance* and Spencer, *The New Negroes and Their Music.* For studies of the visual culture of the Harlem Renaissance, see Nadell, *Enter the New Negroes* and Caroll, *Word, Image, and the New Negro.* The touring performances of the Whitman Sisters (Alberta, Alice, Mabel, and Essie), as George-Graves demonstrates in *Royalty of Negro Vaudeville,* elevated black vaudeville into the realm of the respectable.

36. See, for example, Carby, "Policing"; Edwards, *The Practice of Diaspora;* Holcomb, "Diaspora Cruises"; Maxwell, *New Negro, Old Left;* and Robinson, *Black Movements in America* and *Black Marxism.*

37. Gaines, *Uplifting the Race,* 2.

38. In this respect, see Dwight McBride's caveat for taking middle-class ideology and the discourse of "black respectability" as an object for black queer studies in "Straight Black Studies," 68–73.

39. Thus the Cabaret School marks what Foucault calls "an *insurrection of subjugated knowledges*" (emphasis in original). By "subjugated knowledges," Foucault means both "those blocs of historical knowledge which were present but disguised within the body of functionalist and systematising theory . . . [and also] a whole set of knowledges that have been disqualified as inadequate to their task or insufficiently elaborated." This notion of subjugated, popular knowledges in insurrection (rather than, say, Foucault's notion of "reverse discourse," in which the marginalized or deviant subject enunciates a subjectivity through the language and knowledge

of the dominant discourse) best articulates the Cabaret School's relationship to social scientific disciplinarity and "official knowledge" I describe in this book. See "Two Lectures," 81–82.

40. Foucault, *The History of Sexuality*, vol. I, 17–35. *The Criminal* was revised and expanded in 1897, 1900, 1914, and 1916; *Sexual Inversion* was revised and expanded in 1913 and 1915; and *The Task of Social Hygiene* was revised and expanded in 1927.

41. hooks, "Seductive Sexualities," 193.

42. New York Public Library, Henry W. and Albert A. Berg Collection of English and American Literature.

43. The most influential scholarly treatments of the literary tradition I am dubbing the Cabaret School and its relationship to Harlem's nightlife are Bone, *The Negro Novel*, 58–77; Brown, "Negro Characters," 80–84 and *The Negro in American Fiction*, 131–37; Huggins, *The Harlem Renaissance*, 84–136, 244–301; Lewis, *When Harlem Was in Vogue*, 156–239; and Watson, *The Harlem Renaissance*. For other takes on this cabaret literature, see also Coles and Isaacs, "Primitivism as a Therapeutic Pursuit," 3–12; Brawley, *Negro Genius*, 231–68; Löbberman, "Harlem as a Memory Place"; Mumford, *Interzones*, 133–56; Silberman, "Reading Black Queer Vernacular"; and Stoff, "Claude McKay and the Cult of Primitivism."

44. Hughes, "The Negro Artist and the Racial Mountain," 57, and *The Big Sea*, 225.

45. For more on the spectcaularization of Harlem, see Balshaw, "Black Was White"; Chauncey, *Gay New York*, 244–67; Edwards, *Exotic Journeys*, 142–70; Erenberg, *Steppin' Out*, 252–59; Herring, *Queering the Underworld*, 1–24, 104–49; and Mumford, *Interzones*, 133–56.

46. Davis, "Our Negro 'Intellectuals,'" 286.

47. Chauncey, *Gay New York*, 257.

48. Hughes, *The Big Sea*, 273.

49. Chauncey, *Gay New York*, 259.

50. Hughes, *The Big Sea*, 273.

51. Delgado and Muñoz, *Everynight Life*.

52. de Certeau, *The Practice of Everyday Life*; Lefebvre, *Everyday Life in the Modern World*; and Kelley, *Race Rebels* and *Freedom Dreams*.

53. Gates, "The Black Man's Burden," 233.

54. See, e.g., Brody, "Queering Racial Reproduction"; Cobb, "Insolent Racing, Rough Narrative"; Garber, "A Spectacle in Color"; Hull, *Color, Sex, and Poetry*; Ross, *Manning the Race*; Schwartz, *Gay Voices of the Harlem Renaissance*; Silberman, "Reading Black Queer Vernacular"; Smalls, *The Homoerotic Photography of Carl Van Vechten*; Somerville, *Queering the Color Line* and *Modern Fiction Studies*; Stokes, "Strange Fruits"; James F. Wilson, "Bulldykes, Pansies, and Chocolate Babies," and Wirth, introd.

55. Somerville, *Queering the Color Line*.

56. Davis, *Blues Legacies and Black Feminism*, 39–41; Carby, "The Sexual Politics of Women's Blues," 16; Harrison, *Black Pearls*, 63–111; and Garber, "A Spectacle in Color," 325–26.

57. Smith, *Music on My Mind*, 56. "The Bull Diker's Dream" was recorded on organ by Fats Waller in the late 1920s under the title "The Digah's Stomp." According to Smith it was also known as "The Bowdiger's Dream," "Ladies' Dream," and "Digah's Dream."

58. Katz, *Gay American History*, 39–40.

59. Chauncey, *Gay New York*, 22. In some respects, this suggestion echoes David Halperin's call for expanding our notion of sexual identity with a range of other identities, with the important distinction that where Halperin calls for a more nuanced vocabulary of identities, I am more concerned with processes of identifications. See Halperin, *How to Do the History of Homosexuality*, 43.

60. Sedgwick, *Epistemology of the Closet*, 45.

61. Ibid., 9.

62. Berlant and Warner, "Sex in Public," 322.

63. Moten, "Uplift and Criminality," 332, 331.

64. Berlant, "Intimacy," 2.

65. Foucault, *History of Sexuality*, 99.

66. Kellner, "Langston Hughes's *Nigger Heaven* Blues," 23.

67. Carby, "Policing"; Erenberg, *Steppin' Out*, 132–42.

68. See Williams, *Marxism and Literature*, 115–20, for a discussion of literary traditions, formations, and institutions and their relationship to the social processes and structures of feeling that they undertake to organize. For a useful survey of the formal and thematic articulations of racial uplift in black fiction from 1900–1950, including its revisions during and after the Harlem Renaissance, see the literary genealogy traced in Jarrett, "Racial Uplift." Cf. Gates and Jarrett, *The New Negro*, 6–20.

69. Baker, *Modernism and the Harlem Renaissance*, 91–92; see also Gates, "Harlem on Our Minds."

70. Lewis, *When Harlem Was in Vogue*, xxviii.

71. My understanding of the contradictions and limitations of the Harlem Renaissance's politics of racial representation is shaped by the black feminist and queer critiques made by Carby, *Reconstructing Womanhood*, 163–75; Stavney, "Cross-Dressing Harlem, Re-Dressing Race"; and Schwarz, *Gay Voices of the Harlem Renaissance*, 25–47.

72. Brawley, *Negro Genius*, 117.

73. Brown, *The Negro in American Fiction*, 148–49.

74. For discussions of how literary realism both manages and contains social contradiction, see Glazener, *Reading for Realism*; Jameson, *The Political Unconscious*, 151–84; Kaplan, *The Social Construction of American Realism*; Sundquist, introd.; Thomas, *American Literary Realism*; and Warren, *Black and White Strangers*.

75. See Brown, *The Negro in American Fiction*; Cruse, *Crisis of the Negro Intellectual*; and Wright, "Blueprint for a Negro Writing" for examples of the advancement of African American social realism through the repudiation and disavowal of the Harlem Renaissance. See also Maxwell's discussion of this tendency in his consideration of the aesthetic debate staged between Wright's and Hurston's different approaches to African American literature in *New Negro, Old Left*, 153–78.

76. Bone, preface.

77. Gilroy, *The Black Atlantic*, 37.

78. See ibid., 77–81; cf. Conquergood, "Beyond the Text."

79. Gilroy, *The Black Atlantic*, 36.

80. Ibid., 38.

81. Hughes, "Response," 278.

82. Kirby, "Happenings," 5.

83. Ibid., 5.

84. Here I take my cue from scholars like W. B. Worthen and Jennifer Brody. In a reconsideration of dramatic literature's material history, Worthen asks, "Is it possible to begin to rethink the relation between print and performance by refusing the abstract and universalizing 'logic' of print, and instead putting print and performance into dialogue as materializing practices?" ("The Imprint of Performance," 217). Similarly, in an examination of Ellison's *Invisible Man*, Brody examines "the role that typography plays in eliciting and soliciting (black) sensations and sensations of blackness—in moving us to respond to the calls (as in hailing) of black ink." This analysis of *Invisible Man* is undertaken precisely to envision textual modes of black performance, "to press the issue of the link (or leak) between black ink and embodied forms of blackness (*Punctuation*, 64).

85. For a detailed history of the magazine *Le Chat Noir*, see Segel, *Turn-of-the-Century Cabaret*, 27–35. For a discussion of the magazine *Simplicissimus*, see Segel, *Turn-of-the-Century Cabaret*, 235, and Appignanesi, *The Cabaret*, 31. For more on the literary cabaret in the German tradition, see Lareau, *The Wild Stage*.

86. Anderson, *Imagined Communities*, 16.

87. Harrison, "Cabaret School of Negro Writers," 3; Brawley, *Negro Genius*, 233; Cullen, "Our Book Shelf," 74.

88. Spillers, "Formalism Comes to Harlem," 84.

89. This is an imperative demanded by Du Bois as early as *The Souls of Black Folk*, as well as by more recent scholars like Baker, *Modernism and the Harlem Renaissance*; Barrett, *Blackness and Value*; Bentsen, *Performing Blackness*; Griffin, "When Malindy Sings"; and Moten, *In the Break*.

90. Hughes, *The Weary Blues*, 29; *Collected Poems*, 35.

91. Du Bois, "Books," 82.

92. Du Bois, "The Browsing Reader," 202.

93. See Krasner, *A Beautiful Pageant*, for more on the role of theater, dance, and spectacle in the Harlem Renaissance.

94. Hughes, "The Negro Artist and the Racial Mountain," 59.

95. Baker, *Modernism and the Harlem Renaissance*, 92.

CHAPTER ONE

1. Lasky, *I Blow My Own Horn*, 81.

2. Ibid., 84.

3. For a history of the French establishment, see Castle, *The Folies Bergère*.

4. Lasky, *I Blow My Own Horn*, 83.

5. Hughes, *The Big Sea*, 162.

6. Berlant, "Intimacy," 8.

7. For more on intimacy and its relationship to heteronormativity, national and racial formations, and queer cultural labor, see Zelizer, *The Purchase of Intimacy*; Spahr, "'Love Scattered, Not Concentrated Love'"; Berlant, "Intimacy"; Doyle, *Sex Objects*; Reid-Pharr, *Black Gay Man*; Povinelli, *The Empire of Love*.

8. Cooke, *Afro-American Literature in the Twentieth Century*, 9.

9. Ibid., 136.

10. Goffman, *Behavior in Public Places*, 22.

11. McAuley, *Space in Performance*, 3.

12. Of equal importance, but outside the scope of this discussion, is the history of Latin American and Caribbean nightclubs and their relationship to European cabaret. The international cabaret vogue of the 1910s and 1920s witnessed the elaboration of black performance traditions in cities like Havana, Mexico City, and Buenos Aires, and the movement of performers from various countries through the entertainment corridors of the Western hemisphere. See Edwards, *The Practice of Diaspora*; Moore, *Nationalizing Blackness*; Salessi, "Medics, Crooks, and Tango Queens"; and especially Vázquez, "'Una Escuela Rara'" and "Instrumental Migrations" for entry points into this inquiry.

13. See Roach, *Cities of the Dead* and Webb, "The Black Dandyism of George Walker" for discussions of the methods of performance genealogies. See DuPlessis, *Genders, Races, and Religious Cultures*, 1-28, for a discussion of what she terms "social philology."

14. Webb, "The Black Dandyism of George Walker," 21.

15. See Appignanesi, *The Cabaret*; Cate and Shaw, *The Spirit of Montmartre*; Gendron, *Between Montmartre and the Mudd Club*; Gordon, *Why the French Love Jerry Lewis*; Jelavich, *Berlin Cabaret*; Rearick, *Pleasure of the Belle Époque*; Segel, *Turn-of-the-Century Cabaret*; Senelick, *Cabaret Performance*, vol. 1 and vol. 2.

16. Segel, *Turn-of-the-Century Cabaret*, 36.

17. Senelick, "Text and Violence," 26.

18. Rowland Strong, "Paris Bars Bullfights," *New York Times*, October 22, 1899, 8.

19. Segel, *Turn-of-the-Century Cabaret,* xv. See also Senelick, *Cabaret Performance,* vol. 2, xi–xiv.

20. For studies that foreground the historical significance of Lasky's Folie Bergère, see Erenberg, *Steppin' Out;* Trav S. D., *No Applause—Just Throw Money.*

21. After the economic failure of the Folies Bergère, the theater was reopened as the Fulton Theatre, which was then renamed the Helen Hayes Theatre in 1955. It was torn down in 1982 in order to construct the Times Square Marriott Marquis Hotel (which still stands at that location as of this writing). In 1983, another theater on Forty-fourth Street took the name of the Helen Hayes Theatre.

22. "Folies Bergere Full of Novelties," *New York Times,* April 28, 1911, 13.

23. Ibid.

24. These details are drawn from "Folies Bergere Full of Novelties," *New York Times,* April 28, 1911, 13; and "Plays and Players," *New York Times,* April 23, 1911, X1. Compare to Lasky, *I Blow My Own Horn,* 81–88.

25. Johnson, *Black Manhattan,* 118.

26. "Folies Bergère to End Brief Career," *New York Times,* September 28, 1911, 9. The Terrace Garden at Fifty-eighth Street and Lexington Avenue was the first imitator to appear, about six weeks later. It followed Lasky's and Harris's structure by offering an open-air dinner with an opera performance at 6:00 p.m., followed by a late-night "cabaret" show at which one could continue drinking beer under the stars, all for the price of two dollars. See "Dinner, Opera, Taxi, All for $2 a Seat," *New York Times,* June 12, 1911, 9.

27. Advertisement, *New York Times,* January 15, 1896, 7.

28. Advertisement, *New York Times,* July 8, 1900, 11.

29. "German Actors at Play," *New York Times,* December 18, 1907, p. 9. In this article, the word *cabaret* appears in inverted commas, as if marking not only the foreignness of the word but also its iteration and citationality. *Cabaret* was often marked this way in American newspaper accounts in the years before the word became standardized.

30. Lasky, *I Blow My Own Horn,* 70.

31. For more on black saloon culture in New York City up to the Harlem Renaissance, see Williamson, "Sports and Amusements of Negro New York, Part Two"; Latimer, "History of Negro Saloons"; Ottley and Weatherby, *The Negro in New York;* Johnson, *Black Manhattan;* Anderson, *This Was Harlem.*

32. McNamara, *The New York Concert Saloon.* See also Burrows and Wallace's description of the entertainment of the concert saloon as "a pastiche of French vaudeville, Italian opera, German beer garden, and English theatre" (*Gotham,* 805).

33. Asbury, *The Gangs of New York,* 7.

34. Durante and Kofoed, *Nightclubs,* 12.

35. Bradford, *Born with the Blues,* 163–64.

36. Sante, *Low Life,* 95. See also Sotiropoulos, *Staging Race,* 52–56, 213–24; and Johnson, *Black Manhattan* 118–20, for more on the Marshall Hotel.

37. Hurston, "Characteristics of Negro Expression," 89.

38. Griffin, *"Who Set You Flowin'?"* 48. For more on the history and atmosphere of the jook, see Hazzard-Gordon, *Jookin',* 80–85.

39. See Malone, *Steppin' on the Blues,* 70–90. For more on the movement of black theater and vaudeville circuit performances, including those on the influential Theatre Owner's Booking Association (TOBA), into urban performance spaces, see Jean and Marshall Stearns, *Jazz Dance,* 63–91; Hazzard-Gordon, *Jookin',* 121–62.

40. Johnson, *Black Manhattan,* 77.

41. See Johnson, *The Autobiography of an Ex-Colored Man,* 103–9, and *Black Manhattan,* 75–78; Ottley and Weatherby, *The Negro in New York,* 145n5.

42. Riis, *How the Other Half Lives*, 161–62.

43. Mumford, *Interzones*, 55. Mumford suggests that the name "black and tan" came from Reconstruction-era interracial cooperation in the South, where the Black and Tans referred to a successful black and white political coalition (29–31). The name may have crossed into urban saloon culture shortly after the Civil War, when a notorious and boisterous saloon in a black settlement of Greenwich Village opened under the name Black and Tan. According to an account from the Federal Writers' Project, Black and Tan drew a crowd of "Negroes along with a few Malays, Chinese, and American Indians. Occasionally a white man was seen. . . . The accent and bright colored bandanas of many of the Negro women suggested that they were of southern origin." A basement dance floor at this nightspot featured a four-piece black band with piano, flute, banjo, and violin. Ottley and Weatherby, *The Negro in New York*, 131–32.

44. See, e.g., "Night Life of the World: Black Belt (Harlem, N. Y. City)," *Variety*, February 17, 1926, 4. This is not to say that moral and legal strictures against interracial mixing were not strongly enforced through the 1920s and beyond. Rather, it suggests that nineteenth-century models, discourses, and epistemologies of such policing waned in efficacy, encouraging more modern approaches to limit and contain interracial mixing, particularly through modern administrative regulations like zoning laws and licensing requirements.

45. Peiss, *Cheap Amusements*, 101–2.

46. See *RA* 131; and Chevigny, *Gigs*, 56.

47. Erenberg, *Steppin' Out*, 140.

48. See ibid., 129–30.

49. Berliner, *Ambivalent Desire*; Gendron, *Between Montmartre and the Mudd Club*, 83–116; Dalton and Gates, "Josephine Baker and Paul Colin"; Edwards, *The Practice of Diaspora*; Fabre, *From Harlem to Paris* and "The Harlem Renaissance Abroad"; Shack, *Harlem in Montmartre*; Stovall, *Paris Noir*; and Tischler, "Europa Jazz in the 1920s."

50. Blake, *Le Tumulte Noir*, 113.

51. Hughes, *The Big Sea*, 162.

52. For the "sentimental avant-garde," see Moten, *In the Break*, 25–84. For cabaret's "other performances," cf. McAuley, *Space in Performance*, 277.

53. Ogren, *The Jazz Revolution*; Carby, "Policing."

54. Chevigny, *Gigs*, 57.

55. In 1955, the definition of cabaret was amended to include: "except eating or drinking places, which provide incidental musical entertainment, without dancing, either by mechanical devices, or by not more than three persons." It was later modified again in 1986. NYC admin. code §20-359 (1995). See also Chevigny, *Gigs*, 68–75, 183.

56. Paris, too, was a site of regulatory struggle in the 1920s when French authorities sought to embargo foreign performances in response to the influx of American musicians. The *Amsterdam News* reported that by 1930 it was becoming increasingly difficult for foreign musicians to obtain working cards required under French law. Pressure from the French Musicians Union made issuing such cards to Americans more difficult as economic as well as technological changes (i.e., radio and phonographs) made work scarcer. There were "more than 500 French musicians out of work due to the talkie and the radio which is now being used in cafes." Both black and white American bands were affected; one white orchestra was immediately ousted from a nightclub and replaced with a French band when it was discovered they were performing without the appropriate working cards. The crackdown promised an "extensive inquiry," as "it [was] suspected that the number of American musicians, colored and white, in France without working cards [was] large." Established stars like Josephine Baker and Noble Sissle had no difficulties receiving working cards; such regulations were much more likely to affect less established musicians. See "Musicians in Trouble in Europe," *New York Amsterdam News*, October 8, 1930, 11.

57. Thomas R. Ybarra, "Cabaretting," *New York Times,* April 10, 1912, 12.

58. Waters, *His Eye Is on the Sparrow,* 133, 149-50.

59. Fisher, "The Caucasian Storms Harlem," 394.

60. Román, *Performance in America,* 187-88.

61. Bennet, *Theatre Audiences;* Carlson, *Places of Performance;* McAuley, *Space in Performance.*

62. Cf. Chauduhri, *Staging Place,* 21-53.

63. Blau, *The Audience,* 25.

64. McAuley, *Space in Performance,* 277; Erenberg, *Steppin' Out,* 113-45.

65. Fisher, "The Caucasian Storms Harlem," 398.

66. McAuley, *Space in Performance,* 255.

67. Goffman, *Behavior in Public Places,* 16; emphasis in original. See also 92-94.

68. See, e.g., Powers, *Faces along the Bar,* 93-118; Peiss, *Cheap Amusements* and "'Charity Girls' and City Pleasures"; Clement, *Love for Sale.*

69. Cavan, *Liquor License,* 161.

70. Joseph, *Against the Romance of Community,* 34; emphasis in original.

71. Haskins, *The Cotton Club,* 33.

72. Chartres and Kunstadt, *Jazz,* 196.

73. Hall and Whannel, *The Popular Arts,* 58; emphasis in original.

74. Appignanesi, *The Cabaret,* 12.

75. Louis Mitchell, quoted in Bricktop, *Bricktop,* 94.

76. Bricktop, *Bricktop,* 41.

77. Smith, *Music on My Mind,* 147.

CHAPTER TWO

1. Johnson, *Along This Way,* 380.

2. Johnson, *Black Manhattan,* 78.

3. The year 1926 also saw a number of other literary events that encouraged the emergence of the Cabaret School and provided a theoretical and creative space for its critique, including the publication of Langston Hughes's poetry collection *The Weary Blues* and his manifesto "The Negro Artist and the Racial Mountain," a high-profile forum in the *Crisis* organized by editor W. E. B. Du Bois addressing the terms under which black culture should be represented, Du Bois's own address to the NAACP entitled "The Criteria of Negro Art," and the publication of Wallace Thurman's collectively edited avant-garde literary journal *Fire!!,* whose poems, stories, and plays offered frank and non-moralizing depictions of nonnormative sexuality. As the politics of representation came under increasing assault, the influence of the *Crisis,* in particular, began to diminish, and the journal, once so influential in the promotion of the Harlem Renaissance, became more and more strident in its denunciations of what it viewed as culturally suspect, politically irreverent, or sociologically "negative" depictions of black culture—including Allison Davis's derisive formulation of the "Cabaret School" in 1928 ("Our Negro 'Intellectuals'"). For more on the decline of *Crisis*'s influence after 1926, see Hutchinson, *Harlem Renaissance in Black and White,* 166-69. David Levering Lewis also identifies 1926 as marking a shift in the Harlem Renaissance from a movement largely directed by black civil rights organizations like the NAACP and the Urban League to a less disciplined and less centralized movement organized by the manifold interests and pursuits of various writers. See his preface to the Penguin edition of *When Harlem Was in Vogue,* xxiv, and his introduction to *The Portable Harlem Renaissance Reader,* xxix-xli.

4. For more on the licensing and zoning of Harlem's jazz clubs in 1926, see Chevigny, *Gigs,* 54-80. For an example of the campaign against racial mixing, see "'Black and Tan' Drive Urged by Justices," *Variety,* May 5, 1926, 1.

5. For a focused discussion of the controversy around *Nigger Heaven* and contemporaneous responses to it, see Worth, *"Nigger Heaven* and the Harlem Renaissance."

6. Van Vechten, "Prescription for the Negro Theatre," 98.

7. "Carmen of Harlem to Tell Saga," *Los Angeles Times,* October 6, 1929, B15.

8. See J. Brooks Atkinson, "Wages of Sin in Four Acts," *New York Times,* February 10, 1926, 20; "Carmen of Harlem to Tell Saga," *Los Angeles Times,* October 6, 1929, B15; Edwin Schallert, "Dynamic Play Runs Rampant," *Los Angeles Times,* October 9, 1929, A11; and Johnson, *Black Manhattan,* 205-6. While *Lulu Belle*—complete with its dancing waiters lifted directly from Small's Paradise—filled Van Vechten's prescription, so too did the Greenwich Village Triangle Theatre's 1929 revue *Malinda,* which was described by the *New York Times* as "a pleasant combination of DuBose Heyward, Carl Van Vechten, and Joel Chandler Harris." The musical, by black writer Dennis Donoghue, was about a naïve schoolteacher whisked from Florida by an unscrupulous suitor to perform in a Harlem cabaret and eventually saved from him by a friendly detective. The cast dances through "a maze of gun fights, gin-teas, 'buffet-flat' parlor parties, church picnics, plantation flashbacks and cabaret chorus numbers," including a cabaret "voodoo dance" that "succeeded in surpassing a similar scene in the current Harlem extravaganza, 'Connie's Hot Chocolates.'" "'Malinda' New Revue of South and Harlem," *New York Times,* December 4, 1929, 40.

9. See James Wilson's recovery of the queer cultural appropriations of this play in "That's the Kind of Gal I Am." For two interpretations of *Nigger Heaven* that open up possibilities for seeing the novel itself as a queer manipulation of spectacle and identity, see McCoy, "Inspectin' and Collecting" and Herring, *Queering the Underworld,* 104-27.

10. *Lulu Belle* and *Nigger Heaven* were singled out, for example, in a breathless report issued by the increasingly ineffective Committee of Fourteen, an antiprostitution and morals reform organization. According to the committee, "the colored areas of Harlem seem to be inadequately policed, and its dance halls, cabarets and other places of amusement practically unsupervised." It suggested that what it claimed as a sharp increase in prostitution in 1926 was due to more and more of the city's white population "beginning to discover this section, moved by the witnessing of such plays as 'Miss Lulu Belle,' and the influence of novels such as 'Nigger Heaven.' The interest aroused is not a healthy constructive interest, but more in the nature of morbid curiosity. This is rapidly being capitalized by exploiters of both races." The report called for increased surveillance and policing—especially more investigators "drawn from the colored race"—to complement the recent tightening of the city's commercial ordinances. "Calls Night Clubs Rendezvous of Vice," *New York Times,* July 15, 1927, 6; see also Chevigny, *Gigs;* and Ogren, *The Jazz Revolution.*

11. Fisher, "The Caucasian Storms Harlem," 395.

12. Waters, *His Eye Is on the Sparrow,* 124.

13. Shaw, *Nightlife,* 75.

14. Charters and Kunstadt, *Jazz,* 194.

15. Hartman, *Scenes of Subjection,* 33.

16. Ellington, *Duke Ellington in Person,* 44.

17. Calloway, *Of Minnie the Moocher and Me,* 88. See also Haskins's description of its "jungle décor" in *The Cotton Club,* 33; Shaw's description of its plantation décor in *Nightlife,* 75; and Gottschild's description in *Waltzing in the Dark,* 60-64.

18. In 1931 Clarence Robinson became the first black choreographer for the Cotton Club and later went on to choreograph the musical numbers for the Twentieth Century Fox film *Stormy Weather* (1943), starring Lena Horne and Bill Robinson. Eida Webb became the first black female choreographer at the Cotton Club shortly after him. See Gottschild, *Waltzing in the Dark,* 63.

19. This is not, of course, to say that revue was an intrinsically reactionary form. A number of performers and artists utilized the revue in the service of leftist and antiracist politics. See, e.g., the discussion of black leftist lyricist Andy Razaf's Small's Paradise floorshow, *A Kitchen*

Mechanics' Revue (1930) in Maxwell, *New Negro, Old Left*, 53–59, and a discussion of Popular Front uses of the revue form—including Duke Ellington's *Jump for Joy* (1941)—in Denning's *The Cultural Front*, 283–322.

20. "Innocent amusements" is Hartman's ironic phrase for the "symbolic violence" of slave performances and popular cultural practices that subtended the slave economy and "extended and maintained the relations of domination through euphemism and concealment." See *Scenes of Subjection*, 42.

21. Ottley and Weatherby, *The Negro in New York*, 248.

22. Brown, "Negro Characters," 80.

23. Murray, *Stomping the Blues*, 23–42 passim.

24. McKay, *A Long Way From Home*, 49.

25. Johnson, *Black Manhattan*, 78. For more on the cabaret as a space of professionalization for black musicians, see Dowling, "A Marginal Man in Black Bohemia," 124–30.

26. Charters and Kunstadt, *Jazz*, 196.

27. Ibid., 196.

28. Smith, *Music on My Mind*, 142.

29. Waters, *His Eye Is on the Sparrow*, 125.

30. Quoted in Sylvester, *No Cover Charge*, 48–49. See these pages for more on cutting sessions. For a description of piano cutting, see Shapiro and Hentoff, *Hear Me Talkin' to Ya*, 175.

31. Du Bois, "Books," 81.

32. Johnson, *Along This Way*, 380.

33. Hughes, *The Big Sea*, 225.

34. Huggins, *The Harlem Renaissance*, 90.

35. Lewis, *When Harlem Was in Vogue*, 211.

36. For more on Harlem's residential living conditions and emergence as a slum, see Osofsky, *Harlem*, 108–9.

37. Shapiro and Hentoff, *Hear Me Talkin' to Ya*, 224–25.

38. Waters, *His Eye Is on the Sparrow*, 130.

39. Strayhorn, "The Ellington Effect," 4.

40. Here I follow the example and invitation of Houston Baker Jr.'s analysis of the oratorical performances of Booker T. Washington. Baker turns to Goffman's notion of tight space to theorize the sense of claustrophobia and social anxiety that Washington often described when speaking before white audiences. See *Turning South Again*.

41. Goffman, *Behavior in Public Places*, 198–215.

42. For more on the performance and performativity of racial authenticity, see Johnson, *Appropriating Blackness*, and Favor, *Authentic Blackness*. See also John L. Jackson's discussion of "racial sincerity" as a productive alternative to the tests of racial authenticity in *Real Black*.

43. Fisher, "The Caucasian Storms Harlem."

44. As David Krasner suggests, parody was another way that black theatrical performers were able to loosen the representational constrictions of white spectatorship and the circumscribed opportunities for creative expression. He reminds us to look for resistance and parody even when there is the "appearance of accommodation" in black performance, including the strategies by which black performers simultaneously played to both white and black audiences. Krasner, *Resistance, Parody, and Double Consciousness*, 1.

45. See Vogel, "Performing 'Stormy Weather.'"

46. Haskins, *The Cotton Club*, 57. See Hutchinson, *In Search of Nella Larsen*, 339, 536n63, 565, and565n117 for more on the uneven application of the Cotton Club's segregation policy.

47. Horne, *In Person—Lena Horne*, 50–51.

48. Horne, *Lena*, 55; hereafter cited in text as *Lena*.

49. Shapiro and Hentoff, *Hear Me Talkin' to Ya*, 172.

50. Cf. literary critic James de Jongh's assessment that after Van Vechten, the cabaret "exercised a dominant influence on the literary use of Harlem by black and non-black authors alike during the remaining years of the Harlem Renaissance and has resonated in the literary idea of Harlem ever since" (*Vicious Modernism*, 26) and Cheryl Wall's description of the cabaret scene as "an almost obligatory feature in Harlem novels" ("Passing for What?" 100.) The cabaret was one stock scene among several that shows up often in Harlem Renaissance literature, including church scenes and street scenes.

51. Goffman, *Behavior in Public Places*, 204.

52. For a discussion of *Quicksand* as an exploration of the color line and the no-man's-land it creates for biracial subjects, see Hutchinson, "Subject to Disappearance." For more on the affective particularities—such as irritation, exasperation, pique, and annoyance—of tight spaces in *Quicksand*, see Ngai, *Ugly Feelings*, 174–208. Other works that address the contexts in which Larsen's cabaret scene emerges and functions include Brickhouse, "Nella Larsen and the Intertextual Geography of *Quicksand*," which demonstrates Larsen's careful revision of American literary history in *Quicksand*, including her revision of Van Vechten's *Nigger Heaven*; Esteve, "Nella Larsen's 'Moving Mosaic,'" which contextualizes the cabaret scene in Larsen's more general use of crowds and public space; Gay, "Essence and the Mulatto Traveler," which argues that Larsen attempts but fails to supersede an uplift-versus-primitivism opposition by having her biracial protagonist flee to Europe; Hostetler, "The Aesthetics of Race and Gender in Nella Larsen's *Quicksand*," which examines fashion, color, and race in the novel, including the cabaret scene; and Silverman, "Nella Larsen's *Quicksand*," which considers the scene in the context of discourses of exoticism and primitivism.

53. Larsen, *Quicksand*, 89–90.

54. Ibid., 92.

55. Ibid., 92–93.

56. Helga's complicated gaze upon Audrey mirrors Mary Love's gaze upon Lasca Sartoris when she first sees her at a party in *Nigger Heaven*, including a similar attention to fashion: "Mary stared ahead of her. There he was, dancing with that exotic Negro sense of rhythm which made time a thing in space. In his arms was the most striking woman Mary had ever seen. A robe of turquoise-blue satin clung to her exquisite body, brought out in relief every curve. The dress was cut so low in front that the little depression between her firm, round breasts was plainly visible. Her golden-brown back was entirely nude to the waist. The dress was circled with wide bands of green and black sequins, designed to resemble the fur of the leopard. A tiara of sapphires sparkled in her hair, and a choker of these stones, around her throat." Van Vechten, *Nigger Heaven*, 163.

57. McDowell, "The Changing Same," 78–97.

58. Hurston, "How It Feels to Be Colored Me," 154.

59. Ibid.

60. Silverman compares Hurston's and Larsen's cabaret scenes, to Hurston's disadvantage, in "Nella Larsen's *Quicksand*," 609. Other critiques of Hurston that see this scene as an embrace of primitivism include Mary Helen Washington's introduction to Hurston's "How It Feels to Be Colored Me," 151; and North, *Dialect of Modernism*, 179. Hazel Carby, while not referring specifically to Hurston's urban cabaret scene, juxtaposes Hurston's folk romanticism with Larsen's urban realism, finding Larsen's a more tenable position from which to critique the constraints on women's sexual self-determination (*Reconstructing Womanhood*, 174–75).

61. Barbara Johnson argues that by the end of the essay, Hurston has "conjugated a conflicting and ironic set of responses to her title. Far from answering the question of 'how it feels to be colored me,' she deconstructs the very grounds of answer." See *A World of Difference*, 178. Cheryl Wall describes the double bind in black women writers' use of primitivist discourse and identifies Hurston's simultaneous parody of primitivism and sincere expression of black music's

transfigurative possibilities in this cabaret scene. See *Women of the Harlem Renaissance*, 27-31. And in another recuperative essay, Brian Carr and Tova Cooper reread the cabaret scene within the whole project of "How It Feels to Be Colored Me" in order to remind us of Hurston's careful attention to the contextualization and relationality of racial difference that is often overlooked when this scene is taken out of context. See "Zora Neale Hurston and Modernism at the Critical Limit."

62. Du Bois, *The Souls of Black Folk*, 545-46. For Du Bois's use of the Veil as a metaphor for the color line, see 359-71, 545, passim. Cf. Baker, *Modernism and the Harlem Renaissance*, 57-58, for a discussion of the Veil and these final pages of *The Souls of Black Folk*.

63. Indeed we would not be wrong to read Hurston's entire essay as a direct response to and a revision of the central question of *The Souls of Black Folk*: "How does it feel to be a problem?" Twenty-five years later, Hurston responded with her own take on "How It Feels to Be Colored Me." This perhaps speaks to the contradiction Carla Kaplan has identified in Hurston's work when she observes that in this essay, Hurston "argues that she had 'no separate feeling about being an American citizen and colored,'" none of the 'double consciousness' that Du Bois articulated so famously in *The Souls of Black Folk*. 'I belong to no race or time,' she declared. But all of her anthropological work in the twenties and thirties and her lifelong commitment to bringing African American folklore to the public is devoted to demonstrating precisely the opposite." Seen as a rejoinder to *The Souls of Black Folk*, Hurston's arguments in "How It Feels . . . " take on a very specific address. Kaplan, *Zora Neale Hurston*, 51.

64. Tucker, "Jungle Music," 465. For more on Ellington's relationship to jungle music, see Lock, *Blutopia*, 80-88.

65. Ellington, *Music Is My Mistress*, 420.

66. *The Blacker the Berry* has received much less critical attention than either *Quicksand* or "How It Feels to Be Colored Me." For discussions of Thurman's exploration of race, sexuality, and performance in the novel, see Scott, "Harlem Shadows"; Gaither, "The Moment of Revision"; Jarraway, "Tales of the City."

67. Thurman, *The Blacker the Berry*, 115.

68. Ibid., 120-22.

69. Johnson, *World of Difference*, 177.

70. Thurman, *The Blacker the Berry*, 131.

71. See my discussion in chapter 4 of Claude McKay's and Larsen's use of skin color in the cabaret to further challenge such standardization and homogenization.

72. Thurman, *The Blacker the Berry*, 122.

73. Ibid., 117.

74. See Davis, *Blues Legacies and Black Feminism*, 281-82; Albertson, *Bessie*, 228-29.

CHAPTER THREE

1. For more on the circulation of rumors about Hughes's homosexuality, see Rampersad, *Life of Langston Hughes*, vol. 2, 333-38.

2. Rampersad's biography was preceded by Faith Berry's earlier biography, *Langston Hughes: Before and Beyond Harlem* (later revised and expanded as *Before and Beyond Harlem: A Biography of Langston Hughes*), which argues explicitly that Hughes was homosexual.

3. Rampersad, *Life of Langston Hughes*, vol. 2, 337.

4. Ibid., 336.

5. Rampersad, *Life of Langston Hughes*, vol. 1, 69

6. In 1989, the same year *Looking for Langston* premiered in the United States, St. Martin's Press published *Gay and Lesbian Poetry in Our Time*, an anthology that included four poems by Hughes: "Café: 3 a.m.," "Harlem," "Today," and "Stars"; only the first poem directly takes up themes of sexuality. One avowed effect of this volume, which compiles poems by nearly 100

poets, is to create a tradition and canon of gay and lesbian poetry. But another, counterintuitive, effect, when read alongside Julien's film, is exactly to mix up the boundaries that separate generations, races, genders, periods, poetic forms, and voices, inscribing new queer meanings and possibilities into otherwise nonsexual or desexualized works. Morse and Larkin, *Gay and Lesbian Poetry in Our Time*, 204-6.

7. For contemporaneous media accounts of *Looking for Langston* and the controversy between Hughes's estate and Julien, see Caryn James, "A Trip into the Middle Ages, and a View of Langston Hughes," *New York Times*, October 1, 1989, 61; Lisa Kennedy, "Signs of the Times: Closeting Langston Hughes," *The Village Voice*, October 10, 1989, 39; Douglas Sadownick, "Protest from Poet's Estate Keeps Film Out of Gay Festival," *Los Angeles Times*, July 12, 1989, 2; Vito Russo, "Who Owns the Past?" *The Advocate*, November 21, 1989, 56; Jacqueline Trescott, "'Langston': Poet Versus Premier," *Washington Post*, December 9, 1989, C1; Kevin Thomas, "'Langston' Dramatizes Black Gay Experience," *Los Angeles Times*, January 26, 1990, 10. For scholarly discussions of the controversy over representations of Hughes's sexuality, see Bravmann, "Isaac Julien's *Looking for Langston*"; Gates, "The Black Man's Burden"; Hemphill, "Undressing Icons"; hooks, "Seductive Sexualities"; Jarraway, *Going the Distance*, 92n29; Kenan, *Walking on Water*, 188-90; Mercer, "Traveling Theory"; and Nero, "Re/Membering Langston."

8. Rampersad, *Life of Langston Hughes*, vol. 2, 432.

9. Ibid., 431.

10. Work that pursues traces of Hughes's same-sex desire, possibilities of his same-sex contacts, and the larger queer milieus in which he circulated include Garber, "A Spectacle in Color"; Reimonenq, "Hughes, Langston (1902-1967)"; and Schwartz, *Gay Voices of the Harlem Renaissance*, 68-87. A number of other scholars have explored the various ways in which Hughes's work manipulates gender positions, often taking on the voice of women in ways that call into question the normative construction of racialized gender roles and explore the terrain of black effeminacy; see Barrett, "The Gaze of Langston Hughes"; Borden, "Heroic 'Hussies' and 'Brilliant Queers'"; Jarraway, *Going the Distance*, 69-97; and Ponce, "Langston Hughes's Queer Blues." In these latter works, the authors approach Hughes as an artist concerned in his poetry (as Jarraway and Ponce examine) or his autobiography (as Barrett examines) with the conditions by which sexual, racial, and gender subjectivities becomes possible—and possibly circumvented.

11. For more information on the 135th Street branch of the New York Public Library and its community-building activities, see Hutchinson, *In Search of Nella Larsen*, 132-50, 170-75. Hutchinson notes that "All of this activity at the library benefited from and contributed to the quickening of interest in African American culture on the part of the city's intellectual communities, at the same time that Harlem's nightlife began attracting downtown patronage" (175). For a discussion of the 135th Street branch's refigurations of racial knowledge production and categorization, see Roffman, "Nella Larsen, Librarian at 135th Street."

12. Schomburg, "The Negro Digs Up His Past," 231.

13. Hughes, *The Big Sea*, 211.

14. In thinking of Hughes's poetry and the debates around his sexuality in this way, I am influenced by Diana Taylor's critique of modernity's fetishization of the textual and the alternative approaches to the archive she offers in *The Archive and the Repertoire*, as well as work that challenges the terms of minoritarian historical inquiry, including Butt, *Between You and Me;* Cvetkovich, *An Archive of Feelings;* Harper, "The Evidence of Felt Intuition"; Meyer, "At Home in Marginal Domains"; Muñoz, "Ephemera as Evidence"; Román, *Acts of Intervention*, 1-44, and *Performance in America*, 137-78; and Schneider, "Performance Remains." For further discussion on the history and disciplinarity of concepts such as "proof" and "evidence," see Chandler, Davidson, and Hartoonian, *Questions of Evidence*. For more specific discussion of the debates over evidence, proof, and the archive as it relates to the study of performance, see Postlewait, "Writing History Today." And, with regard to the problem of "proof" for establishing the alleged homosexuality of modern authors, see Churchill, "Outing T. S. Eliot."

15. Cvetkovich, *An Archive of Feelings*, 7.

16. I borrow the phrase "temporal profile" from sociologist of time Eviatar Zerubavel, who uses it to describe the quality and patterns of temporal boundedness, recurrence, punctuality, rhythm, and routine. See *Hidden Rhythms*, 20.

17. Freeman, "Time Binds, or, Erotohistoriography," 59.

18. The title of this chapter intentionally invokes Norman O. Brown's critical experiment, *Closing Time*. Through an interweaving of quotations and fragments from *Finnegans Wake* and *The New Science*, Brown stages a dialogue between James Joyce and Giambattista Vico that rethinks the relationship between fact and fabrication, undoes the authority of empiricism, substitutes a notion of history as cyclical for one that is teleological or developmental, considers which mode of performance—farce, tragedy, operetta (blues?)—might best model history, and argues for the poetic as a location of counterhistoriographic practice.

19. Hughes, *Collected Poems*, 406.

20. Cf. Chauncey, *Gay New York*, 15: "According to Gershon Legman, who published a lexicon of homosexual argot in 1941, *fairy* (as a noun) and *queer* (as an adjective) were the terms most commonly used by 'queer' and 'normal' people alike to refer to 'homosexuals' before World War II. Regulatory agents—police, doctors, and private investigators alike—generally used technical terms such as *invert, pervert, degenerate,* or, less commonly, *homosexual* (or *homosexualist,* or simply *homo*), but they also knew and frequently used the vernacular *fairy* as well."

21. For some of the recent scholarship that theorizes and historicizes notions of queer temporality, see, among others, Dinshaw, *Getting Medieval*, 1–54; Edelman, *No Future*; Freeman, "Time Binds" and "Packing History, Count(er)ing Generations"; Halberstam, *In a Queer Time and Place*; Nealon, *Foundlings*; and Rohy, "Ahistorical."

22. Chauncey, *Gay New York*, 22. See also Erenberg, *Steppin' Out*; Ferguson, *Aberrations in Black*, 39–43; and Mumford, *Interzones*.

23. "Cabaret Raiders Left a Sad Trail," *New York Times*, August 4, 1912, 12.

24. The 1913 and 1914 debates over city closing time can be traced in the following *New York Times* articles: "Jack's All-Night License Revoked," *New York Times*, March 7, 1914, 1; "Gaynor Orders Lid for City April 1," *New York Times*, March 26, 1913, 1; "Gaynor Won't Stop Drinking at Dances," *New York Times*, March 27, 1913, 9; "The White Way Lid Falls at 1 O'Clock," *New York Times*, April 1, 1913, 1; "American Fakers Rival Futurists," *New York Times*, April 13, 1913, 6; "Police Keep Down the 1 O'Clock Lid," *New York Times*, March 5, 1914, 3; "Mayor to Modify 1 A.M. Closing Rule," *New York Times*, March 6, 1914, 3; "Committee to Plan New Closing Policy," *New York Times*, March 9, 1914, 1; "Say Ministers Like New All-Night Plan," *New York Times*, March 10, 1914, 6; "Restaurants Split on Closing Time," *New York Times*, March 12, 1914, 3; "Bishop Fights Plan for Late Closing," *New York Times*, March 17, 1914, 8; "Favor Mitchell Closing Plan," *New York Times*, March 19, 1914; "'All-Night' Plan Ready," *New York Times*, March 20, 1914, 8; "27 Places Now Ask All-Night Licenses," *New York Times*, March 21, 1914, 8; "All Night Licenses for 19 Restaurants," *New York Times*, April 24, 1914, 10; "Restaurant Men Lift Their Own Lid," *New York Times*, April 7, 1914, 9.

25. See Gilfoyle, *City of Eros*, 298–315; and Keire, "The Committee of Fourteen."

26. "Gaynor Orders Lid for City April 1," *New York Times*, March 26, 1913, 1.

27. "Gaynor Won't Stop Drinking at Dances," *New York Times*, March 27, 1913, 9.

28. "Trying to Revoke Licenses," *New York Times*, September 5, 1912, 20.

29. "Mayor to Modify 1 A.M. Closing Rule," *New York Times*, March 6, 1914, 3.

30. "Committee to Plan New Closing Policy," *New York Times*, March 9, 1914, 1. The details of the policy stipulated that cabaret restaurants could take out all-night licenses at the cost of $25 a week if they closed at 2:00 a.m. Failure to close at 2:00 a.m. would result in a revocation of their license. Restaurants without entertainment could take out a license at the cost of $25 per week and stay open until 6:00 a.m. (The dispensation given to these clubs was provided under the logic that late-night workers were entitled to a drink as much as a daytime worker, and

that clubs with performances catered to a decidedly different crowd than these honest laborers. Saloons that demonstrated that they catered to these night workers could apply for all-night licenses. While this legitimate demand would be met, liquor could not be sold in "backrooms" after 1:00 a.m.) Hotels were required to close their bars at 1:00 a.m. but could continue to serve food in their dining rooms. No all-night licenses would be granted for Saturday or Sunday. See "Favor Mitchell Closing Plan," *New York Times*, March 19, 1914, 5.

31. The laws controlling closing time are one thread in a wide regulatory tapestry. McNamara, *The New York Concert Saloon*, for example, provides details on laws passed in 1862 and 1872, later amended in 1875 and 1876, regulating the operation and performances of New York City's concert saloons—an early precursor to the cabaret. Similarly, Chevigny, *Gigs*, provides a history of the regulation of nightlife performance spaces and performers in the twentieth century, beginning with New York City's land-use zoning laws (originally passed in 1916) and "cabaret laws" (passed in 1926), which further licensed modes of performance and social dance. Chevigny also shows how these laws were designed and selectively enforced to contain and control jazz performance and black sociality more generally.

32. "Curfew Will Stay; Hour May Change," *New York Times*, June 9, 1926, 1; "3 a.m. Closing Is Expected by Night Clubs," *Variety*, February 17, 1926, 1, 50; "Night Club Owners Organize for Fight," *New York Times*, January 20, 1927, 8; "Four Night Clubs Accused," *New York Times*, February 12, 1927, 15.

33. Foucault, *Discipline and Punish*, 82.

34. Ibid.

35. The highly selective enforcement of Prohibition is the most visible example of what Foucault calls "'leniency' as a calculated economy of the power to punish" (*Discipline and Punish*, 101). Raids conducted in New York City the day before New Year's Eve in 1928, for example, yielded 93 arrests from two Harlem cabarets alone (out of a total of approximately 200 arrests), and shut down three Greenwich Village clubs. One newspaper account wryly noted that "A check of addresses revealed that none of the 'big' places was included in the unexpected foray, in which city bluecoats joined hands with Federal agents in a sudden interest in the Volstead Act." "200 More Are Held in New York Raids," *Washington Post*, December 31, 1928, 2.

36. Roebuck and Reese, *The Rendezvous*, 257.

37. Calloway, *Of Minnie the Moocher and Me*, 81-82.

38. Smith, *Music on My Mind*, 1-2.

39. Ellington, foreword, x.

40. Hale, "Revolution and the 'Low-Down Folk,'" 55; Rampersad, "Langston Hughes's *Fine Clothes to the Jew*," 145.

41. These reviews are collected in Dace, *Langston Hughes: The Contemporary Reviews*, 85-129, and summarized and contextualized in Rampersad, *Life of Langston Hughes*, vol. 1, 140-46.

42. See Tracy, *Langston Hughes and the Blues*, 141-265.

43. Edwards, *The Practice of Diaspora*, 61.

44. Ethel Ray Nance transcript, Fisk University Black Oral History Collection, 17. See also Lewis, *When Harlem Was in Vogue*, 128.

45. Nance transcript, 17.

46. Hughes, *Collected Poems*, 89.

47. "Everybody Loves My Baby, but My Baby Don't Love Nobody but Me" was a popular song in the 1920s, and its presence in Hughes's poem as part of the ephemera of Harlem's nightlife is not in itself particularly remarkable. However, Hughes specifically notes in his autobiography that he heard Alberta Hunter perform this song at an NAACP benefit performance at Happy Rhone's cabaret on Lenox Avenue in 1924, shortly after his return from Paris. The benefit was an affair of Harlem's literati, and it was there that Hughes met Carl Van Vechten for the first time, a life-altering event for the young poet. Though the title of his poem evokes Ethel

Ray Nance's Fifth Avenue Cat on the Saxophone, the citation of the Spenser and Palmer song could also locate it at Rhone's nightclub on the night of this benefit, perhaps imagining what happens after the middle-class literary and intellectual elites return to their Sugar Hill homes. See Hughes, *The Big Sea*, 202; and Rampersad, *Life of Langston Hughes*, vol. 1, 97-98.

48. Agamben, *The End of the Poem*, 113.

49. Ibid., 112.

50. Brent Edwards suggests that we can read this poem as one of Hughes's Paris poems, noting the formal echo between it and Hughes's poem "Jazz Band in a Parisian Cabaret," written of his time in Paris and included in *Fine Clothes to the Jew*. While locating the cabaret in Paris would change the historical resonance of New York City's closing time, it would not change the affective experience that I argue Hughes archives. More to the point, and resonant with the poem's formal pursuit of the experience of simultaneity, the poem need not refer to a singular time and place. The fact that the poem could mark a black Atlantic intimacy that connects New York and Paris is a particularly fruitful understanding of the work the poem does. See *The Practice of Diaspora*, 65-67.

51. For an example of criticism that sees Hughes's cabaret poems in the *carpe diem* tradition, see Jemie, *Langston Hughes*, 32.

52. Berlant, *The Queen of America Goes to Washington City*, 59-60.

53. Hughes, *Collected Poems*, 116.

54. Ellington, *Music Is My Mistress*, 63; emphasis in original.

55. Smith, *Poetic Closure*, 172-82.

56. Hughes, *Collected Poems*, 113.

57. Jemie, *Langston Hughes*, 37.

58. Hughes, *Collected Poems*, 59.

59. Rampersad, *Life of Langston Hughes*, vol. 1, 104.

60. Nicholas M. Evans helpfully reads this poem as Hughes's negotiation of homosexual identity and his intentional play between queer sexuality as an "open secret" (*I know that you know*) and an "empty secret" (the voiding of homosexual content by a universalizing modernist impulse): "The poem evokes a code that can certainly be interpreted by a knowing minority, yet it occludes that very code with its disappearing 'I' and overall ambiguity, inspiring doubt about the code's very presence." Evans reads the white mist that descends at the end as a kind of closet that obscures Hughes's own sexuality, but we can also see in this poem an attempt to produce an archive of queer feelings that eludes entrapment within the disciplinary registers of modern sexual discourse. See Evans, *Writing Jazz*, 224-28.

61. hooks, "Seductive Sexualities," 200.

62. Quoted in Rampersad, *Life of Langston Hughes*, vol. 2, 137.

63. hooks, "Seductive Sexualities," 197.

64. The phrase "in solution" is Raymond Williams's: "For structures of feeling can be defined as social experiences *in solution*, as distinct from other social semantic formations which have been *precipitated* and are more evidently and more immediately available." *Marxism and Literature*, 133; emphasis in original.

65. Michel de Certeau describes the excision of time from official documentations and spatial representations of the city as creating a temporal "nowhen." This excision fixes and stalls the practices of everyday—or everynight—life and renders illegible the ways in which marginal subjects resist, appropriate, and reimagine the sexual and racial disciplinary organization of the modern city.

CHAPTER FOUR

1. This review has been canonized in the histories of black arts and letters as evidence of the bourgeois affront to the 1920s bohemianism of the younger generation. Indeed, it is even

reprinted in full in the *Norton Anthology of African American Literature*. See Gates and McKay, *Norton Anthology of African American Literature*, 759.

2. Du Bois, "The Browsing Reader," 202.

3. Ibid.

4. Brawley, *Negro Genius*, 245.

5. Huggins, *The Harlem Renaissance*, 126, 122.

6. Mumford, *Interzones*, 145.

7. Cosgrove, introd., 1–2.

8. Bone, *The Negro Novel*, 68.

9. See, e.g., Ferguson, *Aberrations in Black*; Gaines, *Uplifting the Race*, 152–78; Mumford, *Interzones*, 18–49; Ross, *Manning the Race*, 145–99.

10. Gaines, *Uplifting the Race*, xiv.

11. Du Bois, "Talented Tenth," 842.

12. In recent decades, literary scholars and historians have recuperated McKay's work by recasting and recontextualizing its primitivist excess. The publication of McKay's 1923 Russian language book *The Negroes in America*, unavailable in English until 1979, made McKay appealing to a number of historians of 1920s and 1930s American communism. By foregrounding his Marxist-Leninist allegiances and demonstrating his involvement with the Third International, scholars have excavated, recognized, and continued to explore McKay's contribution to revolutionary thought and the activities of the Old Left (see, e.g., Maxwell, *New Negro, Old Left*, 63–124; LeSeur, "Claude McKay's Marxism"; Wald, *Exiles from a Future Time*, 291–97). Other scholars have located McKay in the transatlantic and Caribbean diasporic worlds and performances through which he moved (see, e.g., Chude-Sokei, *The Last "Darky,"* 207–47; Edwards, *The Practice of Diaspora*, 187–240; Hathaway, *Caribbean Waves*, 29–85; Stephens, *Black Empire*, 129–203; and Winston, *A Fierce Hatred of Injustice*). Still others have included McKay in an expanding field of black queer studies (see, e.g., Garber, "A Spectacle in Color"; Maiwald, "Race, Capitalism, and the Third-Sex Ideal"; and Wirth, introd.). For a scholarly undertaking that lucidly synthesizes all three of these revisionary projects, see Holcomb, "Diaspora Cruises," which offers an interpretation of McKay's life and work that keeps the multiplicities of his various subject positions and politics in productive flux.

13. Quoted in Cooper, *Claude McKay*, 247.

14. Holcomb, "Diaspora Cruises."

15. Quoted in Cooper, *Claude McKay*, 247.

16. Negt and Kluge, *Public Sphere and Experience*, 37–38.

17. Gilroy, *The Black Atlantic*, 37.

18. The various reviews and public responses to *Home to Harlem* are surveyed in Cooper, *Claude McKay*, 240–49.

19. De Jongh, *Vicious Modernism*, 26–27.

20. Du Bois, "Books," 81.

21. For more on Du Bois's sociological project in general and his work on *The Philadelphia Negro* more specifically, see Gaines, *Uplifting the Race*, 152–78; Green and Driver, *W. E. B. Du Bois on Sociology and the Black Community*; Katz and Sugrue, *W. E. B. Du Bois, Race, and the City*; Ross, *Manning the Race*, 145–99; and Zamir, *Dark Voices*, 23–109, 148–51.

22. Ross, *Manning the Race*, 154.

23. Foucault, *Discipline and Punish*, 183.

24. Ross, *Manning the Race*, 157.

25. Du Bois, *The Philadelphia Negro*, 311.

26. Ibid., 311n14; emphasis added.

27. Marx, *The Eighteenth Brumaire of Louis Bonaparte*, 75. Stallybrass details how the discursive construction of the lumpen relied on endlessly proliferating representations of "exotic heterogeneity" ("Marx and Heterogeneity," 82). I argue here that McKay, as a writer in the tradi-

tion of an Afro-diasporic modernism, offers a representation of the submerged tenth—or, more broadly, what he would characterize as the flotsam and jetsam of Western industrial life—that confounds this process. See also Edwards's discussion of the lumpenproletariat and international vagabondage in McKay's *Banjo* (*The Practice of Diaspora*, 198-209).

28. It is important to locate the centrality of "the family" in Du Bois's schema within the history of slavery and the self-determination of emancipated slaves to enter into consensual sexual relations and cultivate familial ties. What Du Bois viewed as the structural newness and fragility of the black family (only in institutional existence for two generations) is the underlying logic that figures the cabaret and other urban amusements as such a menacing threat. See Du Bois, "The Negro American Family"; Lewis, *W. E. B. Du Bois*, 195-96.

29. Du Bois, *The Philadelphia Negro*, 308.

30. Gaines, *Uplifting the Race*, 175. It should be noted here that, writing at the dawn of the science of sociology, Du Bois had the acuity to retain a historical perspective that located the cause of black criminality and social deviance of the submerged tenth in the history of slavery, the failure of Reconstruction, and institutionalized white supremacy. Zamir proposes that *The Philadelphia Negro* and Du Bois's earlier historical-sociological study, *The Suppression of the African Slave Trade*, both resist dominant trends in social science methodology: "Du Bois succeeded in deploying empirical practice against the alliance of pseudo-science, liberal optimism, and racism not only because his marginalized position fostered critical understanding, but also because he enlarged his scientific training to include a more historical assessment of the evidence in his work" (*Dark Voices*, 89). David Levering Lewis also characterizes Du Bois's emphasis on historical causality as a "radical subtext" of Du Bois's early sociological work. See Lewis, *W. E. B. Du Bois*, 206.

31. Washington's Seventh Street figures prominently in another important Harlem Renaissance novel, Jean Toomer's *Cane*. Like *Home to Harlem*, *Cane* explores the sexual and social dynamics of urban and migratory modern black life. A prose poem titled "Seventh Street" opens the second part of Toomer's novel. He describes this strip as "a crude-boned, soft-skinned wedge of nigger life breathing its loafer air, jazz songs and love, thrusting unconscious rhythms, black reddish blood into the white and whitewashed wood of Washington" (39). The theaters and cabarets of Washington figure prominently in his stories "Avey," "Theatre," "Box Seat," and "Bona and Paul."

32. de Certeau, *The Practice of Everyday Life*, 97.

33. Ibid., 97.

34. Calloway, *Of Minnie the Moocher and Me*, 119.

35. Johnson, *Black Manhattan*, 162-63.

36. See Baudelaire, *The Painter of Modern Life*; and Benjamin, "On Some Motifs in Baudelaire."

37. For more about the history of the stroll in African American life, see White and White, *Stylin,'* 220-47. Ross characterizes the urban folk novels of the Harlem Renaissance, including *Home to Harlem*, as representing a "footloose mobility" (*Manning the Race*, 349). Similarly, the strolling structure of McKay's novel can be thought of as a local practice of the larger diasporic vagabondage that Edwards (*The Practice of Diaspora*, 198-229), Holcomb ("Diaspora Cruises"), and Hathaway (*Caribbean Waves*, 29-85) identify. Not incidentally, strolling is also the opening and closing device utilized by Carl Van Vechten in *Nigger Heaven*. This structural overlap between these two novels suggests not only that the spatial practices of everynight life and walking in the city are central to understanding representations of the underworld, but also indicate that *Home to Harlem* and *Nigger Heaven* may have been critically yoked together for their formal similarities as well as their content and controversial reception.

38. Ross, *Manning the Race*, 145.

39. Stallybrass and White demonstrate the explicit relationship between policing the

lumpenproletariat and contamination from contact with them in their reading of an 1891 advertisement for Hudson's Soap. "The police and soap," they conclude, "were the antithesis of the crime and disease which supposedly lurked in the slums, prowling out at night to the suburbs; they were the agents of discipline, surveillance, purity" (*The Politics and Poetics of Transgression*, 134). When Du Bois writes, "after the dirtier parts of [*Home to Harlem*] I feel distinctly like taking a bath," he likewise describes his immersion into McKay's novel as a physical contamination that can be purified by a vigorous scrubbing ("The Browsing Reader," 202).

40. Stallybrass and White, *The Politics and Poetics of Transgression*, 134.

41. See Boone, *Libidinal Currents*, 205–87, for a consideration of the ways gay and lesbian modernist literature by Richard Bruce Nugent, Djuna Barnes, Charles Henri Ford and Parker Taylor, and Blair Niles similarly maps sexual spaces in the city through the nocturnal appropriation of walking. Boone, however, does not link these queer nighttime practices to the aesthetic and social street life of African American history.

42. McKay, *Home to Harlem*, 10–11; hereafter cited in text as *HH*.

43. While the literary trope of the "prostitute with a heart of gold" is a well-established tradition within male-authored literature since the early modern era, and while there is nothing at first glance queer about this exchange, I want to offer it as one of the ways McKay complicates the relationship between commerce, sex, and intimacy. One generous approach to this exchange (one McKay may or may not have consciously intended) is to see it as a scene of commercial sex that is not one of pure abjection, exploitation, or objectification, but one that allows for the complexity and contradictory feelings of desire that may be—and usually are—active during such commercial exchanges (not to mention the way such exchanges implicate, in turn, the fiction of noncommercial relationships as somehow transcendent of the material and monetary world). In addition to asking how returning the money to Jake transforms Felice into a proper woman, as Carby does ("Policing," 31), it is also interesting to ask how returning the money transforms Jake, for Felice as well as for the reader. In other words, in seeking to reorient the previous night's intimacy, the return of the money not only transforms Felice from a whore to a respectable woman, but also transforms Jake from a john to a respectable man.

44. See Brody, *Punctuation*, 62–84; and Cobb, "Insolent Racing, Rough Narrative," for considerations of the performative use of ellipses in Ralph Ellison's *Invisible Man* and Richard Bruce Nugent's "Smoke, Lilies and Jade" respectively.

45. Quoted in Cooper, *Claude McKay*, 149–50.

46. McKay, *A Long Way from Home*, 133.

47. Federal Writers' Project, 269.

48. de Certeau, *The Practice of Everyday Life*, 93.

49. McKay, *A Long Way from Home*, 49.

50. McKay, arguably, is as much an heir to this cross-racial literary lineage that leads back to Whitman as Hughes was. For more on Whitman's body politics, homosociality, and notions of "adhesiveness," see Moon, *Disseminating Whitman*.

51. The lyrics McKay records in this scene are "And there is two things in Harlem I don't understan' / It is a bulldycking woman and a faggotty man" (*HH* 36). Bessie Smith's lyrics, as transcribed by Angela Davis, read: "There's two things got me puzzled, there's two things I can't understand / That's a mannish actin' woman and skippin,' twistin,' woman actin' man" (Davis, *Blues Legacies and Black Feminism*, 280). It is clear that McKay is adapting or invoking an actual song credited to Smith. Davis (*Blues Legacies and Black Feminism*, 39–41), Carby ("The Sexual Politics of Women's Blues," 16), and Garber ("Spectacle in Color," 325–26) all argue convincingly that such lyrics describe, document, and recognize queer sexuality in the black underworld without moral disapprobation.

52. Du Bois, "The Problem of Amusement," 226.

53. Ibid., 230.

54. Ibid., 227.

55. Ibid., 231.

56. Ibid., 236–37.

57. Ibid., 237.

58. Du Bois, "The Negro American Family," 213; emphasis in original.

59. Lewis, *W. E. B. Du Bois*, 128.

60. Quoted in Lewis, *W. E. B. Du Bois*, 129; Du Bois, "The Problem of Amusement," 237.

61. Du Bois, "The Problem of Amusement," 237.

62. Du Bois, "The Browsing Reader," 202.

63. Helbling, *The Harlem Renaissance*, 111.

64. Fanon, *Black Skin, White Masks*, 11.

65. Berlant and Warner, "Sex in Public," 325.

66. Baker, *Blues, Ideology, and Afro-American Literature*, 7.

67. McKay, "A Negro Extravaganza," 65.

68. Ibid., 65.

69. In the same *Crisis* review in which Du Bois discussed *Home to Harlem*, he also (favorably) reviewed Nella Larsen's novel *Quicksand* and Melville Herskovitz's sociological study *The American Negro*. Reading these three texts together would have put questions of desire and "color nomenclature" in the forefront of Du Bois's thought. Larsen's *Quicksand* follows Helga Crane's material and psychic conflict as a woman of mixed race rendered unplaceable by the totalizing conventions of the color line. Tellingly, Larsen uses the cabaret in ways remarkably similar to McKay's in order to comment on the possibilities of racial mixing and the ways desire confounds racial identity. When Helga descends into a basement cellar nightclub, for example, "she marveled at the gradations within this oppressed race of hers. A dozen shades slid by. There was sooty black, shiny black, taupe, mahogany, bronze, copper, gold, orange, yellow, peach, ivory, pinky white, pastry white. There was yellow hair, brown hair, black hair; straight hair, straightened hair, curly hair, crinkly hair, woolly hair. She saw black eyes in white faces, brown eyes in yellow faces, gray eyes in brown faces, blue eyes in tan faces" (*Quicksand*, 90). Reviewing these two novels in the same column as Herskovitz's *American Negro* links them explicitly to canonical American sociology. Du Bois focuses on Herskovitz's attempt to reconcile the fact of racial mixing in the United States with the concept of a homogenous Negro population. The consequences of this study, Du Bois claims, are enormous not only "for the race problem in the United States, but also for the whole question of human contact, intermingling of blood and social heredity" ("The Browsing Reader," 202). Clustering these books together on the same page establishes a conversation between fiction and sociology about intimacy, race, and sex.

70. McKay, *A Long Way from Home*, 49.

71. McKay also uses the first-person voice in chapter 17, but there it is presented as a shift in *character* voice: the chapter is a self-contained short story narrated by Ray. In the passage cited above, however, the first-person voice can in no plausible way be ascribed to any character in the novel.

72. Mumford notices a similar shift in voice from third to first person in a letter from Harlem Renaissance author Wallace Thurman to William Rapp, a close friend. Thurman recounts being propositioned in the subway restroom by another man who offered him two dollars, which Thurman accepted. The relationship ended with both Thurman and the anonymous man being arrested by an undercover police officer who jumped out of a mop closet. In his letter, Thurman relates his journey to Harlem in the third person, but shifts to first person at the moment that the man propositions him; in other words, as Mumford puts it, "at precisely the moment when the homosexual act surfaces" (*Interzones*, 90). Both McKay and Thurman employ a shift in pronoun at a moment when articulating the sexual understandings of their selves suggests an inability of narrative conventions to adequately represent the affective possibilities of the scene. Similarly, during the controversy around *Home to Harlem*, Langston Hughes wrote to McKay in support of

the book, claiming that he found *Home to Harlem* "the finest thing 'we've' done yet" (quoted in Cooper, *Claude McKay*, 243). Hughes may have meant "black Americans" in his use of first-person plural, though it seems unlikely given his admiration for the work of Du Bois. Is it possible that his "we've" suggests a different configuration of identity? Those, perhaps, who "love a bar"? Could Hughes be making a reference to this passage of *Home to Harlem*, using the first-person plural and marking it with inverted quotes, to write *himself* into the scene along with McKay?

73. Carby, "Policing"; Erenberg, *Steppin' Out*, 113–45.

74. McKay, *A Long Way from Home*, 150; see also Cooper, *Claude McKay*, 172.

75. See Stallybrass, "Marx and Heterogeneity," for a discussion of the lumpen class as process rather than fixed identity.

CHAPTER FIVE

1. Ellison, "As the Spirit Moves Mahalia," 250.

2. See, e.g., Berlant, *The Queen of America Goes to Washington City*, 221–46; Brooks, *Bodies in Dissent*, 281–342; hooks, "Third World Diva Girls"; Koestenbaum, *The Queen's Throat*, 84–133; and Sedgwick and Moon, "Divinity."

3. One might innocently ask: What is Billie Holiday's relationship to this lineage? Angela Davis convincingly locates Holiday in a feminist blues tradition, though the fit is not always an easy one. Similarly, her cultivated aura of aloofness and her popular song repertoire invite us to think her in relation to Horne, Scott, Dandridge, and others, though this fit is also uneasy, not the least because of the class exclusions that organize this vocal tradition. We might rather think of Holiday's performances as cutting along the bias of either fit—an ill-fitting event that marks the limit or rupture of either tradition (or even tradition itself). See Davis, *Blues Legacies and Black Feminism*, 161–97; Griffin, *In Search of Billie Holliday*; O'Meally, *Lady Day*; and Moten, *In the Break*, 85–169.

4. For more on the NAACP's use of racial "family albums" in its publications, including the *Crisis*, see English, *Unnatural Selections*, 47–64.

5. Baraka, *Blues People*, 88.

6. See Carby, *Cultures in Babylon*, 1–63; and Davis, *Blues Legacies and Black Feminism*; Harrison, *Black Pearls*.

7. Davis, *Blues Legacies and Black Feminism*, xiii.

8. Spillers, "Interstices," 165.

9. Barrett, *Blackness and Value*, 76.

10. Griffin, "When Malindy Sings," 104. Other work on race and vocality that has shaped my reading of Horne includes Kun, *Audiotopias*; Moten, *In the Break*; Sobol, *Digitopia Blues*; Vázquez, "'Una Escuela Rara.'"

11. "Chocolate Cream Chanteuse," *Time*, January 4, 1943, 62.

12. "Lena Horne," *Life*, January 4, 1943, 21. For descriptions of the Savoy-Plaza engagement, see Horne, *Lena*, 146–49; Haskins, *Lena*, 81–83; Lumet-Buckley, *The Hornes*, 168–74; "Lena Horne," *Life*, January 4, 1943, 21; "Song Seller," *Newsweek*, January 4, 1943, 65; and "Chocolate Cream Chanteuse," *Time*, January 4, 1943, 62.

13. John Pope, "Lena Horne," *Lagniappe*, June 25–July 1, 1977, 3.

14. Seymour Peck, "Calling on Lena Horne," *New York Times*, October 27, 1957, X3.

15. For more on Horne's film career, see Bogle, *Toms, Coons, Mulattoes, Mammies, and Bucks*, 176–86, and *Brown Sugar*, 92–97.

16. Haskins, *Lena*, 78.

17. Postlewait, "Autobiography and Theatre History," 248–72.

18. Spillers, "'All the Things You Could Be by Now,'" 427.

19. Bogle, *Toms, Coons, Mulattoes, Mammies, and Bucks*, 9–10. This nineteenth-century racial

discourse of the mulatto stereotype, which continued into twentieth-century literature and film, was a common way that Horne's aloofness and sexual presence has been interpreted. The sexual subjectivity of the mulatta figure is imagined as a perpetual conflict between the "purity" of her white blood and the sexual unrestraint of her black blood. This, as we will see, is part of the representational trap that I argue Horne's aloofness contests. For more on the sexual subjectivity of the mulatto stereotype, see Brody, *Impossible Purities*, 1-58; McDowell, "*The Changing Same*," 51-57, 82-97; Somerville, *Queering the Color Line*, 77-165; and Zackodnik, *The Mulatta and the Politics of Race*.

20. See Dyer, *Stars* and *Heavenly Bodies*. In *Heavenly Bodies*, Dyer briefly discusses the ways in which Horne manipulated her star image to denaturalize dominant ideas of black sexuality (15) and also elaborates, in an extended discussion of Paul Robeson, how racial discourse can shape Hollywood star images (64-136).

21. Michiko Kakutani, "Lena Horne: Aloofness Hid the Pain, Until Time Cooled Her Anger," *New York Times*, May 3, 1981, D1. See also Lena Horne's reflections on her experiences with MGM in the musical compilation *That's Entertainment III* (Warner Home Video, 2004), in which she describes the racial politics of Hollywood casting and her mistreatment by the studio, and Richard Dyer's essay about racial representation in the Hollywood musical, "The Colour of Entertainment."

22. Walter Kerr, "Hail to a Horne of Plenty, *New York Times*, May 24, 1981, D3.

23. I refer here to Carby's "Policing," which outlines the discursive and material structures that shaped and confined working-class black women's sexual subjectivity, as well as ways in which women performers and blues entertainers challenged such representational constraints.

24. See Andrews, *To Tell a Free Story*; Braxton, *Black Women Writing Autobiography*; Butterfield, *Black Autobiography in America*; Mostern, *Autobiography and Black Identity Politics*; Rampersad, "Biography, Autobiography, and Afro-American Culture"; and Stover, *Rhetoric and Resistance in Black Women's Autobiography*.

25. Butterfield, *Black Autobiography in America*, 95.

26. For more on the performativity of autobiography, see Bruss, *Autobiographical Acts*, and Ogren, "Jazz Isn't Just Me." Phillip Auslander, building on the theories of Erving Goffman, further suggests that musicians construct a specific version of their self—a persona—through setting, manner, style, repertoire, genre, gesture, and other aspects of performance. It is this process, I suggest, Horne aimed both to exploit and to evade. See Auslander, "Musical Personae."

27. Postlewait, "Autobiography and Theatre History," 25. Horne's autobiography bears on its title page the signature of her amanuensis, Richard Schickel. Schickel is a documentary filmmaker, movie historian, and film critic who has authored performance biographies of Clint Eastwood, Douglas Fairbanks Jr., and Marlon Brando, among others. It is neither possible nor interesting to determine the extent of Schickel's role in shaping Horne's autobiography. It is, however, worth noting the interracial ensemblic intimacy by which her life story and performance theory are made legible to us today. In Horne's case, the amanuensis is a marker of a complex interracial relationship between a black woman and a white man whom she permits to contribute to the construction of her story.

28. Saussure, *Course in General Linguistics*, 67.

29. Carby, "The Sexual Politics of Women's Blues," 8.

30. Quoted in *Lena*, 196. We might also hear Maxwell's critique with a queer ear, given her own lesbianism and relationship to the closet. That is, her desire for Horne to "project herself beyond herself" might also be heard to comment on Maxwell's own identification with the discursive, psychic, and social constraints on female sexuality in the public sphere. I am indebted to Patricia White for this observation.

31. See *Lena*, 138, 144-45, 183, 193, 226, 271-74.

32. Michiko Kakutani, "Lena Horne: Aloofness Hid the Pain, until Time Cooled Her Anger," *New York Times*, May 3, 1981, D1.

33. Quoted in Bogle, *Brown Sugar,* 96.

34. Denning, *The Cultural Front,* 324.

35. Brecht, "On the Use of Music in an Epic Theatre," 87.

36. Jameson, *Brecht and Method,* 54. See also Diamond, *Unmaking Mimesis,* 43-103.

37. In addition to the live recording of the show (*Lena Horne: The Lady and Her Music,* Qwest Records, 1981), I rely on the following: John Beaufort, "Lena Horne: One-Woman Extravaganza!" *Christian Science Monitor,* May 18, 1981, 23; Haskins, *Lena,* 193-209; Walter Kerr, "Hail to a Horne of Plenty, *New York Times,* May 24, 1981, D3; Rex Reed, "Lena Horne: 'Stormy Weather' Is Her Song and Her Story," *Philadelphia Inquirer,* June 5, 1981, D1; and Frank Rich, "Lena Horne: The Lady and Her Music," *New York Times,* May 13, 1981, C27.

38. Román, *Performance in America,* 179.

39. Frank Rich, "Lena Horne: The Lady and Her Music," *New York Times,* May 13, 1981, C27.

40. For more on the performance strategy of wearing the mask, see Baker, *Modernism and the Harlem Renaissance;* Chude-Sokei, *The Last "Darky";* Krasner, *Resistance, Parody, and Double Consciousness;* Sotiropoulos, *Staging Race;* and Webb, "The Black Dandyism of George Walker." Caryl Phillips's novel *Dancing in the Dark,* which fictionalizes Williams and Walker, also examines the psychic and social compromises of such performance strategies.

41. Lena Horne, "I Just Want to Be Myself," *Show,* September 1963, 64.

42. Dyer, *Heavenly Bodies,* 15.

43. Jameson, *Brecht and Method,* 75.

44. Haskins, *Lena,* 213.

45. Berlant, *The Queen of America Goes to Washington City,* 221-46. See also Regester, "Hazel Scott and Lena Horne," which describes the political commitments of Horne and Scott during the 1940s and 1950s as a practice of diva activism.

46. Horne, "I Just Want to Be Myself," *Show,* September 1963, 113.

47. See *Lena,* 272-74; Haskins, *Lena,* 150-51.

48. Horne, "I Just Want to Be Myself," *Show,* September 1963, 65.

49. Spillers, "'All the Things You Could Be by Now,'" 427.

50. Ibid., 395.

51. Ibid., 396.

52. Michiko Kakutani, "Lena Horne: Aloofness Hid the Pain, until Time Cooled Her Anger," *New York Times,* May 3, 1981, D1.

AFTERWORD

1. For discussions of the history and work of Davis, see Muñoz, *Disidentifications,* 93-115, and Doyle, *Sex Objects,* 121-40. For some descriptions of Davis's club, Bricktops, see Adam Bergman, "In Times Gone By," *Los Angeles Times,* April 3, 2003, E22; Rebecca Epstein, "A Roaring Anniversary," *LA City Beat,* November 25, 2004; and Guy Trebay, "Ready to Fade Into Obscurity. Wait, He's Already There," *New York Times,* May 23, 2004, sec. 9, p. 11.

2. Bricktop, *Bricktop,* 214.

3. Ibid., 119.

4. For discussions of *The Watermelon Woman* and its relationship to queer history and memory, see Cvetkovitch, *An Archive of Feelings,* 239-41; Reid-Pharr, "Makes Me Feel Mighty Real"; and Solomon-Godeau, "On Ghost Writing." Dunye and photographer Zoe Leonard published their constructed archive of the fictional Fae Richards (including photographs, film stills, and newspaper articles) in an artist's book, *The Fae Richards Photo Archive.*

5. Beam, *In the Life;* Hemphill, *Brother to Brother;* Walker, "In Search of Our Mothers' Gardens" and "In Search of Zora Neale Hurston"; Lorde, *Zami.* Alongside these works, I would add the more recent critical explorations of what queer-of-color writer and essayist Thomas Glave calls "moral imagination." Glave describes the queer black literary imagination as a "desire to

conjure oneself as one already was but also as one might be, could be; in the act of conjuring and the emblazoning step toward honing the imagined language of those conjurings into the textual forms of narrative—prose, drama, poetry, or other, newly fused, inventions—creating oneself, *the self*, into being" (*Words to Our Now,* 34). The long tradition of such a black radical imagination and its indissoluble relationship to emancipatory politics is described in Kelley, *Freedom Dreams.*

6. http://www.vaginaldavis.com/new.shtml, accessed June 1, 2004.

7. While here I am situating Bricktops in a vertical relationship to the scene of Harlem cabaret in the 1920s and 1930s, it is also useful to contextualize this performance horizontally in relation to other queer/of color nightlife performances in Los Angeles that, though not explicitly engaged with the history of 1920s Harlem, are nonetheless part of the same queer legacy of public intimacy that I have described throughout this book. Los Angeles performance events such as Marcus Kuiland Nazario's Pop Tarts series, Beth Lapides's Un-Cabaret series, and the cultural events of Tongues, a nonprofit collective created by queer and feminist women of color, for example, have sought over the past two decades to offer alternatives to the corporate, apolitical, and homogenized national gay and lesbian culture. We could add to this list of performances the theatrical events at venues such as the Actor's Gang Ensemble Theatre, the Evidence Room Theatre Project, and Highways performance space. For more on the history of Los Angeles's queer nightlife culture, see Faderman and Timmons, *Gay L. A.;* Hurewitz, *Bohemian Los Angeles;* Cheng, *In Other Los Angeleses;* and Román, *Acts of Intervention,* 177–201.

8. Hemphill, *"Looking for Langston:* An Interview with Isaac Julien," 178.

9. Sartre, *The Imaginary,* 25–29.

10. Ibid., 23.

11. Ibid., 28.

12. Flynn, "The Role of the Image in Sartre's Aesthetic," 432. See also Tims, "Masks and Sartre's Imaginary."

13. Sartre, *The Imaginary,* 18.

14. Morrison, "The Site of Memory," 192.

15. Ibid., 197.

16. Hemphill, *"Looking for Langston:* An Interview with Isaac Julien," 177; emphasis in original.

17. Dinshaw, *Getting Medieval,* 1. In addition to Dinshaw's study, a number of recent works have taken up the project of outlining a queer understanding of history and historiography with which this conclusion is in dialogue. See, e.g. , Bravmann, *Queer Fictions of the Past;* Cvetkovich, *An Archive of Feelings;* Freccero, *Queer/Early/Modern;* Goldberg and Menon, "Queering History"; Herring, *Queering the Underworld;* Nealon, *Foundlings;* and Scott, "Fantasy Echo." See also Schneider, "Performance Remains."

18. Sartre, *The Imaginary,* 125; emphasis in original.

Bibliography

Agamben, Giorgio. *The End of the Poem: Studies in Poetics*. Stanford, Calif.: Stanford University Press, 1999.

Albertson, Chris. *Bessie*. Rev. and exp. ed. New Haven, Conn.: Yale University Press, 2003.

Anderson, Benedict. *Imagined Communities: Reflections on the Origin and Spread of Nationalism*. New York: Verso, 1983.

Anderson, Jervis. *This Was Harlem: A Cultural Portrait, 1900–1950*. New York: Farrar, Straus, and Giroux, 1982.

Andrews, William L. *To Tell a Free Story: The First Century of Afro-American Autobiography, 1760–1865*. Urbana: University of Illinois Press, 1986.

Appignanesi, Lisa. *The Cabaret*. New York: Universe Books, 1976. Reprinted as *Cabaret: The First Hundred Years*, London: Methuen, 1984.

Asbury, Herbert. *The Gangs of New York: An Informal History of the Underworld*. Garden City, N.Y.: Garden City Publishing Company, 1928.

Auslander, Phillip. "Musical Personae." *Drama Review* 50 (2006): 100–119.

Baker, Houston A., Jr. *Blues, Ideology, and Afro-American Literature: A Vernacular Theory*. Chicago: University of Chicago Press, 1984.

———. *Modernism and the Harlem Renaissance*. Chicago: University of Chicago Press, 1987.

———. *Turning South Again: Re-thinking Modernism/Re-reading Booker T.* Durham, N.C.: Duke University Press, 2001.

Balshaw, Maria. " 'Black Was White': Urbanity, Passing and the Spectacle of Harlem." *Journal of American Studies* 33 (1999): 307–22.

Baraka, Amiri [LeRoi Jones]. *Blues People: Negro Music in White America*. New York: Quill, 1963.

Barrett, Lindon. *Blackness and Value: Seeing Double*. Cambridge: Cambridge University Press, 1999.

———. "The Gaze of Langston Hughes: Subjectivity, Homoeroticism, and the Feminine in *The Big Sea*." *Yale Journal of Criticism* 12 (1999): 383–97.

Baudelaire, Charles. *The Painter of Modern Life*. New York: Phaidon, 1995.

Beam, Joseph, ed. *In the Life: A Black Gay Anthology*. Boston: Alyson, 1986.

Benjamin, Walter. "On Some Motifs in Baudelaire." In *Illuminations*, ed. Hannah Arendt, 155–200. New York: Schocken, 1967.

——. "The Work of Art in the Age of Mechanical Reproduction." In *Illuminations,* ed. Hannah Arendt, 217-52. New York: Schocken, 1967.

Bennett, Susan. *Theatre Audiences: A Theory of Production and Reception.* New York: Routledge, 1997.

Bentsen, Kimberly. *Performing Blackness: Enactments of African American Modernism.* New York: Routledge, 2000.

Berlant, Lauren. "Intimacy: A Special Issue." In *Intimacy,* ed. Lauren Berlant, 1-8. Chicago: University of Chicago Press, 2000.

——. *The Queen of America Goes to Washington City: Essays on Sex and Citizenship.* Durham, N.C.: Duke University Press, 1997.

Berlant, Lauren, and Michael Warner. "Sex in Public." In *Intimacy,* ed. Lauren Berlant, 311-30. Chicago: University of Chicago Press, 2000.

Berliner, Brett. *Ambivalent Desire: The Exotic Other in Jazz-Age France.* Amherst: University of Massachusetts Press, 2002.

Berry, Faith. *Before and Beyond Harlem: A Biography of Langston Hughes.* New York: Random House, 1995.

Blake, Jody. *Le Tumulte Noir: Modernist Art and Popular Entertainment in Jazz Age Paris, 1900-1930.* University Park, Pa.: Pennsylvania State University Press, 1999.

Blau, Herbert. *The Audience.* Baltimore: Johns Hopkins University Press, 1990.

Bogle, Donald. *Brown Sugar: Eighty Years of Black Female Superstars.* New York: Da Capo, 1980.

——. *Toms, Coons, Mulattoes, Mammies, and Bucks: An Interpretive History of Blacks in American Films.* New York: Viking, 1973.

Bone, Robert. *The Negro Novel in America.* New Haven, Conn.: Yale University Press, 1958.

——. Preface to *The Negro in American Fiction,* by Sterling Brown. New York: Antheneum, 1968.

Boone, Joseph Allen. *Libidinal Currents: Sexuality and the Shaping of Modernism.* Chicago: University of Chicago Press, 1998.

Borden, Anne. "Heroic 'Hussies' and 'Brilliant Queers': Genderracial Resistance in the Works of Langston Hughes." *African American Review* 28 (1994): 333-45.

Bradford, Perry. *Born with the Blues.* New York: Oak Publications, 1965.

Bravmann, Scott. "Isaac Julien's *Looking for Langston:* Hughes, Biography and Queer(ed) History." *Cultural Studies* 7 (1993): 311-23.

——. *Queer Fictions of the Past: History, Culture, and Difference.* Cambridge: Cambridge University Press, 1997.

Brawley, Benjamin. *Negro Genius.* New York: Dodd, Mead, 1940.

Braxton, Joanne M. *Black Women Writing Autobiography: A Tradition within a Tradition.* Philadelphia: Temple University Press, 1989.

Brecht, Bertolt. "On the Use of Music in an Epic Theatre." In *Brecht on Theatre: The Development of an Aesthetic,* ed. John Willett, 84-90. New York: Hill and Wang, 1957.

Brickhouse, Anna. "Nella Larsen and the Intertextual Geography of *Quicksand.*" *African American Review* 35 (2001): 533-60.

Bricktop [Ada Smith Ducongè]. *Bricktop.* With James Haskins. New York: Atheneum, 1983.

Brody, Jennifer DeVere. *Impossible Purities: Blackness, Femininity, and Victorian Culture.* Durham, N.C.: Duke University Press, 1998.

——. *Punctuation: Art, Politics, and Play.* Durham, N.C.: Duke University Press, 2008.

——. "Queering Racial Reproduction: 'Unnatural Acts' in Angelina Weld Grimké's 'The Closing Door.'" *Text and Performance Quarterly* 23 (2003): 205-23.

Brooks, Daphne A. *Bodies in Dissent: Spectacular Performances of Race and Freedom, 1850-1910.* Durham, N.C.: Duke University Press, 2006.

Brown, Norman O. *Closing Time.* New York: Random House, 1973.

Brown, Sterling. *The Negro in American Fiction.* New York: Antheneum, 1978.

——. "Negro Characters as Seen by White Authors." *Callaloo* 14/15 (1982): 55–89. Originally published in *Journal of Negro Education* 2 (1933): 179–203.

Bruss, Elizabeth. *Autobiographical Acts: The Changing Situation of a Literary Genre.* Baltimore: Johns Hopkins University Press, 1976.

Bullough, Vern L. "The Development of Sexology in the USA in the Early Twentieth Century." In *Sexual Knowledge, Sexual Science: The History of Attitudes to Sexuality,* ed. Roy Porter and Mikulas Teich, 303–22. Cambridge: Cambridge University Press, 1994.

Bulmer, Martin. *The Chicago School of Sociology: Institutionalization, Diversity, and the Rise of Sociological Research.* Chicago: University of Chicago Press, 1984.

Burrows, Edwin G., and Mike Wallace. *Gotham: A History of New York City to 1898.* New York: Oxford University Press, 1999.

Butt, Gavin. *Between You and Me: Queer Disclosures in the New York Art World, 1948–1963.* Durham, N.C.: Duke University Press, 2005.

Butterfield, Stephen. *Black Autobiography in America.* Amherst: University of Massachusetts Press, 1974.

Calloway, Cab. *Of Minnie the Moocher and Me.* With Bryant Rollins. New York: Thomas Y. Crowell, 1976.

Carby, Hazel V. *Cultures in Babylon: Black Britain and African America.* New York: Verso, 1999.

——. "Policing the Black Woman's Body in an Urban Context." In *Cultures in Babylon: Black Britain and African America,* 22–39. New York: Verso, 1999.

——. *Race Men.* Cambridge, Mass.: Harvard University Press, 1998.

——. *Reconstructing Womanhood: The Emergence of the Afro-American Woman Novelist.* New York: Oxford, 1987.

——. "The Sexual Politics of Women's Blues." In *Cultures in Babylon: Black Britain and African America,* 7–21. New York: Verso, 1999.

Carlson, Marvin. *Places of Performance: The Semiotics of Theatre Architecture.* Ithaca, N.Y.: Cornell University Press, 1989.

Caroll, Anne Elizabeth. *Word, Image, and the New Negro: Representation and Identity in the Harlem Renaissance.* Bloomington: Indiana University Press, 2007.

Carr, Brian, and Tova Cooper. "Zora Neale Hurston and Modernism at the Critical Limit." *Modern Fiction Studies* 48 (2002): 293–94.

Castle, Charles. *The Folies Bergère.* New York: Franklin Watts, 1985.

Cate, Phillip Dennis, and Mary Shaw, eds. *The Spirit of Montmartre: Cabarets, Humor, and the Avant-Garde, 1875–1905.* New Brunswick, N.J.: Rutgers University Press, 1996.

Cavan, Sherri. *Liquor License: An Ethnography of Bar Behavior.* Chicago: Aldine, 1966.

Chandler, James, Arnold Davidson, and Harry Hartoonian, eds. *Questions of Evidence: Proof, Practice, and Persuasion across the Disciplines.* Chicago: University of Chicago Press, 1991.

Charters, Samuel B., and Leonard Kunstadt. *Jazz: A History of the New York Scene.* Garden City, N.Y.: Doubleday, 1962.

Chaudhuri, Una. *Staging Place: The Geography of Modern Drama.* Ann Arbor: University of Michigan Press, 1997.

Chauncey, George. *Gay New York: Gender, Urban Culture, and the Making of the Gay Male World, 1890–1940.* New York: Basic, 1994.

Cheng, Meiling. *In Other Los Angeleses: Multicentric Performance Art.* Berkeley and Los Angeles: University of California Press, 2002.

Chevigny, Paul. *Gigs: Jazz and the Cabaret Laws in New York City.* New York: Routledge, 1991.

Chude-Sokei, Louis. *The Last "Darky": Bert Williams, Black-on-Black Minstrelsy, and the African Diaspora.* Durham, N.C.: Duke University Press, 2005.

Churchill, Suzanne W. "Outing T. S. Eliot." *Criticism* 47 (2005): 7–30.

Clement, Elizabeth. *Love for Sale: Courting, Treating and Prostitution in New York City, 1900–1945.* Chapel Hill: University of North Carolina Press, 2006.

Cobb, Michael. "Insolent Racing, Rough Narrative: The Harlem Renaissance's Impolite Queers." *Callaloo* 23 (2000): 328–51.

Coles, Robert A., and Diane Isaacs. "Primitivism as a Therapeutic Pursuit: Notes toward a Reassessment of Harlem Renaissance Literature." In *The Harlem Renaissance: Revaluations,* ed. Armritjit Singh, William S. Shiver, and Stanley Brodwin, 3–12. New York: Garland, 1989.

Conquergood, Dwight. "Beyond the Text: Toward a Performative Cultural Politics." In *The Future of Performance Studies: Visions and Revisions,* ed. Sheron J. Dailey, 25–36. Annandale, Va.: NCA Publications, 1998.

Cooke, Michael G. *Afro-American Literature in the Twentieth Century: The Achievement of Intimacy.* New Haven, Conn.: Yale University Press, 1986.

Cooper, Wayne F. *Claude McKay: Rebel Sojourner in the Harlem Renaissance.* Baton Rouge: Louisiana State University Press, 1987.

Coser, Lewis. "American Trends." In *A History of Sociological Analysis,* ed. Thomas Bottomore and Robert Nesbit, 283–321. New York: Macmillan, 1981.

Cosgrove, Dennis. "Introduction: Mapping Meaning." In *Mappings,* ed. Dennis Cosgrove, 1–23. London: Reaktion Books.

Cruse, Harold. *The Crisis of the Negro Intellectual: A Historical Analysis of the Failure of Black Leadership.* New York: Quill, 1967.

Cullen, Countee. "Our Book Shelf: Poet on Poet." *Opportunity* 4 (February 1926): 73–74.

Cvetkovich, Ann. *An Archive of Feelings: Trauma, Sexuality, and Lesbian Public Cultures.* Durham, N.C.: Duke University Press, 2003.

Dace, Tish, ed. *Langston Hughes: The Contemporary Reviews.* Cambridge: Cambridge University Press, 1997.

Dalton, Karen C. C., and Henry Louis Gates Jr. "Josephine Baker and Paul Colin: African American Dance Seen through Parisian Eyes." *Critical Inquiry* 24 (1998): 903–34.

Davis, Allison. "Our Negro 'Intellectuals.'" *Crisis* 35 (August 1928): 268–69, 284–86.

Davis, Angela Y. *Blues Legacies and Black Feminism: Gertrude "Ma" Rainey, Bessie Smith, and Billie Holliday.* New York: Vintage, 1998.

de Certeau, Michel. *The Practice of Everyday Life.* Translated by Steven Rendall. Berkeley and Los Angeles: University of California Press, 1984.

de Jongh, James. "The Poet Speaks of Places: A Close Reading of Langston Hughes's Literary Use of Place." In *A Historical Guide to Langston Hughes,* ed. Steven C. Tracy, 65–84. Oxford: Oxford University Press, 2004.

———. *Vicious Modernism: Black Harlem and the Literary Imagination.* New York: Cambridge University Press, 1990.

Delgado, Celeste Fraser, and José Esteban Muñoz, eds. *Everynight Life: Culture and Dance in Latin/o America.* Durham, N.C.: Duke University Press, 1997.

Denning, Michael. *The Cultural Front: The Laboring of American Culture in the Twentieth Century.* New York: Verso, 1996.

Diamond, Elin. *Unmaking Mimesis: Essays on Feminism and Theatre.* New York: Routledge, 1997.

Dinshaw, Carolyn. *Getting Medieval: Sexualities and Communities, Pre- and Postmodern.* Durham, N.C.: Duke University Press, 1999.

Donovan, Brian. *White Slave Crusades: Race, Gender, and Anti-vice Activism, 1887–1917.* Champaign: University of Illinois Press, 2006.

Dowling, Robert M. "A Marginal Man in Black Bohemia: James Weldon Johnson in the New York Tenderloin." In *Post-Bellum, Pre-Harlem: African American Literature and Culture, 1877–1919,* ed. Barbara McCaskill and Caroline Gebhard, 124–30. New York: New York University Press, 2006.

Doyle, Jennifer. *Sex Objects: Art and the Dialectics of Desire.* Minneapolis: University of Minnesota Press, 2006.

Du Bois, W. E. B. "Books." *Crisis* 33 (December 1926): 81–82.

———. "The Browsing Reader: Two Novels." *Crisis* 35 (June 1928): 202.

———. "The Criteria of Negro Art." *Crisis* 32 (October 1926): 290–97. Reprinted in *Within the Circle: An Anthology of African American Literary Criticism from the Harlem Renaissance to the Present,* ed. Angelyn Mitchell, 60–68. Durham, N.C.: Duke University Press, 1994.

———. "The Negro American Family." In *W. E. B. Du Bois on Sociology and the Black Community,* ed. Dan S. Green and Edwin D. Driver, 199–213. Chicago: University of Chicago Press, 1978.

———. *The Philadelphia Negro: A Social Study.* New York: Schocken, 1899.

———. "The Problem of Amusement." In *W. E. B. Du Bois on Sociology and the Black Community,* ed. Dan S. Green and Edwin D. Driver, 226–37. Chicago: University of Chicago Press, 1978.

———. *The Souls of Black Folk.* In *Writings: The Suppression of the African Slave-Trade, the Souls of Black Folk, Dusk of Dawn, Essays and Articles,* ed. Nathan Huggins, 357–547. New York: Library of America, 1986.

———. "The Talented Tenth." In *Writings: The Suppression of the African Slave-Trade, the Souls of Black Folk, Dusk of Dawn, Essays and Articles,* ed. Nathan Huggins, 842–61. New York: Library of America, 1986.

Duggan, Lisa. *Sapphic Slashers: Sex, Violence, and American Modernity.* Durham, N.C.: Duke University Press, 2000.

DuPlessis, Rachel Blau. *Genders, Races, and Religious Cultures in Modern American Poetry, 1908–1934.* Cambridge: Cambridge University Press, 2001.

Durante, Jimmy, and Jack Kofoed. *Nightclubs.* New York: Knopf, 1931.

Dyer, Richard. "The Colour of Entertainment." In *Musicals: Hollywood and Beyond,* ed. Bill Marshall and Robyn Stillwell, 23–30. Exeter: Intellect, 2000.

———. *Heavenly Bodies: Film Stars and Society.* 2nd ed. New York: Routledge, 2004.

———. *Stars.* New ed. London, British Film Institute, 1998.

Edelman, Lee. *No Future: Queer Theory and the Death Drive.* Durham, N.C.: Duke University Press, 2004.

Edwards, Brent Hayes. *The Practice of Diaspora: Literature, Translation, and the Rise of Black Internationalism.* Cambridge, Mass.: Harvard University Press, 2004.

Edwards, Justin. *Exotic Journeys: Exploring the Erotics of U.S. Travel Literature, 1840–1930.* Hanover: University of New Hampshire Press, 2001.

Ellington, Edward Kennedy. Foreword to *Music on My Mind: The Memoirs of an American Pianist,* by Willie "the Lion" Smith, with George Hoefer. New York: Da Capo, 1975.

———. *Music Is My Mistress.* New York: Da Capo, 1973.

Ellington, Mercer, with Stanley Dance. *Duke Ellington in Person: An Intimate Memoir.* Boston: Houghton Mifflin, 1978.

Ellison, Ralph. "As the Spirit Moves Mahalia." In *The Collected Essays of Ralph Ellison,* ed. John F. Callahan, 250–55. New York: Modern Library of America, 1995.

English, Daylanne K. *Unnatural Selections: Eugenics in American Modernism and the Harlem Renaissance.* Chapel Hill: University of North Carolina Press, 2004.

Erenberg, Lewis. *Steppin' Out: New York Nightlife and the Transformation of American Culture, 1890–1930.* Chicago: University of Chicago Press, 1981.

Esteve, Mary. "Nella Larsen's 'Moving Mosaic': Harlem, Crowds, and Anonymity." *American Literary History* 9 (1997): 268–86.

Evans, Nicholas M. *Writing Jazz: Race Nationalism, and Modern Culture in the 1920s.* New York: Garland, 2000.

Fabre, Michel. *From Harlem to Paris: Black American Writers in France, 1840–1980.* Champaign: University of Illinois Press, 1991.

———. "The Harlem Renaissance Abroad: French Critics and the New Negro Literary Move-ment." In *Temples for Tomorrow: Looking Back at the Harlem Renaissance,* ed. Genevieve Fabre and Michel Feith, 314–32. Bloomington: Indiana University Press, 2001.

Faderman, Lillian, and Stuart Timmons. *Gay L.A.: A History of Sexual Outlaws, Power Politics, and Lipstick Lesbians.* New York: Basic, 2006.

Fanon, Frantz. *Black Skin, White Masks.* Translated by Charles Lam Markmann. New York: Grove, 1967.

Favor, J. Martin. *Authentic Blackness: The Folk in the New Negro Renaissance.* Durham, N.C.: Duke University Press, 1999.

Federal Writers' Project. "The Harlems." In *The WPA Guide to New York City: The Federal Writers' Project Guide to 1930s New York,* 253–68. New York: Pantheon, 1982.

Ferguson, Roderick. *Aberrations in Black: Toward a Queer of Color Critique.* Minneapolis: University of Minnesota Press, 2004.

Fisher, Rudolph. "The Caucasian Storms Harlem." *American Mercury* 11 (1927): 393–98.

Floyd, Samuel, ed. *Black Music in the Harlem Renaissance: A Collection of Essays.* New York: Greenwood, 1990.

Flynn, Thomas. "The Role of the Image in Sartre's Aesthetic." *Journal of Aesthetics and Art Criticism* 33 (1975): 431–42.

Foley, Barbara. "Jean Toomer's Washington and the Politics of Class: From 'Blue Veins' to Seventh-street Rebels." *Modern Fiction Studies* 42 (1996): 289–321.

Foucault, Michel. *Discipline and Punish: The Birth of the Prison.* New York: Pantheon, 1977.

———. *The History of Sexuality,* vol. 1: *An Introduction.* New York: Vintage, 1978.

———. "Two Lectures." In *Power/Knowledge: Selected Interviews and Other Writings, 1972–1977,* ed. Colin Gordon, 78–108. New York: Pantheon, 1980.

Freccero, Carla. *Queer/Early/Modern.* Durham, N.C.: Duke University Press, 2006.

Freeman, Elizabeth. "Packing History, Count(er)ing Generations." *New Literary History* 31 (2000): 727–44.

———. "Time Binds; or, Erotohistoriography." *Social Text* 84–85, vol. 23 (2005), 59.

Gaines, Kevin Kelly. *Uplifting the Race: Black Leadership, Politics, and Culture in the Twentieth Century.* Chapel Hill: University of North Carolina Press, 1996.

Gaither, Renoir. "The Moment of Revision: A Reappraisal of Wallace Thurman's Aesthetics in *The Blacker the Berry* and *Infants of the Spring.*" *College Language Association Journal* 37 (1993): 81–93.

Garber, Eric. "A Spectacle in Color: The Lesbian and Gay Subculture of Jazz Age Harlem." In *Hidden from History: Reclaiming the Gay and Lesbian Past,* ed. Martin Duberman, Martha Vicinus, and George Chauncey Jr., 318–31. New York: Penguin, 1989.

Gates, Henry Louis, Jr. "The Black Man's Burden." In *Fear of a Queer Planet: Queer Social Theory,* ed. Michael Warner, 230–38. Minneapolis: University of Minnesota Press, 1993.

———. "Harlem on Our Minds." *Critical Inquiry* 24 (1997): 1–12.

Gates, Henry Louis, Jr., and Gene Andrew Jarrett, eds. *The New Negro: Readings on Race, Representation, and African American Culture, 1892–1938.* Princeton, N.J.: Princeton University Press, 2007.

Gates, Henry Louis, Jr., and Nellie Y. McKay, eds. *Norton Anthology of African American Literature.* New York: W. W. Norton, 1996.

Gavin, James. *Intimate Nights: The Golden Age of New York Cabaret.* New York: Grove Weidenfeld, 1991.

Gay, Jeffrey. "Essence and the Mulatto Traveler: Europe as Embodiment in Nella Larsen's *Quicksand.*" *Novel: A Forum on Fiction* 27 (1994): 257–70.

Gendron, Bernard. *Between Montmartre and the Mudd Club: Popular Music and the Avant-Garde.* Chicago: University of Chicago Press, 2002.

George-Graves, Nadine. *Royalty of Negro Vaudeville: The Whitman Sisters and the Negotiation of Race, Gender and Class in African American Theatre, 1900-1940*. New York: St. Martin's, 2000.

Gilfoyle, Timothy. *City of Eros: New York City, Prostitution, and the Commercialization of Sex, 1790-1920*. New York: W. W. Norton, 1992.

Gilroy, Paul. *The Black Atlantic: Modernity and Double Consciousness*. Cambridge, Mass.: Harvard University Press, 1993.

Glave, Thomas. *Words to Our Now: Imagination and Dissent*. Minneapolis: University of Minnesota Press, 2007.

Glazener, Nancy. *Reading for Realism: The History of a U.S. Literary Institution, 1850-1910*. Durham, N.C.: Duke University Press, 1997.

Goffman, Erving. *Behavior in Public Places: Notes on the Social Organization of Gatherings*. New York: Free Press, 1963.

Goldberg, Jonathan, and Madhavi Menon. "Queering History." *PMLA* 120 (2005): 1608-17.

Gordon, Rae Beth. *Why the French Love Jerry Lewis: From Cabaret to Early Cinema*. Stanford, Calif.: Stanford University Press, 2001.

Gottschild, Brenda Dixon. *Waltzing in the Dark: African American Vaudeville and Race Relations in the Swing Era*. New York: Palgrave Macmillan, 1999.

Green, Dan S., and Edwin D. Driver, eds. *W. E. B. Du Bois on Sociology and the Black Community*. Chicago: University of Chicago Press, 1978.

Griffin, Farah Jasmine. *In Search of Billie Holiday: If You Can't Be Free, Be a Mystery*. New York: Ballantine, 2001.

——. "When Malindy Sings: A Meditation on Black Women's Vocality." In *Uptown Conversations: The New Jazz Studies*, ed. Robert G. O'Meally, Brent Hayes Edwards, and Farah Jasmine Griffin, 102-25. New York: Columbia University Press, 2004.

——. *"Who Set You Flowin'?" The African American Migration Narrative*. New York: Oxford University Press, 1996.

Halberstam, Judith. *In a Queer Time and Place: Transgender Bodies, Subcultural Lives*. New York: New York University Press, 2004.

Hale, Robert C. "Revolution and the 'Low-Down Folk': Poetic Strategies for the Masses in William Wordsworth's *Lyrical Ballads* and Langston Hughes's *Fine Clothes to the Jew*." *Langston Hughes Review* 13 (1995): 54-67.

Hall, Stuart, and Paddy Whannel. *The Popular Arts*. New York: Pantheon, 1965.

Halperin, David. *How to Do the History of Homosexuality*. Chicago: University of Chicago Press, 2002.

Harper, Phillip Brian. "The Evidence of Felt Intuition: Minority Experience, Everyday Life, and Critical Speculative Knowledge." *GLQ* 6 (2000): 641-57.

Harrison, Daphne Duval. *Black Pearls: Blues Queens of the 1920s*. New Brunswick: Rutgers University Press, 1988.

Harrison, Hubert H. "Cabaret School of Negro Writers Do Not Represent One-Tenth of Race." *Pittsburgh Courier*, May 28, 1927, 3.

Hartman, Saidiya. *Scenes of Subjection: Terror, Slavery and Self-Making in Nineteenth Century America*. New York: Oxford University Press, 1997.

Haskins, James. *The Cotton Club*. New York: Random House, 1977.

——. *Lena: A Personal and Professional Biography of Lena Horne*. With Kathleen Benson. New York: Stein and Day, 1984.

Hasse, John Edward. *Beyond Category: The Life and Genius of Duke Ellington*. New York: Simon & Schuster, 1993.

Hathaway, Heather. *Caribbean Waves: Relocating Claude McKay and Paule Marshall*. Bloomington: Indiana University Press, 1999.

Hazzard-Gordon, Katrina. *Jookin': The Rise of Social Dance Formations in African-American Culture*. Philadelphia: Temple University Press, 1992.

Helbling, Mark. *The Harlem Renaissance: The One and the Many*. Westport, Conn.: Greenwood, 1999.

Hemphill, Essex. "Undressing Icons." In *Brother to Brother: New Writings by Black Gay Men*, ed. Essex Hemphill and Joseph Beam, 181–83. Boston: Alyson, 1991.

———. *"Looking for Langston:* An Interview with Isaac Julien." In *Brother to Brother: New Writings by Black Gay Men*, ed. Essex Hemphill and Joseph Beam, 174–83. Boston: Alyson, 1991.

Hemphill, Essex, and Joseph Beam, eds. *Brother to Brother: New Writings by Black Gay Men*. Boston: Alyson, 1991.

Herring, Scott. *Queering the Underworld: Slumming, Literature, and the Undoing of Lesbian and Gay History*. Chicago: University of Chicago Press, 2007.

Higginbotham, Evelyn Brooks. *Righteous Discontent: The Women's Movement in the Black Baptist Church, 1880–1920*. Cambridge, Mass.: Harvard University Press, 1993.

Holcomb, Gary E. "Diaspora Cruises: Queer Black Proletarianism in Claude McKay's *A Long Way from Home*." *Modern Fiction Studies* 49 (Winter 2003): 714–45.

hooks, bell. "Seductive Sexualities: Representing Blackness in Poetry and on Screen." In *Yearning: Race, Gender and Cultural Politics*, 193–202. Boston: South End Press, 1990.

———. "Third World Diva Girls." In *Yearning: Race, Gender, and Cultural Politics*, 89–102. Boston: South End Press, 1990.

Horne, Lena. *In Person—Lena Horne*. As told to Helen Arstein and Carlton Moss. New York: Greenberg, 1950.

———. *Lena*. With Richard Schickel. Garden City, N.Y.: Doubleday, 1965.

Hostetler, Ann E. "The Aesthetics of Race and Gender in Nella Larsen's *Quicksand*." *PMLA* 105 (1990): 35–46.

Huggins, Nathan. *The Harlem Renaissance*. New York: Oxford University Press, 1971.

Hughes, Langston. *The Big Sea*. New York: Hill and Wang, 1940.

———. "Blessed Assurance." In *Short Stories of Langston Hughes*. ed. Akiba Sullivan Harper, 231–36. New York: Hill and Wang, 1997.

———. *The Collected Poems of Langston Hughes*. Edited by Arnold Rampersad and David Roessel. New York, Vintage: 1994.

———. *Fine Clothes to the Jew*. New York: Knopf, 1927.

———. "The Negro Artist and the Racial Mountain." In *Within the Circle: An Anthology of African American Literary Criticism from the Harlem Renaissance to the Present*, ed. Angelyn Mitchell, 55–59. Durham, N.C.: Duke University Press, 1994.

———. "Response to 'The Negro in Art: How Shall He Be Portrayed.'" *Crisis* 31 (1926): 278.

———. "Seven People Dancing." Langston Hughes Papers, James Weldon Johnson Collection, Beinecke Rare Book and Manuscript Library, Yale University. Manuscript 3485. n.d.

———. *The Weary Blues*. New York: Knopf, 1926.

Hull, Gloria T. *Color, Sex, and Poetry: Three Women Writers of the Harlem Renaissance*. Bloomington: Indiana University Press, 1987.

Hurewitz, Daniel. *Bohemian Los Angeles and the Making of Modern Politics*. Berkeley and Los Angeles: University of California Press, 2007.

Hurston, Zora Neale. "Characteristics of Negro Expression." In *Within the Circle: An Anthology of African American Literary Criticism from the Harlem Renaissance to the Present*, ed. Angelyn Mitchell, 79–94. Durham, N.C.: Duke University Press, 1994.

———. "How It Feels to Be Colored Me." In *I Love Myself When I Am Laughing, and Then Again When I Am Looking Mean and Impressive: A Zora Neale Hurston Reader*, ed. Alice Walker, 152–55. New York: Feminist Press, 1979.

Hutchinson, George. *The Harlem Renaissance in Black and White*. Cambridge, Mass.: Harvard University Press, 1995.

———. *In Search of Nella Larsen: A Biography of the Color Line*. Cambridge: Harvard University Press, 2006.

———. Introd. to *The Cambridge Companion to the Harlem Renaissance*, ed. George Hutchinson. Cambridge: Cambridge University Press, 2007.

———. "Subject to Disappearance: Interracial Identity in Nella Larsen's *Quicksand*." In *Temples for Tomorrow: Looking Back at the Harlem Renaissance*, ed. Genevieve Fabre and Michel Feith, 177–92. Bloomington: Indiana University Press, 2001.

Jackson, John L., Jr. *Real Black: Adventures in Racial Sincerity*. Chicago: University of Chicago Press, 2005.

Jameson, Frederic. *Brecht and Method*. London: Verso, 2000.

———. *The Political Unconscious: Narrative as a Socially Symbolic Act*. Ithaca, N.Y.: Cornell University Press, 1981.

Jarraway, David. *Going the Distance: Dissident Subjectivity in Modernist American Literature*. Baton Rouge: Louisiana State University Press, 2003.

———. "Tales of the City: Marginality, Community, and the Problem of (Gay) Identity in Wallace Thurman's 'Harlem' Fiction." *College English* 65 (2002): 36–52.

Jarrett, Gene Andrew. "Racial Uplift and the Politics of African American Fiction." In *A Concise Companion to American Fiction, 1900–1950*, ed. Peter Stoneley and Cindy Weinstein, 205–27. Maden, Mass.: Blackwell, 2008.

Jelavich, Peter. *Berlin Cabaret*. Cambridge, Mass.: Harvard University Press, 1993.

Jemie, Onwuchekwa. *Langston Hughes: An Introduction to the Poetry*. New York: Columbia University Press, 1973.

Johnson, Barbara. *A World of Difference*. Baltimore: Johns Hopkins University Press, 1987.

Johnson, E. Patrick. *Appropriating Blackness: Performance and the Politics of Authenticity*. Durham, N.C.: Duke University Press, 2003.

Johnson, E. Patrick, and Mae Henderson. *Black Queer Studies: A Critical Reader*. Durham, N.C.: Duke University Press, 2005.

Johnson, James Weldon. *Along This Way: The Autobiography of James Weldon Johnson*. 1933. New York: Penguin, 1990.

———. *The Autobiography of an Ex-Colored Man*. New York: Hill and Wang, 1960.

———. *Black Manhattan*. New York: Antheneum, 1977.

———. Preface to *The Book of American Negro Poetry*, ed. James Weldon Johnson. New York: Harcourt, Brace, and World, 1931.

Jones, William H. *Recreation and Amusement among Negroes in Washington, D.C.: A Sociological Analysis of the Negro in an Urban Environment*. Washington, D.C.: Howard University Press, 1927. Reprint, Westport, Conn.: Negro University Press, 1970. Page references are to the 1970 edition.

Joseph, Miranda. *Against the Romance of Community*. Minneapolis: University of Minneapolis Press, 2002.

Kaplan, Amy. *The Social Construction of American Realism*. Chicago: University of Chicago Press, 1988.

Kaplan, Carla. *Zora Neale Hurston: A Life in Letters*. New York: Doubleday, 2002.

Katz, Jonathan Ned. *Gay American History: Lesbian and Gay Men in the U.S.A.: A Documentary History*. New York: Meridian, 1976.

Katz, Michael B., and Thomas J. Sugrue, eds. *W. E. B. Du Bois, Race, and the City:* The Philadelphia Negro *and Its Legacy*. Philadelphia: University of Pennsylvania Press, 1998.

Keire, Mara L. "The Committee of Fourteen and Saloon Reform in New York City, 1905–1920." *Business and Economic History* 26 (1997): 573–83.

Kelley, Robin D. G. *Freedom Dreams: The Black Radical Imagination*. Boston: Beacon, 2002.

———. *Race Rebels: Culture, Politics, and the Black Working Class*. New York: Free Press, 1994.

Kellner, Bruce. "Langston Hughes's *Nigger Heaven* Blues." *Langston Hughes Review* 11 (1992): 21–27.

Kenan, Randall. *Walking on Water: Black American Lives at the Turn of the Twenty-First Century.* New York: Vintage, 2000.

Kirby, Michael. "Happenings: An Introduction." In *Happenings and Other Acts,* ed. Mariellen R. Sanford, 1–28. New York: Routledge, 1995.

Koestenbaum, Wayne. *The Queen's Throat: Opera, Homosexuality, and the Mystery of Desire.* New York: Poseidon, 1993.

Krasner, David. *A Beautiful Pageant: African American Theatre, Drama, and Performance in the Harlem Renaissance, 1910–1927.* New York: Palgrave Macmillan, 2003.

———. *Resistance, Parody, and Double Consciousness in African American Theatre, 1895–1910.* New York: St. Martin's, 1997.

Kun, Josh. *Audiotopias: Music, Race, and America.* Berkeley and Los Angeles: University of California Press, 2005.

Lareau, Alan. *The Wild Stage: Literary Cabarets of the Weimar Republic.* Columbia, S.C.: Camden House, 1995.

Larsen, Nella. *Quicksand.* In *The Complete Fiction of Nella Larsen: Passing, Quicksand, and the Stories,* ed. Charles R. Larson, 29–162. New York: Anchor, 2001.

Lasky, Jesse. *I Blow My Own Horn.* With Don Weldon. Garden City, N.Y.: Doubleday, 1957.

Latimer, Richard. "History of Negro Saloons." Federal Writers' Program, New York. Reel 2. Schomburg Center for Research in Black Culture, New York Public Library.

Lefebvre, Henri. *Everyday Life in the Modern World.* Translated by Sacha Rabinovitch. London: Allen Lane, 1971.

Leonard, Zoe, and Cheryl Dunye. *The Fae Richards Photo Archive.* San Francisco: Artspace, 1996.

LeSeur, Geta. "Claude McKay's Marxism." In *The Harlem Renaissance: Revaluations,* ed. Amritjit Singh, William S. Shiver, and Stanley Brodwin, 219–31. New York: Garland, 1989.

Levine, Lawrence. *Highbrow/Lowbrow: The Emergence of Cultural Hierarchy in America.* Cambridge, Mass.: Harvard University Press, 1988.

Lewis, David Levering, ed. *The Portable Harlem Renaissance Reader.* New York: Viking, 1974.

———. *W. E. B. Du Bois: Biography of a Race, 1869–1919.* New York: Henry Holt, 1993.

———. *When Harlem Was in Vogue.* New York: Penguin, 1996.

Löbberman, Dorothea. "Harlem as a Memory Place: Reconstructing the Harlem Renaissance in Space." In *Temples for Tomorrow: Looking Back at the Harlem Renaissance,* ed. Geneviève Fabre and Michel Feith, 210–21. Bloomington: Indiana University Press, 2001.

Lock, Graham. *Blutopia: Visions of the Future and Revisions of the Past in the Work of Sun Ra, Duke Ellington, and Anthony Braxton.* Durham, N.C.: Duke University Press, 1999.

Lorde, Audre. *Zami: A New Spelling of My Name.* Trumansburg, N.Y.: Crossing Press, 1982.

Lowe, Lisa, and David Lloyd. Introd. to *The Politics of Culture in the Shadow of Capital,* ed. Lisa Lowe and David Lloyd, 1–32. Durham, N.C.: Duke University Press, 1997.

Lumet-Buckley, Gail. *The Hornes: An American Family.* New York: Knopf, 1986.

Mackey, Thomas. *Pursuing Johns: Criminal Law Reform, Defending Character, and New York City's Committee of Fourteen, 1920–1930.* Columbus: Ohio State University Press, 2005.

Maiwald, Michael. "Race, Capitalism, and the Third-Sex Ideal: Claude McKay's *Home to Harlem* and the Legacy of Edward Carpenter." *Modern Fiction Studies* 48 (2002): 825–57.

Malone, Jacqui. *Steppin' on the Blues: The Visible Rhythms of African American Dance.* Urbana: University of Illinois Press, 1996.

Marx, Karl. *The Eighteenth Brumaire of Louis Bonaparte.* New York: International Publishers, 1963.

Maxwell, William J. *New Negro, Old Left: African-American Writing and Communism between the Wars.* New York: Columbia University Press, 1999.

McAuley, Gay. *Space in Performance: Making Meaning in the Theatre.* Ann Arbor: University of Michigan Press, 2000.

McBride, Dwight. "Straight Black Studies: On African American Studies, James Baldwin, and Black Queer Studies." In E. Patrick Johnson and Mae Henderson, eds. *Black Queer Studies: A Critical Reader.* Durham: Duke University Press, 2005. 68–89.

McCoy, Beth. "Inspectin' and Collecting: The Scene of Carl Van Vechten." *Genders* 28 (1998). http://www.genders.org/g28/g28_inspectin.txt.

McDowell, Deborah. *"The Changing Same": Black Women's Literature, Criticism, and Theory.* Bloomington, Indiana University Press, 1995.

McKay, Claude. *Home to Harlem.* Boston: Northeastern University Press, 1987.

———. *A Long Way from Home.* New York: Arno, 1969.

———. *The Negroes in America.* Edited by A. L. McLeod. Port Washington, N.Y.: Kennikat, 1979.

———. "A Negro Extravaganza." *Liberator* 4 (December 1921), 24–26. Reprinted in *The Passion of Claude McKay: Selected Poetry and Prose, 1912–1948,* ed. Wayne F. Cooper, 62–65. New York: Schocken, 1973. Page references are to the 1973 edition.

McNamara, Brooks. *The New York Concert Saloon: The Devil's Own Nights.* New York: Cambridge University Press, 2002.

Mercer, Kobena. "Traveling Theory: The Cultural Politics of Race and Representation." Interview by Lorraine Kenny. *Afterimage* 18 (1990): 7–9.

Meyer, Richard. "At Home in Marginal Domains." *Documents* 18 (2000): 19–32.

Mitchell, Michele. *Righteous Propagation: African Americans and the Politics of Racial Destiny after Reconstruction.* Chapel Hill: University of North Carolina Press, 2004.

Moon, Michael. *Disseminating Whitman: Revision and Corporeality in Leaves of Grass.* Cambridge, Mass.: Harvard University Press, 1991.

Moore, Jacqueline M. *Booker T. Washington, W. E. B. Du Bois, and the Struggle for Racial Uplift.* Wilmington, Del.: Scholarly Resources, 2003.

———. *Leading the Race: The Transformation of the Black Elite in the Nation's Capital, 1880–1920.* Charlottesville: University Press of Virginia, 1999.

Moore, Robin. *Nationalizing Blackness: Afrocubanismo and Artistic Revolution in Havana, 1920–1940.* Pittsburg: University of Pittsburg Press, 1997.

Morrison, Toni. "The Site of Memory." In *Inventing the Truth: The Art and Craft of Memoir,* ed. William Zinsser, 183–200. New York: Mariner, 1998.

Morse, Carl, and Joan Larkin, eds. *Gay and Lesbian Poetry in Our Time.* New York: St. Martin's, 1989.

Moses, William Jeremiah. *The Golden Age of Black Nationalism, 1850–1925.* New York: Oxford University Press, 1988.

Mostern, Kenneth. *Autobiography and Black Identity Politics: Racialization in Twentieth-Century America.* New York: Cambridge University Press, 1999.

Moten, Fred. *In the Break: The Aesthetics of the Black Radical Tradition.* Minneapolis: University of Minnesota Press, 2003.

———. "Uplift and Criminality." In *Next to the Color Line: Gender, Sexuality, and W. E. B. Du Bois,* ed. Susan Gillman and Alys Eve Weinbaum, 317–49. Minneapolis: University of Minnesota Press, 2007.

Mumford, Kevin. *Interzones: Black/White Sex Districts in Chicago and New York in the Early Twentieth Century.* New York: Columbia University Press, 1997.

Muñoz, José Esteban. *Disidentifications: Queers of Color and the Performance of Politics.* Minneapolis: University of Minnesota Press, 1999.

———. "Ephemera as Evidence: Introductory Notes to Queer Acts." In *Women & Performance* 8 (1996): 5–16.

Murdy, Anne-Elizabeth. *Teach the Nation: Public School, Racial Uplift, and Women's Writing in the 1890s.* New York: Routledge, 2003.

Murray, Albert. *Stomping the Blues.* New York: Da Capo, 1976.

Nadell, Martha Jane. *Enter the New Negroes: Images of Race in American Culture.* Cambridge, Mass.: Harvard University Press, 2004.

Nealon, Christopher. *Foundlings: Lesbian and Gay Emotional History before Stonewall.* Durham, N.C.: Duke University Press, 2001.

Negt, Oskar, and Alexander Kluge. *Public Sphere and Experience: Toward an Analysis of the Bourgeois and Proletarian Public Sphere.* Translated by Miriam Hansen. Minneapolis: University of Minnesota Press, 1993.

Nero, Charles I. "Re/Membering Langston: Homophobic Textuality and Arnold Rampersad's *Life of Langston Hughes.*" In *Queer Representations: Reading Lives, Reading Cultures,* ed. Martin Duberman, 188–96. New York: New York University Press, 1997.

Ngai, Sianne. *Ugly Feelings.* Cambridge, Mass.: Harvard University Press, 2005.

North, Michael. *The Dialect of Modernism: Race, Language and Twentieth-Century Literature.* New York: Oxford University Press, 1997.

Ogren, Kathy. "'Jazz Isn't Just Me': Jazz Autobiographies as Performance Personas." In *Jazz in Mind: Essays on the History and Meaning of Jazz,* ed. Reginald T. Buckner and Steven Weiland, 112–27. Detroit: Wayne State University Press, 1991.

———. *The Jazz Revolution: Twenties America and the Meaning of Jazz.* New York: Oxford University Press, 1989.

O'Meally, Robert. *Lady Day: The Many Faces of Billie Holiday.* New York: Arcade, 1991.

Osofsky, Gilbert. *Harlem: The Making of a Ghetto: Negro New York, 1890–1930.* New York: Harper & Row, 1971.

Ottley, Roi, and William Weatherby, eds. *The Negro in New York: An Informal Social History.* Dobbs Ferry, N.Y.: Oceana, 1967.

Peiss, Kathy. "'Charity Girls' and City Pleasures: Historical Notes on Working Class Sexuality, 1880–1920." In *Passion and Power: Sexuality in History,* ed. Kathy Peiss and Christina Simmons, 57–69. With Robert A. Padgug. Philadelphia: Temple University Press, 1989.

———. *Cheap Amusements: Working Women and Leisure in Turn-of-the-Century New York.* Philadelphia: Temple University Press, 1986.

Perpener, John O. *African American Concert Dance: The Harlem Renaissance and Beyond.* Urbana: University of Illinois Press, 2001.

Phillips, Caryl. *Dancing in the Dark.* New York: Knopf, 2006.

Ponce, Martin Joseph. "Langston Hughes's Queer Blues." *Modern Language Quarterly* 66 (2005): 505–37.

Postlewait, Thomas. "Autobiography and Theatre History." In *Interpreting the Theatrical Past: Essays in the Historiography of Performance,* ed. Thomas Postlewait and Bruce A. McConachie, 248–72. Iowa City: University of Iowa Press, 1989.

———. "Writing History Today." *Theatre Survey* 41 (2000): 83–106.

Povinelli, Elizabeth. *The Empire of Love: Toward a Theory of Intimacy, Genealogy, and Carnality.* Durham, N.C.: Duke University Press, 2006.

Powers, Madelon. *Faces along the Bar: Lore and Order in the Workingman's Saloon, 1870–1920.* Chicago: University of Chicago Press, 1999.

Rampersad, Arnold. "Biography, Autobiography, and Afro-American Culture." *Yale Review* 73 (1983): 1–16.

———. "Langston Hughes's *Fine Clothes to the Jew.*" *Callaloo* 26 (1986): 144–48.

———. *The Life of Langston Hughes,* vol. 1, *1902–1941: I, Too, Sing America.* New York: Oxford University Press, 2002.

———. *The Life of Langston Hughes,* vol. 2, *1941–1967: I Dream a World.* New York: Oxford University Press, 2002.

Rearick, Charles. *Pleasure of the Belle Époque: Entertainment and Festivity in Turn-of-the-Century France.* New Haven, Conn.: Yale University Press, 1985.

Regester, Charlene B. "Hazel Scott and Lena Horne: African-American Divas, Feminists, and Political Activists." *Popular Culture Review* 7 (1996): 81-95.

Reid-Pharr, Robert F. *Black Gay Man: Essays.* New York: New York University Press, 2001.

———. "Makes Me Feel Mighty Real: *The Watermelon Woman* and the Critique of Black Visuality." In *F Is for Phony: Fake Documentary and Truth's Undoing,* ed. Alexandra Juhasz and Jesse Lerner, 130-42. Minneapolis: University of Minnesota Press, 2006.

Reimonenq, Alden. "Hughes, Langston (1902-1967)." In *The Gay and Lesbian Literary Heritage: A Reader's Companion to the Writers and Their Works, from Antiquity to the Present,* rev. ed., ed. Claude J. Summers, 349-50. New York: Routledge, 2002.

Riis, Jacob. *How the Other Half Lives: Studies among the Tenements of New York.* Edited and with an introduction by David Leviatin. New York: Bedford/St. Martin's, 1996.

Roach, Joseph. *Cities of the Dead: Circum-Atlantic Performance.* New York: Columbia University Press, 1996.

Robbins, Richard. *Sidelines Activist: Charles S. Johnson and the Struggle for Civil Rights.* Jackson: University Press of Mississippi, 1996.

Robinson, Cedric. *Black Marxism: The Making of the Black Radical Tradition.* Chapel Hill: University of North Carolina Press, 2000.

———. *Black Movements in America.* New York: Routledge, 1997.

Roebuck, Julien, and Wolfgang Reese. *The Rendezvous: A Case Study of an Afterhours Club.* New York: Free Press, 1976.

Roffman, Karin. "Nella Larsen, Librarian at 135th Street." *Modern Fiction Studies* 53 (2007): 752-87.

Rohy, Valerie. "Ahistorical." *GLQ* 12 (2006): 61-83.

Román, David. *Acts of Intervention: Performance, Gay Culture, and AIDS.* Bloomington: Indiana University Press, 1998.

———. *Performance in America: Contemporary U.S. Culture and the Performing Arts.* Durham, N.C.: Duke University Press, 2005.

Ross, Marlon B. *Manning the Race: Reforming Black Men in the Jim Crow Era.* New York: New York University Press, 2004.

Salessi, Jorge. "Medics, Crooks, and Tango Queens: The National Appropriation of a Gay Tango." In *Everynight Life: Culture and Dance in Latin/o America,* ed. Celeste Fraser Delgado and José Esteban Muñoz, 141-74. Durham, N.C.: Duke University Press, 1997.

Sante, Luc. *Low Life: Lures and Snares of Old New York.* New York: Farrar, Strauss, and Giroux, 1991.

Sartre, Jean-Paul. *The Imaginary.* Translated by Jonathan Webber. New York: Routledge, 2004.

Saussure, Ferdinand de. *Course in General Linguistics.* Translated by Wade Baskin. Edited by Charles Bally and Albert Sechehaye. New York: MacGraw-Hill, 1966.

Schneider, Rebecca. "Performance Remains." *Performance Research* 6 (2001): 100-108.

Schomburg, Arthur. "The Negro Digs up His Past." In *The New Negro,* ed. Alain Locke, 231-37. New York: Charles and Boni, 1925.

Schwarz, A. B. Christa. *Gay Voices of the Harlem Renaissance.* Bloomington: Indiana University Press, 2003.

Scott, Daniel. "Harlem Shadows: Re-Evaluating Wallace Thurman's *The Blacker the Berry.*" *MELUS* 29 (2004): 323-339.

Scott, Joan W. "The Evidence of Experience." In *The Lesbian and Gay Studies Reader,* ed. Henry Abelove, David Halperin, and Michele Aina Barale, 397-415. New York: Routledge, 1993.

———. "Fantasy Echo: History and the Construction of Identity." *Critical Inquiry* 27 (2001): 284-304.

Sedgwick, Eve Kosofsky. *The Epistemology of the Closet.* Berkeley and Los Angeles: University of California Press, 1990.

Sedgwick, Eve Kosofsky, and Michael Moon. "Divinity: A Dossier, a Performance Piece, a Little Understood Emotion." In *Tendencies,* edited by Eve Kosofsky Sedgwick, 215–51. Durham, N.C.: Duke University Press, 1993.

Segel, Harold B. *Turn-of-the-Century Cabaret: Paris, Barcelona, Berlin, Munich, Vienna, Cracow, Moscow, St. Petersburg, Zurich.* New York: Columbia University Press, 1987.

Seitler, Dana. "Queer Physiognomies; or, How Many Ways Can We Do the History of Sexuality?" *Criticism* 46 (2004): 71–102.

Senelick, Laurence. *Cabaret Performance,* vol. 1: *Europe, 1890–1920.* New York: Performing Arts Journal, 1989.

———. *Cabaret Performance,* vol. 2: *Europe, 1920–40.* Baltimore: Johns Hopkins University Press, 1993.

———. "Text and Violence: Performance Practices of the Modernist Avant-Garde." In *Contours of the Theatrical Avant-Garde: Performance and Textuality,* ed. James M. Harding, 15–42. Ann Arbor: University of Michigan Press, 2000.

Shack, William. *Harlem in Montmartre: A Paris Jazz Story between the Great Wars.* Berkeley and Los Angeles: University of California Press, 2001.

Shapiro, Nat, and Nat Hentoff, eds. *Hear Me Talkin' to Ya: The Story of Jazz as Told by the Men Who Made It.* Toronto: Rinehart, 1955.

Shaw, Charles G. *Nightlife:* Vanity Fair's *Intimate Guide to New York after Dark.* New York: John Day Company, 1931.

Shaw, Stephanie. *What a Woman Ought to Be and Do: Black Professional Women Workers during the Jim Crow Era.* Chicago: University of Chicago Press, 1996.

Silberman, Seth Clark. "Reading Black Queer Vernacular in the 'Streetgeist and Folklore' of Harlem's Renaissance." In *Public Space, Private Lives: Race, Gender, Class and Citizenship in New York, 1890–1929,* ed. William Boelhower and Anna Scacchi, 129–52. Amsterdam: VU University Press, 2004.

Silverman, Debra B. "Nella Larsen's *Quicksand:* Untangling the Webs of Exoticism." *African American Review* 27 (1993): 599–614.

Singh, Amritjit. "Black-White Symbiosis: Another Look at the Literary History of the 1920s." In *Harlem Renaissance Re-examined,* rev. and exp. ed., ed. Victor A. Kramer and Robert A. Russ, 65–74. Troy, N.Y.: Whitson, 1997.

Smalls, James. *The Homoerotic Photography of Carl Van Vechten: Public Face, Private Thoughts.* Philadelphia: Temple University Press, 2006.

Smith, Barbara Herrenstein. *Poetic Closure: A Study of How Poems End.* Chicago: University of Chicago Press, 1968.

Smith, Willie "the Lion." *Music on My Mind: The Memoirs of an American Pianist.* With George Hoefer. New York: Da Capo, 1975.

Sobol, John. *Digitopia Blues: Race, Technology and the American Voice.* Banff: Banff Centre Press, 2002.

Solomon-Godeau, Abigail. "On Ghost Writing: The Fae Richards Archive." *artUS* 1 (2004): 25–33.

Somerville, Siobhan B. *Queering the Color Line: Race and the Invention of Homosexuality in American Culture.* Durham, N.C.: Duke University Press, 2000.

———, ed. Special issue, *Modern Fiction Studies* 48, no. 4 (2002).

Sotiropoulos, Karen. *Staging Race: Black Performers in Turn of the Century America.* Cambridge, Mass.: Harvard University Press, 2006.

Spahr, Julianna. " 'Love Scattered, Not Concentrated Love': Bernadette Mayer's Sonnets." *differences* 12 (2001): 98–120.

Spencer, Jon Michael. *The New Negroes and Their Music: The Success of the Harlem Renaissance.* Knoxville: University of Tennessee Press, 1997.

Spillers, Hortense. "'All the Things You Could Be by Now if Sigmund Freud's Wife Was Your Mother': Psychoanalysis and Race." In *Black, White, and in Color: Essays on American Literature and Culture*, 376–427. Chicago: University of Chicago Press, 2003.

———. "Formalism Comes to Harlem." In *Black, White, and in Color: Essays on American Literature and Culture*, 81–92. Chicago: University of Chicago Press, 2003.

———. "Interstices: A Small Drama of Words." In *Black, White, and in Color: Essays on American Literature and Culture*, 152–75. Chicago: University of Chicago Press, 2003.

Stallybrass, Peter. "Marx and Heterogeneity: Thinking the Lumpenproletariat." *Representations* 31 (1990): 69–95.

Stallybrass, Peter, and Allon White. *The Politics and Poetics of Transgression*. Ithaca, N.Y.: Cornell University Press, 1986.

Stavney, Anne. "Cross-Dressing Harlem, Re-Dressing Race." *Women's Studies* 28 (1999): 127–56.

Stearns, Jean, and Marshall Stearns. *Jazz Dance: The Story of American Vernacular Dance*. New York: Da Capo, 1968.

Stephens, Michelle Ann. *Black Empire: The Masculine Global Imaginary of Caribbean Intellectuals in the United States, 1914-1962*. Durham, N.C.: Duke University Press, 2005.

Stoff, Michael B. "Claude McKay and the Cult of Primitivism." In *The Harlem Renaissance Remembered*, ed. Arna Bontemps, 126–46. New York: Dodd, Mead, 1972.

Stokes, Mason. "Strange Fruits: Rethinking the Gay Twenties." *Transition* 12 (2002): 56–79.

Stovall, Tyler. *Paris Noir: African Americans in the City of Lights*. New York: Houghton Mifflin, 1996.

Stover, Johnnie M. *Rhetoric and Resistance in Black Women's Autobiography*. Gainesville: University Press of Florida, 2003.

Strayhorn, Billy. "The Ellington Effect." *Downbeat*, November 5, 1952.

Sundquist, Eric J. "Introduction: The Country of the Blue." In *American Realism: New Essays*, ed. Eric J. Sundquist, 3–24. Baltimore: Johns Hopkins University Press, 1982.

Sylvester, Robert. *No Cover Charge: A Backward Look at the Night Clubs*. New York: Dial, 1956.

Taylor, Diana. *The Archive and the Repertoire: Performing Cultural Memory in the Americas*. Durham, N.C.: Duke University Press, 2004.

Taylor, Henry Louis, Jr., and Walter Hill, eds. *Historical Roots of the Urban Crisis: African Americans in the Industrial City, 1900-1950*. New York: Garland, 2000.

Terry, Jennifer. *An American Obsession: Science, Medicine, and Homosexuality in Modern Society*. Chicago: University of Chicago Press, 1999.

Thomas, Brooks. *American Literary Realism and the Failed Promise of Contract*. Berkeley and Los Angeles: University of California Press, 1997.

Thomas, H. Nigel. "Black American Writers and White Readers." In *Claude McKay: Centennial Studies*, ed. A. L. McLeod, 160–71. New Delhi: Sterling, 1992.

Thurman, Wallace. *The Blacker the Berry*. New York: Simon and Schuster, 1929.

Thurman, Wallace, et al. *Fire!!* 1, November 1926.

Tims, W. Keith. "Masks and Sartre's Imaginary: Masked Performance and the Imaging Consciousness." Ph.D. diss., Georgia State University, 2007.

Tischler, Barbara L. "Europa Jazz in the 1920s and the Musical Discovery of Harlem." In *The Harlem Renaissance: Revaluations*, ed. Armritjit Singh, William S. Shiver, and Stanley Brodwin, 185–93. New York: Garland, 1989.

Toomer, Jean. *Cane*. New York: Boni and Liveright, 1923.

Tracy, Stephen C. "Langston Hughes and Afro-American Vernacular Music." In *A Historical Guide to Langston Hughes*, ed. Steven C. Tracy, 85–118. Oxford: Oxford University Press, 2004.

———. *Langston Hughes and the Blues*. Champaign: University of Illinois Press, 1988.

Trav S. D. *No Applause—Just Throw Money: The Book That Made Vaudeville Famous*. New York: Faber and Faber, 2001.

Tucker, Mark. "Jungle Music." In *The New Grove Dictionary of Jazz,* 2nd ed., vol. 2, ed. Barry Kernfeld. New York: Macmillan, 2002.

Van Vechten, Carl. *Nigger Heaven.* New York: Knopf, 1926.

——. "Prescription for the Negro Theatre." *Vanity Fair,* October 1925, 46, 92, 98. Reprinted in *"Keep A-Inching Along": Selected Writings of Carl Van Vechten about Black Art and Letters,* ed. Bruce Kellner, 29–34. Westport, Conn.: Greenwood, 1979. Page references are to the 1925 edition.

Vázquez, Alexandra. "Instrumental Migrations: The Transnational Movement of Cuba and Its Music." Ph.D. diss., New York University, 2006.

——. "'Una Escuela Rara': Havana Meets Harlem in Montmartre." *Women and Performance* 16 (2006): 27–49.

Vogel, Shane. "Performing 'Stormy Weather': Ethel Waters, Lena Horne, and Katherine Dunham." *South Central Review* 25 (2008): 93–113.

Wald, Alan M. *Exiles from a Future Time: The Forging of the Mid-Twentieth Century Literary Left.* Chapel Hill: University of North Carolina Press, 2002.

Walker, Alice, "In Search of Our Mothers' Gardens." *Ms.,* May 1974, 64, 66, 68, 70, 105.

——. "In Search of Zora Neale Hurston [Looking for Zora]." *Ms.,* March 1975, 74, 76, 78, 79, 85, 89.

Wall, Cheryl. "Passing for What? Aspects of Identity in Nella Larsen's Novels." *Black American Literature Forum* 20 (1986): 97–111.

——. *Women of the Harlem Renaissance.* Bloomington: Indiana University Press, 1995.

Warren, Kenneth. *Black and White Strangers: Race and American Literary Realism.* Chicago: University of Chicago Press, 1993.

Waters, Ethel. *His Eye Is on the Sparrow.* With Charles Samuels. New York: Doubleday, 1950.

Watson, Steven. *The Harlem Renaissance: Hub of African-American Culture, 1920-1930.* New York: Pantheon, 1995.

Webb, Barbara L. "The Black Dandyism of George Walker: A Case Study of Genealogical Method." *Drama Review* 45 (2001): 7–24.

White, Ronald C., Jr. *Liberty and Justice for All: Racial Reform and the Social Gospel, 1877-1925.* San Francisco: Harper & Row, 1990.

White, Shane, and Graham White. *Stylin': African American Expressive Culture from Its Beginnings to the Zoot Suit.* Ithaca: Cornell University Press, 1998.

Williams, Raymond. *Marxism and Literature.* New York: Oxford University Press, 1977.

Williamson, Simon. "Sports and Amusements of Negro New York, Part Two: Amusements." 1937. Federal Writers' Program, New York. Reel 5. Schomburg Center for Research in Black Culture, New York Public Library.

Wilson, James F. "Bulldykes, Pansies, and Chocolate Babies: Performance, Race, and Sexuality in the Harlem Renaissance." Ph.D. diss., City University of New York, 2000.

——. "'That's the Kind of Gal I Am': Drag Balls, Lulu Belles, and 'Sexual Perversion' in the Harlem Renaissance." In *Staging Desire: Queer Readings of American Theatre History,* ed. Kim Marra and Robert A. Schanke, 262–87. Ann Arbor: University of Michigan Press, 2002.

Winston, James. *A Fierce Hatred of Injustice: Claude McKay's Jamaican Poetry of Rebellion.* London: Verso, 2001.

Wirth, Thomas H. Introd. to *Gay Rebel of the Harlem Renaissance: Selections from the Work of Richard Bruce Nugent,* ed. Thomas Wirth. Durham, N.C.: Duke University Press, 2002.

Wolcott, Victoria W. *Remaking Respectability: African American Women in Interwar Detroit.* Chapel Hill: University of North Carolina Press, 2001.

Woodson, Carter G. *Free Negro Heads of Families in the United States in 1830.* Washington, D.C.: Association for the Study of Negro Life and History, 1925.

Worth, Robert F. *"Nigger Heaven* and the Harlem Renaissance." *African American Review* 29 (1995): 461–73.

Worthen, W. B. "The Imprint of Performance." In *Theorizing Practice: Redefining Theatre History*, ed. W. B. Worthen and Peter Holland, 213-34. London: Palgrave Macmillan, 2003.

Wright, Richard. "Blueprint for Negro Writing." In *Within the Circle: An Anthology of African American Literary Criticism from the Harlem Renaissance to the Present*, ed. Angelyn Mitchell, 97-106. Durham, N.C.: Duke University Press, 1994.

Zackodnik, Teresa C. *The Mulatta and the Politics of Race*. Jackson: University Press of Mississippi, 2004.

Zamir, Shamoon. *Dark Voices: W. E. B. Du Bois and American Thought, 1888-1903*. Chicago: University of Chicago Press, 1995.

Zelizer, Vivian A. *The Purchase of Intimacy*. Princeton, N.J.: Princeton University Press, 2005.

Zerubavel, Eviatar. *Hidden Rhythms: Schedules and Calendars in Social Life*. Berkeley and Los Angeles: University of California Press, 1985.

Index

Note: Page numbers in *italics* indicate illustrations or tables.

245

42232380R00170

Made in the USA
Lexington, KY
13 June 2015